HUMAN SECURITY IN NEPAL: CONCEPTS, ISSUES AND CHALLENGES

Edited by
Bishnu Raj Upreti
Rajan Bhattarai
Geja Sharma Wagle

ADROIT

Citation:
Upreti BR, Bhattarai R, Wagle GS, editors. 2015. Human Security in Nepal: Concepts, Issues and Challenges. New Delhi: Adroit Publishers.

Published by:
ADROIT PUBLISHERS
4675/21, Ganpati Bhawan, Ansari Road,
Daryaganj, New Delhi-110 002
Phones : 011-23266030
E-mail : adroitpublishers@gmail.com

ISBN: 978-81-87393-16-0

Cover design/layout: Bhanu Design Unit

Printed in India on behalf of M/s Adroit Publishers by
Akhil Sharma E-mail : akhil21@gmail.com

This book was first published as a research-based monograph by the Nepal Institute for Policy Studies (NIPS) and the South Asia Regional Coordination Office of the NCCR North-South programme, an international research programme co-funded by the Swiss National Science Foundation (SNSF), the Swiss Agency for Development and Cooperation (SDC), and the participating institutions in Switzerland.

Original citation: Upreti BR, Bhattarai R, Wagle GS, editors. 2013. Human Security in Nepal: Concepts, Issues and Challenges. Kathmandu: Nepal Institute for Policy Studies (NIPS) and South Asia Regional Coordination Office of NCCR (North-South).

Printed at Thompson Press (India) Limited, New Delhi.

Dedication

To the millions of people who are suffering from human insecurity.

ACKNOWLEDGEMENT

The issue of security is a little-debated matter in our academic domain. When it comes to dealing with human security, we often confront questions like: What constitutes human security? Why has it become so pertinent for a country like Nepal? How can human security be made tenable?

These and many other questions on human security came to our mind before we decided to publish this book. This is our small attempt to address some of those questions and generate debate and discussion on the increasingly changing security dynamics of Nepal.

This book is the collective outcome of the efforts of several people. Though it is not possible to list them all individually, we would like to extend our sincere thanks to them collectively.

It would be unfair not to acknowledge some of the persons who were very instrumental in bringing the book into shape.

Our first and foremost gratitude goes to the authors of the individual chapters, who despite their extremely busy schedules accepted our request to write a chapter. Without them, we cannot even think of the book.

We would like to extend our sincere thanks to Ms. Ramala Bhandari of the Nepal Institute for Policy Studies (NIPS) who took the burden of logistical support throughout the preparation of this book. Likewise, we extend our thanks to the staffs from the South Asia Regional Office of the National Centre of Competence of Research (NCCR) North-South, especially Mr. Siddhi Manadhar, Mr. Suman Babu Paudel and Mr. Safal Ghimire for their support at different stages of the preparation of this book.

We would like to express our gratitude to Dr Sally Carlton of NIPS who worked hard to review all the chapters, prepared comments to send to the individual writers, as well edited the chapters for English language.

We thank Ms Jyoti Khatiwada from Heidel Press, Dillibazar, for her hard work on formatting and designing the book.

We invite constructive and valuable comments and suggestions from our esteemed readers.

Editors
2015

List of contents

Acknowledgements 5

Acronyms and abbreviations 11

Chapter 1 Setting the context 17
Bishnu Raj Upreti, Rajan Bhattarai, Geja Sharma Wagle

Chapter 2 Human security: Concepts and criticism 29
Rajan Bhattarai

Chapter 3 Poverty: A threat to human security 55
Yuba Raj Khatiwada

Chapter 4 Social protection for human security 87
Sony KC, Bishnu Raj Upreti

Chapter 5 Food security: A fundamental basis for human security 121
Yamuna Ghale, Nirmal Kumar Bishokarma

Chapter 6 Health and human security 155
Damodar Adhikari

Chapter 7 Changing migration patterns and their impacts on human security in Nepal 201
Anita Ghimire

Chapter 8 Climate change: A challenge to human security 231
Batu Krishna Uprety

Chapter 9 Political insecurity and armed conflict: A threat to human security 259
Geja Sharma Wagle

About the authors 291

List of tables

Table 4.1 Two discernable patterns of social protection 97
Table 4.2 Why social risk management framework for social protection 98
Table 4.3 Understanding social risk management framework 100
Table 4.4 Impacts of social transfers 103
Table 4.5 Various social protection programmes 104
Table 4.6 Karnali employment programme: Progress report from five districts (2009/10) 106
Table 4.7 Social protection as a human security issue in relation to the MDGs 114
Table 5.1 Evolution of international instruments 124
Table 5.2 Some major instruments related to poverty and hunger ratified by the Government of Nepal 130
Table 5.3 Major food security policies and programmes in Nepal 133
Table 6.1 Health and human security: A global scenario 157
Table 6.2 Trends in key health indicators and MDGs targets 162
Table 6.3 Key maternal care indicators 164
Table 6.4 Immunisation indicators 164
Table 6.5 Treatment status (Maternal and child health) 165
Table 6.6 Trends in the nutritional status of children under five years of age 168
Table 6.7 Breast and complementary feeding 168
Table 6.8 Key indicators related to HIV/AIDS and current status (%) 170
Table 6.9 Trends in four or more ANC visits by wealth quintile in percentage 172
Table 6.10 Trends in deliveries attended by Doctors, Nurses and Auxiliary Nurse Midwives (ANMs) by wealth quintile in percentage 173

Table 6.11	Proportion of fully immunised children aged 12-23 months by wealth quintile in percentage	174
Table 6.12	Prevalence of diabetes in South Asia (projected in 1998)	177
Table 6.13	Risk factors for non-communicable diseases (2007-2008, population aged 15-64 years)	178
Table 6.14	Budget vs expenses status-DOHS and irregularities clearance status	189
Table 9.1	The number of deceased, disappeared, displaced and abducted persons from 13 february 1996 due to the armed conflict (Numbers as of july, 2011)	269
Table 9.2	Agreements among major political parties and important decisions of the Government of Nepal and Parliament	273
Table 9.3	Facts and figures regarding the maoist army combatants' registration, verification, regrouping process and number of arms	275
Table 9.4	Killings and human rights violations after the signing of the Comprehensive Peace Agreement (CPA)	277

List of figures

Figure 1.1	Link of different security issues within the overarching concept of human security.	20
Figure 1.2	Overview and the interrelationship between different chapters	24
Figure 4.1	The 3P framework: Functions of the institution and resilience opportunity	101

Figure 4.2 Factors that makes human security when linked to social protection 109
Figure 4.3 European Union, Social protection reduces poverty by 50 per cent 112
Figure 6.1 The health and human security link 159
Figure 6.2 Relationship between NCDs and poverty 176
Figure 8.1 The emission gap 238
Figure 8.2 Average annual maximum temperatures (1975-2006) 241
Figure 8.3 Precipitation trends (1971-2006) 241
Figure 8.4 Climate vulnerable districts of Nepal 242
Figure 8.5 Rice yield (kg/ha) and rainfall (mm) 245
Figure 9.1 Civil wars peaked in the early 1990s and then declined 264

List of diagram

Diagram 5.1 State obligations 127
Diagram 5.2 Power concentration 142

List of boxes

Box 8.1 Greenhouse gases 233
Box 8.2 Major events on climate change 236
Box 8.3 Major national initiatives on climate change 255

Abbreviations and acronyms

AEPI	Army Environmental Policy Institute
AMMAA	Agreement on the Monitoring of Management of Arms and Armies
ANC	Antenatal Care
ANMs	Auxiliary Nurse-Midwives
APF	Armed Police Force
ARI	Acute Respiratory Infections
ASEAN	Association of South East Asian Nations
BAP	Bali Action Plan
BCC	Behaviour Change and Communication
BMI	Body Mass Index
BOD	Burden of Diseases
BPKIHS	BP Koirala Institute of Health Sciences
BS	Bikram Sambat[1]
CBS	Central Bureau of Statistics
CCC	Climate Change Council
CCMD	Climate Change Management Division
CDMs	Clean Development Mechanisms
CER	Certified Emission Reduction
CIFD	Commission to Investigate Forced Disappearances
	CMR Child Mortality Rate
CPA	Comprehensive Peace Agreement
CPN	Communist Party of Nepal
CPN (UML)	Communist Party of Nepal (Unified Marxist

---

[1] Bikram Sambat is a system of making years according to the lunar calendar and is widely practiced in Nepal by the government and other media. It is 56 years ahead of the Gregorian calendar.

	Leninist)
CVD	Cardio Vascular Disease
DALY	Disability Adjusted Life Years
DANIDA	Danish International Development Agency
DDR	Disarmament, Demobilisation and Reintegration
DFID	Department for International Development
DWSS	Department of Water, Sanitation and Sewerage
EDPs	External Development Partners
EHCS	Essential Health Care Services
ES	Environmental Security
FAO	Food and Agriculture Organisation
FCHVs	Female Community Health Volunteers
FSW	Female Sex Workers
GDP	Gross Domestic Production
GHGs	Green House Gases
GLOF	Glacier Lake Outburst Flood
GtCO2eq	Gigatonnes of Carbon dioxide Equivalent
HDI	Human Development Index
HDR	Human Development Report
HFOMC	Health Facility Operation and Management Committee
HIV/AIDS	Human Immunodeficiency virus (HIV) Acquired Immunodeficiency Syndrome (AIDS)
HPI	Human Poverty Index
HPs	Health Posts
HR	Human Resources
ICESCR	International Covenant on Economic, Social and Cultural Rights
IEA	International Energy Agency
IFAD	International Fund for Agricultural Development
IMF	International Monetary Fund

INSEC	Informal Sector Services Centre
IYCF	Infant and Young Child Feeding
JICA	Japan International Cooperation Agency
KP	Kyoto Protocol
LBW	Low-Birth Weight
LDC	Least Developed Country
MCCICC	Multi-stakeholder Climate Change Initiatives Coordination Committee
MDGs	Millennium Development Goals
MIS	Maternity Incentive Scheme
MMR	Maternal Mortality Rate
MoF	Ministry of Finance
MoHA	Ministry of Home Affairs
MoHP	Ministry of Health and Population
MPI	Multidimensional Poverty Index
MPRF	Madhesi People's Rights Forum
NA	Nepal Army
NAGA	Nutrition Assessment and Gap Analysis
NAPA	National Adaptation Programme of Action
NATO	North Atlantic Treaty Organisation
NC	Nepali Congress
NCASC	National Centre for AIDS and STD Control
NEA	Nepal Electricity Authority
NGOs	Non-Governmental Organisations
NHR	National Human Rights Commission
NID	National Intelligence Department
NOC	Nepal Oil Corporation
NP	Nepal Police
NPC	National Planning Commission
NRM	Natural Resource Management
NSP	National Security Policy

NTFPs	Non-Timber Forest Products
OCHA	Office for the Coordination of Humanitarian Affairs
OHCHR-N	Office of the High Commissioner for Human Rights-Nepal
OPHI	Oxford Poverty and Human Development Initiative
ORT	Oral Rehydration Treatment
PDD	Project Design Document
PHCCs	Primary Health Care Centers
PPCR	Pilot Programme for Climate Resilience
PRSP	Poverty Reduction Strategy Paper
PWID	People Who Inject Drugs
REDD	Reducing Emissions from Deforestations and Forest Degradation
RETs	Renewable Energy Technologies
SAARC	South Asian Association for Regional Cooperation SAFTASouth Asian Free Trade Agreement
SARS	Severe Acute Respiratory Syndrome
SBAs	Skilled Birth Attendants
SC	Special Committee
SDIP	Safe Delivery Incentive Programme
SHPs	Sub-Health Posts
SPA	Seven Party Alliance
SREP	Scaling up Renewable Energy Programme
SSR	Security Sector Reform
SWAp	Sector-Wide Approach
TC	Technical Committee
TRC	Truth and Reconciliation Commission
UCPN (M)	Unified Communist Party of Nepal (Maoist)
UN	United Nations

UNDP	United Nations Development Programme
UNEP	United Nations Environment Programme
UNFCCC	United Nations Framework Convention on Climate Change
UNICEF	United Nations Children's Fund
UNMIN	United Nations Mission in Nepal
VAT	Value-Added Tax
WB	World Bank
WCED	World Commission on Environment and Development
WFP	World Food Program
WHO	World Health Organisation
WSSD	World Submit on Sustainable Development
WTO	World Trade Organization

Chapter 1

Setting the context

Bishnu Raj Upreti, Rajan Bhattarai, Geja Sharma Wagle

Nepal is undergoing through a painful process of transition. The Comprehensive Peace Agreement (CPA) (2006), which is the foundation of the Interim Constitution (2007), dissolved Constituent Assembly and the government, has envisioned the fundamental restructuring of the state that include state's vital institutions like judiciary, legislative and executive (including security and bureaucracy). In this context, intense discussions and debate are going on about the concepts, procedures, applications and limitations of the restructuring of the state institutions. Security is one of such which is sensitive in nature, kept close for long (to discuss security issues by non-security persons was viewed as encroachment and threat to the security itself), less availability of the expertise and low interests of people (because of self censorship or practiced as risk aversion strategy). The debate on the security sector was opened only after the signing of the CPA but again it was limited to small circle of people, mainly with ex-officials of security forces and bureaucrats and they too were concentrated in traditional security issues (focusing on military and state not the people). In Nepal, the security policy has basically been guided by ad hoc and non- tranparent policies and programmes. The National Security Council under the Ministry of Defense has never been institutionalized and supported to engage in organized study, planning, policy development or execution. These facts are compounded by limited awareness of security policy, strategy and security sector governance issues in the country including among the governing elites. Lack of knowledge and lucid analysis prevails, with little understanding of newer ideas in security studies.

Therefore, it can be argued that holistic debate of security is still largely missing or started in superficial level (at the stage of referral or what question, but not focused on why and how). Hence, there is a blatant need of widening discussions on national security issues and its various dimensions and agendas that include the non-traditional security issues focusing to the question why and how. As the concept of human security has evolved in the early years of last decade, it has broadened the definitions and agendas of security by incorporating political, social, economic, cultural and environmental issues. Furthermore, it has also shifted the concept of security from traditional state-centric approach to the people-centric approach. Therefore, it has become important to bring this issue at public discourse and sensitize at the political, policy and decision making levels. Our hope is that this book will contribute to some extent, fill the gap and facilitate the public debate on human security.

1.1 Expanding the security debate in Nepal

Though the concept of human security was formally introduced by Special Advisor to UNDP Dr Mahbub ul Haq with publication of Human Development Report in 1994 and it had extensively dealt this issue (UNDP 1994). Human security concept is getting popular together with the growing newer and unconventional security challenges in the world, because the conventional security arrangements, though getting priority at the political levels, are not able to safeguard the vital interests (food, shelter, water, etc.) of people, families and communities. This debate has gained momentum once UNDP published its Human Development Report in 1994. Later, the UN had created separate Human Security Commission and the UN has aggressively promoted the concept through international conferences, meetings and workshops. In 1999 an international network was also established among the 'like-minded states' and organised series of ministerial meetings to promote the concept of HS.

Though the concept was already introduced in 1994, it took almost 2 decades for Nepal to introduce the concept and engage in this debate. However, we are still not able to reorient our development policies and plannings towards the human security perspective. Since the concept was first introduced as an alternative perspective from the traditional state-centric security approach to the people-centric security approach, several efforts were made by leading researchers, scholars and academicians specifically developing and refining conceptual frameworks and methodological approaches for human security (Alkire 2003). In this context, the Human Security Commission has also played important role in promoting the HS debate in the world (CHS 2003).

The figure 1.1 shows the overlapping and or complementary components of the human security. Components of human security, as shown in the figure 1.1, are ecosystem and climate security, water and energy security, food and health security, environmental security, nuclear and biological security, individual security, societal security and national security. In this context, human security is a holistic concept to be achieved through ensuring different security aspects presented in the figure 1.1. However, majority of the policy makers, decision makers and security officials in Nepal (like in many other countries) are not yet able to internalize the importance of and interrelationship between different components of security (figure 1.1 and 1.2) mainly focus on the national security of achieving security from the use of forces (i.e. military).

Figure 1.1 Link of different security issues within the overarching concept of human security

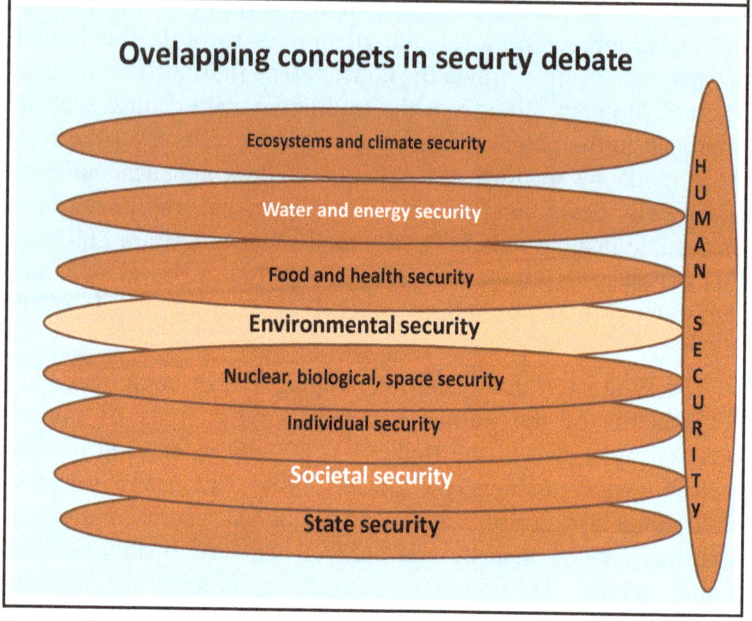

Source: Designed by Bishnu Raj Upreti

1.2 Incorporation of non-traditional security issues in security policy/debate

Often security is linked with the conflict, violence, crime, burglary, unwanted encroachment or interference and so forth, in sum, more on the reactive side. The armed conflict database of Peace Research Institute OSLO, PRIO (2009) shows that the security discourses in the past 6 decades was dominated by the conflict across the world. In the post World War-II, the security discourse was dominated mainly by the Cold War between the USA and the then USSR (that was mainly reflected on expanding influences in other countries through military invasion). Hence, other aspects of security as presented in the figure 1.2 were not getting attention until the disintegration of the USSR in 1991. In the 1950s the inter-state conflicts were very intensive compared to the intra-state conflicts and it was continued until 1979. And after 1980s, it is in the decreasing trend (HSRP 2011). From the decade of the 1980s the unconventional security issues like environmental security was brought into the security debate and in the 1990s the concept of human security was introduced by broadening its definitions and incorporating wider agendas such as climate security, water security, food security and health security. Countries like Canada, Norway and Japan appeared to be the champion of human security in the earlier years.

They have promoted the concept of 'freedom from fear' and 'freedom from want'. However, many other countries like Romania, Republic of Moldova, Ukraine, Australia, Finland, the UK, the Netherlands have also taken up human security issue and included it in their national security policies. For example, Romania included economic migration and displacement, protection of citizens, national identity and recognition, creation of civil society and empowerment, family ties, employment and income generation, public health, garbage management, control of aggressive/violent social behaviour, protection of minority rights and sustainable development as societal security issues in its security policy. Republic of Moldova has incorporated recognition of linguistic, ethnic, religious and cultural identities and rights, immigration, livelihood concerns of poor and minorities, as some of the important societal security issues in its national security policy. Ukraine has also included language, effectiveness of socio-economic infrastructures, management of population, gender equality as societal security issues in the national security policy. In the national security policy of Australia mass migration, environmental security threats, resource management and distribution, problems and insecurity created by climate change effects, risks related to population, food insecurity, water and energy insecurity and economic crisis are included. Similarly, Finland, Germany, the United Kingdom and the Netherlands have included unconventional security issues (human security, societal security) in their national security policies.[1]

---

1 See a) Finish Security and Defense Policy 2009 (the Prime Minister's Office Publication 13/2009), b) Securing an Open Society: Canada's

Scholars and researchers have started highlighting the need of expanding the security debate on unconventional security issues in Nepal since the end of last decade (Matthew and Upreti 2009). The examination of the inter-linkages between skewed/irrational exploitation of environmental resources like water, land, forest and civil wars/armed insurgency as a major source of insecurity in Nepal (Upreti 2004; Mathew and Upreti 2005), the environmental security and sustainable development (Upreti 2012a), the food and water security (Upreti 2012b), health security (Khatri 2012) are some of the examples of security debate to non-traditional security in Nepal. Interestingly, the newly appointed Chief of the Army Staff Gen. Gaurav Samsher Rana highlighted the need of incorporating non-traditional security threats into the national security policy while making his speech after assumption of his newly appointed position.[2]

Originally, the 7 components of HS were included as: economic security, food security, health security, environmental security, personal security, community security and political security. Because of the practical relevance, the HS has been broadened and getting wider attention. Even though the original components were limited to 7, over the time the components of HS needed to be expanded and cover many other areas and issues which are increasingly posing threats to the nation-state and the human being such as water security, climate security and so forth.

Report of the Conference of the Parties serving as the meeting of the parties to the Kyoto Protocol on its Seventh Session, held

---

National Security Policy April 2004 (Canada Privy Council Office) c) Defense Policy Guidelines for the area of responsibility of the Federal Minister of Defense, Germany, 21 May 2003, d) National Security Strategy of the Netherlands, Ministry of Interior and Kingdom Relations, May 2007, e) The New Zealand Defense Force Strategic Plan 2007-2011, Ministry of Defense f) National Security Strategy of the United Kingdom: Security in the Interdependent World (The Cabinet Office, March 2008), for details about the inclusion of societal security in their national security policies and strategies.

2 General Rana, in his first Principal Staff Officers meeting immediately after the assumption as CoAS presented the strategy paper, where security challenges were highlighted in details and many of such challenges were related to non-traditional security issues.

in Durban from 28 November to 11 December 2011, clearly highlighted that climate security is a major security concern today for the world (Climate Change Secretariat 2011). Climate related disasters like flood, glacier melt, sea level rise, prolonging drought, increasing frequency of hurricane and storms etc are posing greater risks and threats to humanity. A Special Report of Working Groups I and II of the Intergovernmental Panel on Climate Change and the World Meteorological Organisation entitled 'Managing the Risks of Extreme Events and Disasters to Advance Climate Change Adaptation - Summary for Policymakers' (IPCC 2012) amply highlights the looming disaster risks and threats to human security. World Bank (WB 2010) in its World Development Report has highlighted the relationship between climate change and development.

Similarly, the Food and Agriculture Organization's Report 'The State of Food Insecurity in the World' indicates the global challenges posed by food insecurity (FAO 2008). Several authors and scholars then started examining the relationship between environmental security and climate change (Floyd 2008; Matthew and Upreti 2009) and significance of the environmental security debate for climate change. In the recent decade security of migrant population is another security concern, which has been depicted in the series of World Migration Reports (IOM 2011).

Increasing civil strife, armed conflicts and intra-state wars are becoming day to day reality in the present world; restoring peace is becoming one of the main HS concerns (HSRP 2011). Further, when state governments fail to judicially deal with the scarce resources and concerns of poor and marginalised people are ignored for long civil strife and conflict is unavoidable and it will be more in developing world (Kahl 2006; WB 2011). The World Development Report of the World Bank entitled 'Conflict, Security and Development' vividly highlighted the interrelationship between development, security and conflict.

1.3 Organization of the book chapters

Linking the thematic subjects into security and transforming the stand- alone concept into integrated human security concept is extremely difficult task for the authors. All contributors in one way or another encountered this situation in different degree. However, based on the peer review, comments, feedback and re-iterative process of rewriting made the content of individual chapter well grounded relating it into human security concept. Despite our constant efforts, we were not able to find relevant experts to write water security chapter linking with human security. In the following section a brief overview of each chapter is presented:

Figure 1.2 Overview and the interrelationship between different chapters

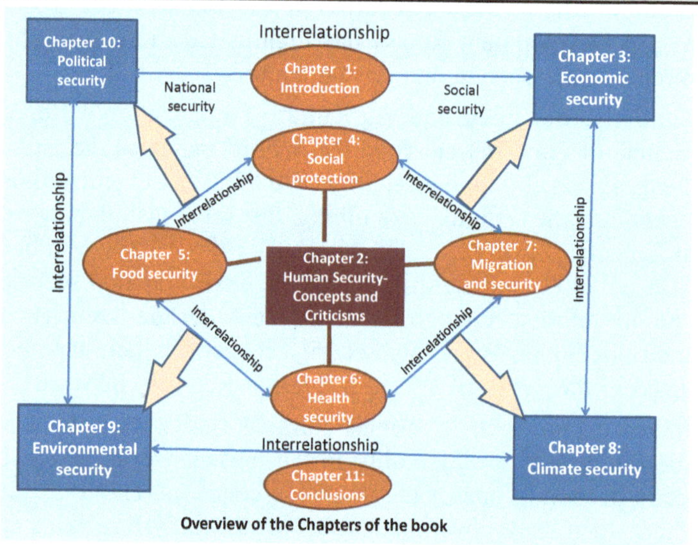

Source: Designed by Bishnu Raj Upreti

The Chapter 1 has set the context by briefly introducing the conceptualisation and evolution of human security in general and the development of the debate in Nepal. Then this chapter presents some example of counties incorporating components of human security and societal security in their national security policies. It also highlights the need and relevance of human security in the changing context.

In Chapter 2 Rajan Bhattarai presents concepts and criticisms of HS and presents evolution of the concept at global, regional and national levels. In this chapter, readers can find different concepts, arguments, perspectives and critiques of human security by the well known writers and critics in the field of human security. This Chapter is the central framework of the book.

In Chapter 3 Yuba Raj Khatiwada, based on his a wide range of experiences in the areas of policy making, examines poverty and inequality from human security perspective and succinctly presents the link between human development and human security, politics of poverty, causes and consequences. The chapter offers the link between the development and poverty and its relation with security.

Sony KC and Bishnu Raj Upreti in Chapter 4 discusses the relationship between social protection and human security and highlight the need of social security to protect weakest section of society, who are more vulnerable from the systematic shocks, chronic deficiency of basic needs. The authors argue that to achieve security in general and human security in particular social protection is one of the preconditions.

Yamuna Ghale and Nirmal Kumar Bishokarma in Chapter 5 present food insecurity as security challenge in Nepal. The authors succinctly inter- relate food security with human security and argue that food security is a fundamental right of people and achieving human security and national security is not possible without ensuring food security. The authors also present food security situation in Nepal in terms of access, affordability, availability and food security challenges.

Another important aspect of HS is health security, which is becoming a major security threat in the world. A report entitled 'Fifty Facts: Global Health Situation and Trends 1995-2025' of World Health Organisation presents worrying scenario if the states do not take serious action in time (WHO 1995). In Chapter 6, Damodar Adhikari analyses health security in Nepal from human security perspective. He brings overview of the health security situation in Nepal and demographic challenges (ageing population, migration, child mortality, women trafficking, etc.), nutritional issues and new health challenges. His important argument is that health security is one of the fundmantal basis to achieve other security, as it is related to the people's health.

Anita Ghimire in Chapter 7 discusses migration and security. She presents patterns of migration and nexus between migration and human security. The author highlights the complication of migration for foreign employment and associated insecurity to be addressed by the nation.

Batu Krishna Uprety in Chapter 8 offers climate change and its relation with human security in Nepal and efforts made in addressing challenges of climate change. In this chapter ongoing climate change debate is presented and efforts made in adaptation and mitigation is discussed. A quick overview of progress made in Nepal so far in addressing concerns of climate change is also presented.

Geja Sharma Wagle in Chapter 9 presents the political security debate and examines the relationship between human security and political security with special focuses on the decade long armed-conflict, peace process and post-conflict challenges in Nepal.

References

Alkire S. 2003. *A Conceptual Framework for Human Security*. Crise Working Paper 2. Oxford: University of Oxford.

CHS [Commission on Human Security]. 2003. *Human Security Now*. New York: Commission on Human Security/UNOPS (United Nations Office for. Project Services). Also available at: http://www.humansecurity-chs.org/ finalreport/index.html; accessed on 3 July 2012.

Climate Change Secretariat. 2011. *Report of the Conference of the Parties serving as the meeting of the Parties to the Kyoto Protocol on its seventh session, held in Durban from 28 November to 11 December 2011*. Bonn: Climate Change Secretariat.

FAO [Food and Agriculture Organization]. 2008. The State of Food Insecurity in the World, Rome: Food and Agriculture Organization. Available at: http://www.fao.org/publications/sofi/en/; accessed on 27 April 2010.

Floyd R. 2008. The environmental security debate and its significance for climate change. *The International Spectator* 43(3):51-65.

HSRP [Human Security Report Project]. 2011. Human Security Report 2009/2010: The causes of peace and the shrinking costs of war. Simon Fraser University, Canada. New York and London: Oxford University Press.

IOM [International Organisation for Migration]. 2011. World Migration Report: *Communicating Effectively about Migration.* Geneva: International Organisation for Migration.

IPCC [Intergovernmental Panel on Climate Change]. 2012. *Managing the Risks of Extreme Events and Disasters to Advance Climate Change Adaptation- Summary for Policymakers*. A Special Report of Working Groups I and II of the Intergovernmental Panel on Climate Change. Geneva: World Meteorological Organisation.

Kahl C. 2006. *States, Scarcity, and Civil Strife in the Developing World.* Princeton: Princeton University Press.

Khatri SK. 2012. Health and Human Security in Nepal and Possible Trajectories for 2025. In: Non-traditional Security Challenges in Nepal (ed.) National Bureau of Asian Research. NBR Special Report (36). Seattle and Washington: The National Bureau of Asian Research. Pp. 5-20.

Matthew R and Upreti BR. 2009. Environmental Change and Human Security in Nepal. *In*: Matthew RA, Barnett J, McDonald B, P'Brien KL, editors. *Global Environmental Change and Human Security.* Arvine: MIT Press, pp137-154.

Mathew R and Upreti BR. 2005. Nepal: Environmental Stress, Demographic Changes and the Maoists. Environmental Change and Security Programme Report, Issue 11. Woodrow Wilson International Centre for Scholars. Pp-29-39.

PRIO [Peace Research Institute, Oslo]. 2009. *Armed Conflict Dataset*. Oslo: PRIO.

UNDP [United Nations Development Programme]. 1994. *Human Development Report*. New York: Oxford University Press.

Upreti BR. 2012a. Environamntal Security and Sustainable Devleopment (Chapter 12). In: Rita Floyd and Richard Matthew (eds.) *Environmental Security*.

Upreti BR. 2012b. Water and Food Insecurity: Non-traditional Security Challenges for Nepal. In: Non-traditional Security Challenges in Nepal (ed.) National Bureau of Asian Research. NBR Special Report (36). Seattle and Washington: The National Bureau of Asian Research. Pp. 21-34.

Upreti BR. 2004. The Price of Neglect: From Resource Conflict to Maoist Insurgency in the Himalayan Kingdom. Kathmandu: Bhrikuti Academic Publications.

WB [World Bank]. 2010. *World Development Report, 2010. Development and Climate Change*. Washington, D.C.: World Bank.

WB [World Bank]. 2011. *Conflict, Security and Development*. Washington DC: World Bank.

WHO [World Health Organisation]. 1995. *Fifty Facts: Global Health Situation and Trends 1995-2025*. New York: World Health Organisation. Also available at: http://www.who.int/whr

****

Chapter 2

Human security: Concepts and criticism

Rajan Bhattarai, PhD

1.1 Introduction

What is human security? There is still no consensual definition. Different scholars have come up with different definitions for the term. The ambiguity about the concept of security has long been felt by academicians as well as practitioners. Several questions have been raised which include issues related to 'Security for whom', 'Of what values', 'From what threats' and 'By what means'. Answers to these questions rely on the different conceptions and definitions of security. Realists and Neo-Realists such as Hobbes, Waltz and Kissinger argue that the referent object of security is the state, that the state and the military are the means to achieve maximum security in an anarchical world (Howard 1983). Similarly, Bajpai argues that nation states are often the main actors in international politics and give priority to protection (Bajpai 2002). It is a state-centric theory of international relations. Such scholars believe that the international system is governed by anarchy and that there is no central authority. Realist theory claims to rely upon an ancient tradition of thought which includes writers such as Thucydides, Machiavelli and Rousseau. According to classical Realists like Arnold Wolfers, Klaus Knorr and Henry Kissinger, world politics represent a struggle for power between states (Howard 1983). Therefore, their arguments hold that rising nations will seek to expand their roles and influence and will become less benign when their capabilities increase. The primary function of a nation- state is to survive and enhance its power in an anarchical and conflictual international system and develop its capability (military and otherwise) to ensure the security of the state (Sabur 2003). As highlighted by Bajpai, Neo-Realists argue that in a Hobbesian world, the state is the primary provider of security: if the state is secure, then those who live within it are also secure. Two values associated with the state are central: territorial integrity and national independence (Bajpai 2002).

Likewise, Neo-Realists like Kenneth Waltz argue that the state of the structure must be taken into account in explaining state behaviour (Waltz 1979). The Neo-Realists question the classical Realists about the similar behaviour exhibited by both the United States of America (USA) and the Union of Soviet Socialist Republics (USSR) during the Cold War period, despite the superpowers' different political orders. According to the Neo-Realists, during the Cold War, the fact that both superpowers followed similar behavioural patterns stems from the systemic forces which homogenise foreign policy behaviour (ibid). However, Neo-Realists have also had difficulties in finding a common definition of 'security'. Security is a contested concept with no precise definition. It generates unsolvable debate about its meaning and application; as Richard Little points out, it contains an ideological element which renders empirical evidence irrelevant as a means of resolving the dispute (Little 1981). Macdonald and Jervis attempted to tackle the ambiguity of the concept, but again concluded that security is an 'inadequate' concept (Macdonald 1981).

In the post-Cold War era, the state-centric security agenda did not disappear; rather a new security agenda has come to be included. However, both the Realists and Neo-Realists have failed to recognise that security issues go beyond the state and military. The lack of awareness of non-military issues related to security (such as socio-economic structures, the ethnic composition of a nation-state and its relations with the security environment) is the major constriction of the Realist and Neo- Realist school of thoughts. Protecting citizens' interests and their lives from 'freedom from fear' and 'freedom from want' are missing in their arguments.

Even countries like Canada, Japan and the European Union and the United Nations Development Programme (UNDP), have differences about the definition of human security. As viewed by one scholar, the concept of human security really is in the eye of the beholder (Paris 2001). Generally, human security is defined as a people-centric approach to security, which is necessary for national, regional and global stability. It concentrates on the safety of people and communities. The broad aim of human security is to mitigate threats to the insecurity of individuals including socio- economic and political conditions such as food, health, environmental, community and personal safety. The Cold War and the dominance of the Realist School in international relations placed emphasis on the primacy of the state in security discourse. This emphasis ensured that nation-states became the building blocks of the international system (Chari and Gupta 2003) and that the traditional concept of security was state-centric.

For its part, UNDP has called for a transition from a narrow concept of national security to the all-encompassing concept of human security. It distinguishes between the perception of rich and poor countries. UNDP (1994) emphasised that the rich seek security from the threat of crime and drug wars in their streets, the spread of deadly diseases like HIV/AIDS, soil degradation, rising levels of pollution, the fear of losing their jobs and other anxieties that emerge as the social fabric disintegrates. People in poor countries demand liberation from the continuing threat of hunger, disease and poverty whilst also facing the same problems that threaten industrial countries (UNDP 1994).

Once the reference point of security is changed to individuals, the notion of 'safety' is extended to become a condition beyond mere existence (survival) to a life worth living; hence, to the wellbeing and dignity of human beings (Tadjbakhsh and Chenoy

2007). It is a concept of security which extends beyond the conventional domain of military threats to include those that fall outside of this domain. Non-military threats are rooted in social, economic, sociological and political choices made by the country, but are frequently left out of the decision-making process. Very often these threats jeopardise a country's economic development, social fabric and political stability (Chari and Gupta 2003). Critics of human security argue that its vagueness undermines its effectiveness.

The issue of security for a nation is different from the issue of security for an individual. Since the Westphalia Treaty in 1648 after a war that lasted 30 years, under the Hobbesian model of the state, it has been said that the state would provide security for its citizens living within its borders. The state has to assure security to its people. However, many states today are partly or completely failing to fulfill their social contract to protect people. Some states even threaten their own people through repression, genocide or massacre. Mack (2004) claims that in the last one hundred years, far more people have died at the hands of their own governments than have been killed by foreign armies (Mack 2004). As Thakur further claims, over the last century thirty million people were killed in international wars, seven million in civil wars and 170 million people were killed by their own governments (Thakur 2000).

Human security is not just the absence of war; it also covers wider areas which include people's right to a secure environment in which to live and grow access to jobs and political participation. Human security also refers to the security of the individual or people in terms of their political, social, environmental, economic and cultural rights and choices. There are many countries around the world where people are still deprived of their basic rights, and are forced to compromise their freedom for the sake of 'national interests' and sovereignty. Today, almost all the world's countries are faced with threats of one or another forms resulting from migratory movement, environmental degradation, terror attacks, the outbreak of contagious diseases, ethnic, racial or religious conflicts, abject poverty and inequality. The impact of these different threats is far greater and deeper from the threats generated by traditional inter-state rivalries and conflicts. This has resulted in the suffering of hundreds of thousands people who have been deprived from enjoying their fundamental rights to life and livelihood. In other words, protecting citizens' lives has increasingly become more prominent and vital, both in national security discourse and in the global security environment. This has presented new challenges to nation-states.

An emerging trend within this evolution has been a move towards greater emphasis on the concept of human security (Dabelko, Lonergan and Matthew 2000). Anne Hammerstad wrote, "According to the human security approaches, security is about the social, political, environmental and economic conditions conducive to live in a free and dignified manner" (Hammerstad 2000). Human security is not in opposition to earlier trends of redefining security (Mathew 1989). In fact, it is an outgrowth of these trends. Indeed, many early attempts to broaden the definition of 'security' used language very similar to that found in today's discussions on 'human security.' For example, Norman Myers argues that security applies most at the level of the individual citizen. It amounts to human wellbeing: not only protection from harm and injury but access to water, food, shelter, health, employment and other basic requisites that are the due of every person on the Earth. It is the collectivity of these citizens' needs - overall safety and quality of life - that should figure prominently in the nation's view of security (Myers 1993).

As the fundamental basis for human security is the security of human beings, it can be argued that international security is dependent upon the security of individuals. As Nef points out, if the safety of individuals is the key to global security, then if this safety is threatened, so is international security (Nef 1999). In this perspective, the status of the individual is transformed from that of a simple citizen of his or her state into that

of an actor involved in international relations. The individual becomes an 'agent' who can be actively engaged in defining potential security threats and who can participate in efforts to mitigate them. The survival, well-being and dignity of the individual become the ultimate goal and constructs such as the state, the institutions of political democracy and the market are relegated to secondary status as a means to achieve that goal. If primary threats stem from economic failure, violation of human rights and political discrimination, then the guarantee of national security no longer lies in military power but in favourable social, political and economic conditions, the promotion of human development and the protection of human rights (Tadjbakhsh and Chenoy 2007).

The 1994 United Nations Human Development Report, prepared by Mahbub ul Haq, urged that the focus of security had to be changed from state-centric security to human security. UNDP's focus was on 'freedom from want' under which the report subdivided issues to be securitised into seven categories: economic, food, health, environment, personal, community and political security. The state has the duty to provide the mode of security needed by minority groups, individuals and system (UNDP 1994). The issue of non-traditional security was further advanced by the importance given to it in the report of the Commission on Global Governance (CGG 1995). The report tried to shift the direction of the security discussion by focusing on issues of human life and human dignity rather than on weapons and territory.

Likewise, the countries which are the leading advocates of the human security (primarily Canada and Japan) have always emphasised the issues from their own perspectives. In 1996, the Government of Canada came out with its own version of human security that places greater emphasis on 'freedom from fear' (The Government of Canada 1996). This Canadian version of security included the protection of people from war and conflict and promoted the agenda of peace. Canada's human security policy is based on five priorities: a) public safety (building international expertise with the capacity to counter growing cross-border threats posed by terrorism, drug trafficking and spread of crime); b) protection of civilians (the establishment of legal norms, the reduction of the human costs of armed conflict, human rights field operations and the deployment of military forces in extreme situations to control atrocities and war crimes; c) conflict prevention (strengthening the capacity of the international community to resolve violent conflicts, building national and local capacity to manage political and social tensions without resorting to violence, by using targeted economic sanctions to reduce the chances of civil war breaking out); d) governance and accountability (fostering improved accountability of public and private sector institutions with emphasis on building an effective International Criminal Court (ICC) and promoting reform of security institutions including military, police and judiciary, reducing corruption, promoting freedom of expression and encouraging corporate social responsibility); and e) peace support operations (bolstering international capacity, undertaking peace missions, dealing with issues related to women, providing policy and civil experts to undertake complex missions) (Huliaras and Tzifakis 2007).

To reach these objectives, the Canadian Government launched a human security programme in 1996. Through the promotion of the agenda of human security, Canada believes it can enhance its role on the international stage. It had earlier played a leading role in the campaign banning the deployment of landmines, with 122 countries gathering in Ottawa in 1997 to sign the Ottawa Convention on the Prohibition, Use, Stockpiling, Production and Transfer of Anti-Personnel Landmines and their destruction. Similarly, Canada has been at the forefront of setting up the ICC which it has regarded as part of promoting the issue of 'freedom of fear'. Likewise, Japan established a Commission on Human Security in 1999 and set up the largest trust fund in the United Nations. Japan has become one of the leading countries to provide leadership and funding for human security. The Japanese approach to human security promotes measures designed to protect people from threats to their livelihoods and dignity while supporting self-empowerment. The Japanese human security policy took as a model in a ministerial-level programme which proved successful in the areas of Overseas Development Assistance (ODA) and which became very popular with the Japanese public (Yeo 2004). However, despite Japan's claim that its foreign policy is based on human security, it continues to pursue traditional security interests in the region. Thus, the human security agenda in Japanese foreign policy is a complement and not a replacement of traditional security concerns (ibid).

Since its introduction in the early 1990s, the concept of human security has drawn wide attention from both its advocates and critics. Both sides have made arguments and counter-arguments about its concept, viability and academic usability. Various security experts and scholars have analysed the concepts of human security and its prospects. In the meantime, many scholars have expressed their reservations and criticised the concept and its academic usability. The views expressed by some of the prominent scholars on human security are given below.

Human security advocate, Caroline Thomas believes that human security is an integrative concept allowing for the bridging and interconnection of sector-specific threats to people in the international system, rather than states. For Thomas, human security means the provision of basic material needs and the realisation of human dignity including emancipation from oppressive power structures, whether global, national or local in origin or scope (Thomas 2004). She further adds that a distinction is made between quantitative aspects of human security, which incorporate basic needs (food, shelter, education and health care) and qualitative aspects encompassing dignity, personal autonomy, control over one's life, participation in the community, chance and opportunity. The concept provides a language and rationale for raising the concerns of the majority of humanity. The ultimate utility of the concept is in the practical application of knowledge to interconnections between threats. For policy purposes, bottom-up participatory approaches to politics are necessary (ibid).

Another security writer, Amitav Acharya, argues that we need to avoid casting the human security debate within the existing paradigms of international relations. Instead, human security is in itself a holistic paradigm which offers opportunities for creative synthesis and theoretical eclecticism. As for its policy utility, the concept addresses issues that the narrow definition of security no longer reflects in terms of real world development.

Tadjbakhsh and Chenoy (2007) argue that governments can no longer survive - much less achieve legitimacy - solely by addressing economic growth; nor can they maintain social and political stability solely by providing for defense against external military threats. Democratitisation empowers new actors, such as civil society, that must be accounted for in the security framework (ibid).

A South Asian scholar Kanti Bajpai opines that threats to security and capacities to deal with them vary according to time, so that a universalist conceptual definition is a misguided idea. Human security study as a policy science must focus on audits of threats and possible responses. Having commissioned unpublished public opinion survey conducted among 10,000 people in India on national and human security and how insecure Indians feel, Bajpai proposes to draw a Human Security Index based on eleven measures of threats (Tadjbakhsh and Chenoy 2007).

Keith Krause argues that the focus should be on freedom from fear because firstly, a broad definition is simply an itemised wish-list and secondly, there are no clear gains from linking security and development. Thus, the narrow definition of human security allows for clear policy goals and actions to combat direct threats to the individual (such as organised violence) (Krause 2004).

Another advocator of human security, Ramesh Thakur, states that human security is improved when the 'quality of life' of people in a society can be upgraded; that is, the enhancement of what he calls 'human welfare'. It is threatened when this 'quality of life', which is left open to definition, is degraded by threats such as unchecked demographic growth, diminished resources and scarcity, or access issues and other global threats. The reformulation of national security into human security has 'profound consequences' for international relations, foreign policy and people's conception of other people's cultures. The traditional security conception privileges the military in terms of resource allocation but non-traditional concerns merit the gravity of the security level (Tadjbakhsh and Chenoy 2007).

Some scholars even question the academic usability of

human security. The prominent security scholar Barry Buzan writes that no clear analytical value is derived from the concept of human security which confuses international security with social security and civil liberties. Human security thus presents a reductionist vision of international security and hence has limited academic usability. The concept collapses the differences between international and domestic security agendas without analysing existing linkages. Yet the concept may allow for discussion of human rights issues which were previously considered sensitive, but this amounts to little more than 'political pondering' (Buzan 2004).

Another security writer, Rolland Paris, opines that human security discourse is currently dominated by 'circular discussion' deliberating definition. She further expresses that the vagueness is very problematic for academic study given the inability to analytically separate the components of the concept, rendering a determination of causal relationships impossible. Ultimately, the vagueness of the definition serves a political purpose in uniting a diverse coalition of actors (Tadjbakhsh and Chenoy 2007).

Even amongst scholars who support the concept of human security there are minimalist and maximalist approaches. Most academics support the broad view of human security and recognise the maximalist definition with its added value including going beyond classical violent threats (Tadjbakhsh and Chenoy 2007). MacLean highlighted human security does not merely 'envelop' matters of individual benefit (such as education, health care, protection from crime) but rather denotes protection from the unstructured violence that often accompanies many aspects of non-traditional security, such as violence emanating from environmental scarcity, or mass migration (MacLean 2002).

2.2 The evolving process of human security

The United Nations has shifted its strategy for dealing with conflict from containment to prevention after the collapse of the USSR and the end of the Cold War. In a euphoric mood after the end of the bi-polar world system, then Secretary-General of the United Nations Boutros Boutros- Ghali issued an agenda for peace, peace-making and peace-keeping;[1] however, it was dashed by the proliferation of a number of conflicts in many parts of the world. Most of these conflicts were internal and were caused by what were seen as non-traditional threats such as internal socio-political conditions, rapidly deteriorating economic conditions, environmental threats, identity politics and powerful organised crime rings (Buzan et al. 1998). The UN has since this time focused on people as the referent object of security, whereas earlier its focus was on the state. The adoption of the 1948 Universal Declaration of Human Rights and the subsequent creation of the International Covenant on Civil and Political Rights (1966), the International Covenant on Economic, Social and Cultural Rights (1966) and the Convention on the Rights of the Child (1989) can all be seen as elements of this alternative perception of security. Each of these three covenants focuses on various vulnerabilities and threats experienced by individuals. The UN's adaptation of these covenants laid the ground work for broadening the concept into new areas more directly linked to people's concerns.

The concept of human security was first cultivated by former Pakistani Finance Minister Mahbul ul Haq, with the support of Nobel Laureate Amartya Sen, with the launching of UNDP's 1994 Human Development Report (HDR). It was the first document which articulated the issue in conceptual terms with clear policies and programmes. The 1994 HDR was the product of a high-level roundtable organised on 'Economics of Peace' in January 1990 in Costa Rica, in which Mr. Ul Haq and many others participated. At the end of the roundtable, a statement was issued which stated that the post-Cold War world needed "a new concept of global security" with the "orientation of defense and foreign policy objectives changed from an almost exclusive concern with military security [...] to a broader concern for the overall security of individuals

---

1 See the statement issued by Secretary-General of the UN Broutros-Ghali in 1992, accessed on 15 January 2012, http://www.foreignaffairs.com/articles/52044/fouad-ajami/the-mark-of-bosnia-boutros-ghalis- reign-of-indifference

from social violence, economic distress and environmental degradation. This would require paying attention to the causes of individual insecurity and the obstacles to the realisation of the full potential of individuals".[2]

Likewise, the HDR states that the traditional approach of security has been widened to incorporate the safety of individuals and groups from threats such as hunger, disease and political instability and protection from "sudden and hurtful disruption in patterns of daily life" (UNDP 1994). The report further identified seven core elements of human security: economic security, food security, health security, environmental security, personal security, community security and political security (ibid). The evolution of human security also had the support of various countries including Canada, Japan and Norway. These three governments led the way in institutionalising human security concerns into their respective foreign policies. Huliaras and Tzifakis (2007) emphasised that human security means safety from both violent and non-violent threats. It is a condition or state of being characterised by freedom from pervasive threats to people's rights, their safety, even their lives. Likewise, the Ministry of Foreign Affairs of Japan urges states, international organisations, non- governmental organisations and civil society to work towards eliminating threats to each and every person.

2.3 Global commissions, reports and human security

It is important to note that the linkages between human security and peace and development issues are not new. Issues of development, peace and security have been on the agenda since the last quarter of the twentieth century. Such linkages can be found in numbers of reports produced by high profile global commissions in the 1980s and 1990s. Some of these important reports include:

The first global commission known as the Brandt Commission

---

[2] See the statement of the North South Roundtable 1990, UNDP, Human Development Report Office, National Human Development Reports Unit, http//hdr.undp.org accessed 18 January 2012.

report North-South: A Programme for Survival, published in 1980, called for a new concept of security which would transcend the narrow notions of military defense and look more towards conditions conducive to peaceful relations (Brandt Commission 1980). The Commission criticised the military-focused security system which ignored the development agenda, particularly in developing countries. It noted that the glaring disparity between the living conditions of the rich and those of the poor would ultimately lead to crisis. Further elaboration on the question of the survival of humankind was provided in the next Brandt Commission report of 1983, entitled Common Crisis, North-South: Cooperation for World Recovery. In the report's introduction, Brandt argued that we may be arming ourselves to death without actually going to war - by strangling our economies and refusing to invest in the future (ibid). The crisis facing the human race, Brandt stated, would lead to the development of 'common interests' between the industrialised North and the underdeveloped South. In reference to the growing gap, the report argues that the rich have a moral obligation to the poor, in particular towards those whose conditions have become more desperate. Brandt suggested that deepening cooperation in order to eliminate the situation in which a child dies of hunger of disease every two seconds (ibid).

Immediately after the Brandt Commission Report, another commission was formed to address the growing issue of disarmament and development: The Report of the Palme Commission in 1982 which stressed the need to identify the relationship between disarmament and development and its resultant impacts on security. The report further noted that security could not be attained through nuclear détente. This argument contradicts the Realist view of security which was the dominant school of thought during the Cold War period. The report focused on disarmament, development and capacity building. The Report concludes that the world can either continue to pursue the arms race with characteristic vigour or move consciously and with deliberate speed towards a more stable and balanced social and economic development. It cannot do both (Palme Commission 1982). The report argued for disarmament and security to prevent Third World countries from further decline. The report argued for "common security, with socioeconomic and political rather than military factors as the basis for enhancing it. Common security requires that people live in dignity and peace, that they have enough to eat, are able to find work and live in a world without poverty and destitution" (ibid). The Palme Commission's recommendations on common security are very much reflected in the discourse on international relations, especially after the end of the Cold War.

In the late 1980s, when growing militarisation and the arms race was impacting on development expenditure (particularly in developing countries and by the most authoritarian and dictatorial regimes), another international commission was formed to recommend concrete steps to curb growing military expenditure. The Commission, which was initiated in 1987 by the then Prime Minister of Malaysia Mahathir Mohammad, aimed to examine the problems in the countries of the South in order to help the people and governments of the South to be more effective in overcoming their numerous problems, in achieving their ambitions, in developing their countries in freedom and in improving the lives and living conditions of their people (The South Commission 1990).

The report stressed expanding South-South cooperation, clearly stating that the responsibility for the development of the South lies in the South and in the hands of the people in the South (The South Commission 1990). The focus of the report was on the pervasive impact of militarisation on development, the human and social costs of the arms race, the abandonment of democracy and human rights, the breeding of corruption and the perverse implications for political systems of the growth of military culture. Military expenditure in developing countries on average amounted to 25 per cent of the world's total of the time. Their arms imports alone averaged USD 22 billion per year during the 1980s. But only a few developing countries rightly claim that their military expenditure is proportionate either to any external threats or to the resources at their disposal (ibid). The increasing military expenditures were reflected in the development crisis of developing countries. The Report recommended "development as the first thing first", in order to fulfill the basic needs of the mass of the people and make a firm commitment to the removal of poverty and hunger (ibid).

After publication of the UNDP's Human Security Report in 1994, another report was published in 1995 under the leadership of Shridath Ramphal on Global Security. The Ramphal Commission on Global Governance report, called 'Our Neighbourhood', stated that global security must be broadened from the traditional focus on the security of states to include the security of people and the security of the planet (Ramphal Commission 1995), thus presaging the intensive link that was to develop between security and the environment. This wider idea of security has gradually drawn a large number of scholars and institutions across the world to examine the empirical and operational validity in a range of issues including that of security related to human, energy, environment and food. The Report further emphasised that global security policy should be to prevent conflict and war and to maintain the integrity of the planet's life-support systems by eliminating the economic, social and environmental, political and military conditions that generate threats to the security of people and the planet (ibid).

In 2000, the UN formed another commission to submit a report particularly focusing on the UN's role on Peace Making, Peace Building and Peace Keeping. As UN has been engaging in this area for several decades, it wanted to review its work at the beginning of new century. For this, it formed a commission under the leadership of Mr. Lakhdar Brahimi. Known as the Brahimi Report on UN Peacekeeping Operation (Brahimi Report 2000), the report emphasises the role of the UN Peacekeeping Operations in making and reinforcing peace and security in various parts of the world. It also stresses the necessity of restructuring the peacekeeping system under the United Nations. The paper engages with practical operational issues such as the composition and mandate of a potential UN standing army, as well as policy-level changes considering the new format of conflict.

Another key global initiative in the area of human security was taken in 2003 with the formation of the Commission on

Human Security. The 'Human Security Now' (CHS 2003) report is another contribution towards making human security the focus issue in security. The Commission's report focuses on promoting democratic principles as a step towards attaining human security and development. The Report draws policy conclusions on a variety of subjects, including protecting people in violent conflict, the proliferation of arms, encouraging fair trade and markets to benefit the extremely poor, ensuring universal access to basic health care and universalising basic education (Brahimi Report 2000).

Furthermore, the UN Secretary-General's High-level Panel on Threats, Challenges and Changes report, A More Secure World: Our Shared Responsibility (UN 2004), focuses on the changing nature of threats on security. The Report identified six major challenges in security that include economic and social threats such as poverty, deadly infectious diseases, environmental degradation, inter-state conflict, internal conflict, civil war and genocide, weapons of mass destruction, terrorism and trans-national organised crime. The Report states that development has to be the first line of defence for a collective security that takes prevention seriously.

Combating poverty will not only save millions of lives, but also strengthen states' capacity to combat terrorism, organised crime and proliferation. Development makes everyone more secure (ibid).

Another development towards promoting human security by linking it with the overall development issues is the 2005 UN Secretary-General's Report in Larger Freedom that deals extensively with threats to security. It states that all people have the right to security and to development (UN 2005). The Report identifies various challenges and threats to security and also provides mechanisms and methods in respond to those challenges.

All these reports have contributed to the changing nature of security threat perceptions at the global level and have helped identify key challenges. They also clearly provide policies for dealing with these challenges by linking security with poverty reduction and socio-economic development, environmental protection, promoting human rights and democracy, fighting against terrorism, organised crime and threats from contagious diseases and the negative impacts of climate change. All the reports recommend certain policy initiatives and strategies which, if taken on board, could significantly improve the situation of human security globally. All these arguments have a common element: the shift from state-centric security systems to collective security. Focus has been given to the economic development, particularly in developing countries.

The Report also warn that insecurity emanates from vulnerabilities and that vulnerabilities need not necessarily derive from external factors but also from internal factors. Global security vulnerabilities today have not come from somewhere else; they are basically due to the failure of the state(s). Furthermore, this problem has been heightened by the failure of state machineries and governance systems to deliver goods and services, bringing elements of anarchy and chaos into state management.

2.4 Human security in South Asia

The concept of human security is fast emerging as a major discussion point in South Asian security debates. The biggest regional challenge to human security issues is the static mindset of policy-making elites who continuously put emphasis on the military aspects of security which better serve their interests. Bajpai traces the genealogy of the concept of human security to Mahbub-ul-Haq's work at the United Nations Development Programme (UNDP) and the Canadian government, as well as to academics who have led a middle powers' initiative. The individual is the central variable of human security (Bajpai 2000).

Commenting on the nuclearisation of South Asia, Bidwai opines that embracing the doctrine of nuclear deterrence means seeking security through insecurity, terror and threat to cause havoc on a mass scale with pitiless disregard for life (Bidwai 2000). On the deteriorating democratic polity in South Asian countries, Chari states that South Asian politics are in a state of violent flux (Chari 2000). The weakening of secular ideology has strengthened religion-based parties, leading to a struggle between liberal and revivalist sentiments. Lama holds the view that the region's overuse of resources invariably leads to questions relating to sustainability of both livelihood and ecological balance. Among the types of migratory phenomena that characterise South Asia, the most notable has been the one triggered by poverty-related displacement, which is often gradual and sometimes visible if triggered by environmental dislocation (Lama 2003).

Countries in the South created institutional mechanisms to deal with the region's increasing non-traditional security threats a long time ago; however, due to the failure of their implementation by the ruling elites, the region remains one of the most vulnerable in the world.

Activities which intend to provoke a state of terror in the general public for political purposes are regarded as terrorist activities. In recent decades, the world has been marred by an increase of such activities and South Asia is no exception. Despite the volatile situation, the region has still failed to agree on a common definition and joint action plan to prevent terrorism. The SAARC convention on terrorism, which was signed in 1987, still remains non-operational as some member countries have failed to legislate domestic enabling laws, despite the fact that at the Islamabad Summit in January 2004, governments of the regions went as far as to add protocol to control the financing of terrorist activities in the region (Khatri 2004). After 19 years, the convention still remains a paper document that has little impact on development in the region. The intra-state conflicts in South Asia have been pervasive. This region has come to be known as having some of the largest numbers of armed groups, the longest insurgencies and the rising number of fatalities resulting from terrorist- related violence in the world. According to the report 'Military Balance 2002-2003', prepared by the International Institute of Strategic Studies, Bangladesh, out of the 18 identified groups, three are in Bangladesh, eight in India, five in India/Pakistan and one each in Nepal and Sri Lanka (ibid).

Most of the groups are transnational in character, which often leads to accusations of cross-border terrorism. The same report claimed that conflicts in South Asia have lasted longer than in any other region of the world. Of eight armed conflicts in the region, only one (East Pakistan) ended in the same calendar year and another (Baluch) lasted for 4 years (1973-77). The others have lasted more than 10 years including the Chittagong Hill Tract Movement in Bangladesh, Mizo, Naga, the Assam and the Maoist movements in India and Ealam in Sri Lanka. Similarly, the number of fatalities resulting from terrorist-related violence is large: the report stated that Asia accounts for 75 per cent of all terrorism casualties worldwide. It is interesting to note that in South Asia alone, the annual number of fatalities in terrorist-related violence surpasses the death toll in the Middle East, which is often seen as the traditional place of terrorism. Even after 9/11, the number of fatalities in terrorist-related violence has increased significantly in the region. A recent report identified at least 54 groups that are proscribed under various terrorism laws in South Asian countries, including 32 in India, one in Nepal, 11 in Pakistan, one in Sri Lanka and nine in Bangladesh.[3]

Khatri (2004) emphasised that the non-traditional security approach is increasingly gaining currency in South Asia due to two factors. The first has to do with the shifting emphasis on security studies from inter-state to intra-state issues (Khatri 2004). A compelling reason for the paradigm shift was the recognition that inter-states wars alone do not account for the insecurity that nations face today. Between 1990 and 2002, there were 58 different major armed conflicts in 46 different locations throughout the world, out of which all but three were internal conflicts (Eriksson et.al 2003). Intra-state conflicts, along with the tendency of states to inflict violence on their own citizens, accounted for the largest number of deaths. According to one estimate, some 151 million persons were killed by governments,

---

3 See P.V. Raman, 'RCSS Data Chapter on Profiles of "Terrorist" Groups in South Asia.' This is part of the RCSS project on "Understanding and Responding to 'Terrorism in the South' that is currently being completed by the Center.

in addition to the death toll from war and civil war (which is said to account another 39 million). A majority of deaths were perpetrated by governments on their own citizens; among them totalitarian states was responsible for 84 per cent of these deaths and authoritarian states for most of the rest (Rummel 1994). The situation has been no different in South Asia, which is also marred by cross-border migration, the trafficking of women and refugee crises (Sabur 1999).

The conflictual situation of the region has triggered many other social and environmental crises. For instance, due to the escalation of violence in rural areas, forced migration has been taking place which has precipitated large numbers of internal refugees in the region. Environmental insecurity is another serious threat that the region is facing today. Due to growing urbanisation and the depletion of natural resources, people are finding it hard to get basic facilities such as drinkable water, public spaces and fresh air to breathe. As a result of the lack of these basic needs, countries of the region are facing serious health-related crises. The challenge of 'non- traditional security threats' that South Asian countries are experiencing today is immense and there is a need to take action at both regional and local levels.

2.5 Conceptual critiques of human security

Prominent academicians such as Khong (2001), Ayoob (2004), Paris (2001), Mac Farlane (2004) and Krause (2004) have extensively criticised the concept of human security. Critics basically point out that human security is a vague concept, claiming it is too broad and does not have clear parameters. Furthermore, it involves renaming many problems that have already been recognised in other context. Human security proponents make dangerous attempts to prove false causal assumptions linking socio- economic issues to political outcomes. As Ayoob argues, what is gained by combining these issues under a new label (Ayoob 2004). Similarly criticising the vagueness of the concept, Paris believes that human security does not have any definite parameters, therefore anything and everything could be considered a risk to security (Paris 2001). Human security, when broadened to include issues like climate change, terrorism and threats from disease, complicates the international machinery for reaching decisions or taking action on the threats identified (Owens and Arneil 1999).

Another critic, Buzan (1998) argues that human security as a concept aspires to explain almost everything and consequently, in reality explains nothing. It is academically confusing because it seems to support all hypotheses and their opposites at the same time (Paris 2001). Human security is a very complex issue and it makes security more complicated without having explanatory power. Khong argue that if theory building is difficult enough in security studies with 200 states, what do we learn from the behaviour of 6 billion diverse people? (Khong 2001). Critics further argue that securitisation means prioritising an issue, making it worthy of special attention and resources, including an immediate resolution through possible military means. Consequently, the prioritisation of 'soft' issues takes away from the urgency of traditional security issues (ibid). Similarly, human security also challenges the sovereignty of a state's role to provide security to its citizens. Furthermore, critics say that human security challenges the role of the sovereign state as the sole provider of security. It is a new tool for existing governing agencies to shape and control civil population. Any expansion of security definitions will result in an increased use of force, justified by the international community as their responsibility, even though human security is regarded as an individual- centric approach and its focus is on people rather than the state. However, as each and every person is a citizen of a certain state, without the role of the state it would be impossible to create a security environment for that particular citizen of that particular country. Therefore, as Buzan further argues, human security remains state-centric despite the supranational dimensions of the concept, allowing for the prominent role of the state as a necessary condition for individual security (Buzan et al. 1998).

2.6 Conclusion

The literature of human security has evolved over the years from an early focus on incorporating individual- and people-centric approaches into the definition of 'security' to a new focus on how social, economic and environmental change can cause or amplify violent conflict. More radical critiques have emerged. Feminists, critical theorists and postmodernists argue that dominant groups within societies have imposed particular interpretations of 'reality'. These have the effect of promoting interests of some sections of society at the expense of others, underpinning a fundamentally unjust political and economic order (Sheehan 2006).

Despite such diverse - and at times, heterogeneous - perspectives on the definition of human security threats, human security still represents some strikingly common features. Firstly, it is not state-centric and does not substantiate state-centric theories. Rather, it is a people-centric view which includes threats that are perceived as threats to the safety of human beings and individuals. It, at the same time, does not eliminate the idea of state security. Secondly, human security threats have no particular geographical focus. As the issues are more human-centric, non- traditional challenges, the threats and dangers are multidimensional and multidirectional, requiring a multilateral approach to deal with. Thirdly, since the threats and dangers are diverse and related with development, democracy and environmental protection, these issues cannot be managed by traditional defense policies or military-based strategies alone. Military organisations may have a role, but effective management requires the involvement of a range of non-military actors including the state, civil society groups, NGOs, INGOs, the UN, international financial institutions, regional organisations and international organisations.

References

Ayoob M. 2004. Third World Perspectives on Humanitarian Intervention and International Administration. *Global Governance* 10: 99-118.

Bajpai K. 2002. Beyond Comprehensive Security: Human Security. *In:* Bajpai K, editor. *Comprehensive Security: Perspectives from India's Regions*. New Delhi: New India Foundation.

Bajpai K. 2000. *Human Security: Concept and Measurement.* Kroc Institute Occasional Paper 19.:OP:1. Notre Dame: Kroc Institute for International Peace Studies. Also available at: http://www.hegoa.ehu.es/dossierra/seguridad/Human_security_concept_and_measurement.pdf; accessed on 12 August 2012.

Bidwai P. 2000. Pokhran in Retrospect: The High Costs of Nuclearism. *The Times of India*. New Delhi, 13 May.

Brahimi Report. 2000. *The Report of the Panel on United Nations Peace Operations* New York: United Nations.

Brandt Commission. 1980. *North South: A Programme for Survival.* Cambridge: The MIT Press.

Buzan B, Waever O, de Wilde J. 1998. *Security: A New Framework For Analysis*. Boulder: Lynne Rienner.

Buzan B. 2004. A Reductionist, Idealistic Notion that Adds Little Analytical Value. *In* Burgess P, Owens T, editors. *What is Human Security? Comments by 21 authors, Special Issue of Security Dialogue* 35(3): 369-70.

CGG [Commission on Global Governance]. 1995. *Our Global Neighbourhood: The Report of the Commission on Global Governance.* Oxford: Oxford University Press.

Chari PR, Gupta S. 2003. *Human Security in South Asia: Gender, Energy, Migration and Globalisation*. New Delhi: Social Science Press.

Chari PR. 2001. *Security & Governance in South Asia*. New Delhi: Manoharan.

CHS [Commission on Human Security]. 2003. *Human Security Now*. New York: Commission on Human Security/UNOPS (United Nations Office for. Project Services). Also available at: http://www.humansecurity-chs.org/ finalreport/index.html; accessed on 3 March 2012.

Dabelko G, Lonergan S, Matthew R. 2000. *State-of-the-art review on environment, security and development co-operation* Paris: Organisation for Economic Co-operation and Development (OECD). Also available at: http://www. iisd.org/pdf/2002/envsec_oecd_review.pdf; accessed on 22 January 2012.

Eriksson M, Sollenberg M, Wallenstein P. 2003. Patterns of major armed conflict, 1990-2002. In: *SIPRI Yearbook 2003. Armament, Disarmament and International Security*. Oxford: Oxford University Press.

Hammerstad A. 2000. Whose Security? UNHCR, Refugee Protection and State Security after the Cold War. *Security Dialogue* 31 (4):391-403.

Howard M. 1983. *The Causes of War. London:* Temple Smith. Also available at:http://www.un.org/peace/reports/peace_operations/; accessed on 22 February 2012.

Huliaras A, Tzifakis N. 2007. Contextual Approach to Human Security. *International Journal* 62(3): *559-575.* Also available at: http:// ekemprogram. org/ seeurope_ en/ images/ stories/ pdf/ contextualapproachestohumansecurity.pdf; accessed 22 February 2012.

Khatri S. 2004. What is New Security Agenda for South Asia? *In:* Baral LR, editor. *Non-Traditional Security State, Society, and Democracy in South Asia.* New Delhi: Adroit Publishers.

Khong YF. 2001. Human Security: A Shotgun Approach to Alleviating Human Misery? *Global Governance* 7(3): 231-236.

Krause K. 2004. The Key to a Powerful Agenda, if Properly Defined. *In* Burgess P, Owens T, editors. *What is Human Security? Comments by 21 authors, Special Issue of Security Dialogue* 35 (3): 367-368.

Lama MP. 2003. Poverty, Migration and Conflict: Challenges to Human Security in South Asia. *In:* Chari PR, Gupta S, editors. *Human Security in South Asia: Energy, Gender, Migration and Globalisation.* New Delhi: Social Science Press.

Little R. 1981. Ideology and Change. *In:* Buzan B, Jones RJB, editors. *Change and Study of International Relations.* London: Frances Printer.

Macdonald H. 1981. The Place of Strategy and the Idea of Security. *Millennium - Journal of International Studies* 10 (3):229-239.

MacFarlane SN. 2004. A Useful Concept that Risks Losing its Political Salience. *In* Burgess P, Owens T, editors. *What is Human Security? Comments by 21 authors, Special Issue of Security Dialogue* 35 (3): 368-369.

Mack A. 2004. A Signifier of Share Values. *In:* Burgess P, Owens T, editors. *What is Human Security? Comments by 21 authors. Special Issue of Security Dialogue* 35 (3): 366-367.

Mathew J. 1989. Redefining Security. *Foreign Affairs* 68 (2):162-177.

McLean G. 2002. Redefining Security Policy: Canada's Human Security Initiative. *In* D. Mutimer, editor. *A New Canadian International Security Policy?.* Toronto: Center for International and Security Studies.

Myers N. 1993. *Ultimate security: The environmental basis of political stability.* New York: W.W. Norton and Co.

Nef J. 1999. *Human Security and Mutual Vulnerability: The Global Political Economy of Development and Underdevelopment.* [2nd edition]. Ottawa: International Development Research Centre.

Owens S, Arniel B. 1999. The Human Security Paradigm Shift: A New Lens on Canadian Foreign Policy? Report of the University of British Columbia Symposium on Human Security. *In:* Tehranian M, editor. *Worlds Apart: Human Security and Global Governance.* London: I. B. Tauris.

Palme Commission. 1982. *Common Security: A Blueprint for Survival.* New York: Simon and Schuster.

Paris R. 2001. Human Security: Paradigm Shift or Hot Air?. *International Security* 26(2): 87-102.

Ramphal Commission. 1995. *Our Neighbourhood.* New York: Oxford University Press.

Rummel RJ. 1994. Dimensions of Conflict Behaviour within and between Nations. *In: General Systems: Yearbook of the Society for General Systems* VIII 8 (1963): 1-50.

Sabur AKM A. 1999. Indo-Pakistan Security Relationship and the Kargil Crisis. *BIISS Journal* 20 (3): 235-270.

Sabur AKM A. 2003. Evolving a Theoretical Perspective on Human Security: The South Asian Context. *In:* Chari PR, Gupta S, editors. *Human Security in South Asia: Gender, Energy, Migration and Globalisation.* New Delhi: Social Science Press.

Sheehan M. 2006. *International Security: An Analytical Survey.* New Delhi: Viva Books.

Tadjbakhsh S, Chenoy A. 2007. *Human Security Concepts and Implications.* London: Routledge.

Thakur R. 2000. *Security in the New Millennia. RCSS Newsletter 6(4).* Colombo: Regional Centre for Strategic Studies.

The Government of Canada. 1999. *Human Security: Safety for People in a Changing World.* Also available at: http//www.defiat.maeci.gc.ca/foreign/humansecurity/secur-e.htm; accessed on 12 January 2012.

The South Commission. 1990. *The Challenges in the South.* New York: Oxford University Press.

Thomas C. 2004. A Bridge Betweenbetween the Interconnected Challenges Confronting the World. *In*: Burgess P, Owens T, editors. *What is Human Security? Comments by 21 Authors, Special Issue of Security Dialogue* 35(3): 353–354.

UN [United Nations]. 2004. *A more secure world: Our shared responsibility Report of the High-level Panel on Threats, Challenges and Change.* New York: United Nations. Also available at: http://www.un.org/secureworld/; accessed on 3 March 2012.

UN [United Nations]. 2005. *In larger freedom: towards development, security and human rights for all.* Fifty-ninth session Agenda items 45 and 55. New York: United Nations.

UNDP [United Nations Development Programme]. 1994. *Human Development Report*. New York: Oxford University Press.

Waltz KN. 1979. *Theory of International Politics*. Reading, Mass: Addison-Wesley Pub. Co.

Yeo D. 2004. *Whither Human Security? An Argument for Complementarily and Co-operation in Canadian and Japanese Human Security Policies*. Also available at: http://www.humansecuritygateway.com/document; accessed on 15 January 2012.

****

Chapter 3

Poverty: A threat to human security

Yuba Raj Khatiwada, PhD

Overview

Nepal has long been facing a high incidence of poverty, a low level of human development and weak human security propelled by the decade- long armed conflict, disasters, climate change and vulnerability. The country's low economic growth rate, unequal distribution of productive assets and income and limited social security coverage means many people are vulnerable. In addition, amid weak institutions to protect human life various ethnic and other forms of violence have undermined human rights of people. As such, poverty has been both the cause and the result of weak human security conditions, even after the victory of the Nepali people over the centuries-old feudal system and other forms of exploitation.

Despite Nepal being an independent country for centuries, its people have never been free; not foreign powers, but their own rulers have suppressed and exploited them. Nepal has experienced many political revolutions from 1950 to 2006. They encompass freedom from family autocratic rule, the restoration of multi-party democracy, the ousting of the monarchy and the evolution of the nation into a federal democratic republic. These changes clearly reflect the Nepali people's untiring struggle for democracy with the expectation that a new political regime will make people free from fear and want, deliver development to people and empower them. Still, many aspirations for development are yet to be achieved.

At present, every fourth Nepali lives in absolute poverty (CBS 2011a). Such abject poverty is often related to inequality and is frequently accompanied by a sense of powerlessness and exclusion. Conflict has become both the cause and the consequence of poverty. Poverty is also the cause and the consequence of a massive human rights deficit. Along with many other factors, abject poverty, weak human rights conditions and a low level of economic empowerment have undermined human security in Nepal.

Nepal is also far behind in terms of human development. As measured by the Human Development Index (HDI), Nepal is at the bottom of medium HDI countries, a position which also reflects the country's human security situation. As such, human development and human security are related issues as the latter is related to downside risks of well-being and the former is an upward-oriented concept for the same. While human development aims to expand people's opportunities in order to make progress fair to everyone, human security deliberately focuses on downside risks and takes into account a variety of elements that inhibit human development (JICA 2006). Since want and fear the two components of human security (UNDP 1994) are inseparable phenomena, the promotion of human development and security require an integrated approach that incorporates both of these factors in order to create an environment for dignified and decent living.

Human security can never be achieved without meeting the basic needs for decent living. It has to emanate from political, social and economic empowerment of the people rather than from a welfare program of the state. Safety from the threats of hunger, disease, crime and repression, as well as protection from sudden and harmful disruptions in the pattern of people's daily lives - whether in our homes, jobs, communities or environment - can only be achieved by strengthening human capabilities and empowering people to live a dignified, healthy and decent life.

This article is organised in the following manner. Section two delves into the broader concept of poverty, human development and human security and the interrelationship between these phenomena. Section three highlights the linkage between poverty and human security in Nepal. Section four considers the environment as a link between human security and poverty. Section five is focused on the regional and global context of linking poverty and human security. The final section, Section six, concludes the chapter.

3.2 Interrelationship between poverty, human development and human security

3.2.1 Poverty: A multi-dimensional concept

Poverty is often narrowly defined as a lack of essential items such as food, clothing, water and shelter needed for proper living. WSSD (1996) broadly defined poverty as a condition characterised by the severe deprivation of basic human needs, including food, safe drinking water, sanitation facilities, health, shelter, education and information. To measure poverty in any statistical way, however, more rigid definitions have been used including the concepts of 'relative poverty' and 'absolute poverty' which are based on income or consumption.[1] The United Nations defines poverty as a denial of choices and opportunities; a violation of human dignity, which constitutes a lack of basic capacity to participate effectively in society along with insecurity, powerlessness and the exclusion of individuals, households and communities (UN 1998).

The World Bank (WB 2000) defines poverty as deprivation in wellbeing, comprising many dimensions. It includes low

---

1 Relative poverty is the simplest way to determine the extent of poverty in individual countries. It refers to a lack of usual or socially acceptable levels of resources or income compared to others within a society or country. Absolute poverty, however, sets a 'poverty line' at a certain amount of income or consumption per year, based on the estimated value of a 'basket of goods' (food, housing, clothing, etc.) necessary for proper living.

income and the inability to acquire the basic goods and services necessary for survival with dignity. Poverty also encompasses low levels of health and education, poor access to clean water and sanitation, inadequate physical security, lack of voice and insufficient capacity and opportunity to better one's life.

Just as defining poverty is a debated issue, so too is its measurement. The dollar-a-day definition of absolute poverty has been globally taken as an indicator for international and inter-temporal poverty monitoring. Besides, countries have their own poverty lines defined in terms of the fulfillment of daily calorie requirements and other basic needs, an idea comparable to defining poverty in terms of income or consumption. But the wider definition of poverty encompasses, along with income or assets, other well-being indicators such as shelter, education, health and water. A lack of choices, voicelessness, exclusion and disempowerment are also often linked with poverty.

Inclusion of the above-mentioned indicators under the measurement of poverty is, however, not easy, despite several efforts made towards this. Recently, the Oxford Poverty and Human Development Initiative (OPHI) constructed the Multi-dimensional Poverty Index (MPI) to measure poverty in a broader way (Alkire and Santos 2010). Following the Human Development Index (HDI) and related indices, MPI has covered three dimensions of poverty - health, education and standards of living - with 10 indicators, two each for health and education and six for standard of living dimension.[2] Conceptually, MPI has a foundation similar to the Human Development Index (HDI) or Human Poverty Index (HPI), but operationally it belongs to the family of income- or consumption-based poverty measures. Either way, if we closely look into the components

---

2 The 10 indicators used for depicting the three dimensions of MPI are as follows: (a) Health (child mortality and malnutrition); (b) education (enrolment from one to eight years of education mean years of schooling); and (c) standard of living (access to (i) drinking water, (ii) sanitation, (iii) electricity, (iv) types of cooking fuel (v) floor, (vi) ownership of any of seven assets including radio, television, phone, bike, motor bike, car or tractor.

of multiple poverty, they are similar to the components of the evolving concept of human security.

The above-mentioned definitions give different meanings to the intensity of poverty in Nepal. Based on the dollar-a-day definition, which has now been revised up to 1.25 dollars per day, 19.7 per cent of the households in Nepal were in 2010 categorised as living in absolute poverty. According to the national poverty line definition, the same accounts for 25 per cent (NPC 2010a). Following (Alkire and Santos 2010) Multidimensional Poverty Index approach, as many as 65 per cent of households live in poverty. As these poverty numbers are derived from different definitions, they are not directly comparable; they only show that as we move towards a wider definition of poverty, a larger number of Nepali households fall under the poverty category.

3.2.2 Human security: An evolving concept of well-being

The Commission on Human Security[3] defines human security as the protection of 'the vital core of all human lives in ways that enhance human freedom and fulfillment' (CHS 2003), Human security thus means protecting fundamental freedom - protecting people from critical threats and situations that menace their well-being. In a broader sense, it implies creating political, social, environmental, economic, military and cultural systems that together give people the building blocks for survival, livelihoods and dignity. Human security - far more than the absence of violent conflict - encompasses human rights, good governance and access to economic opportunity, education and health care. It is a concept that comprehensively addresses both 'freedom from fear' and 'freedom from want' and thus creates an environment for faster poverty reduction and human development.

---

3 In response to issues such as global insecurity and poverty, the violation of human rights, at the United Nations Millennium Summit the UN Secretary-General Kofi Annan called upon the world community to advance the twin goals of 'freedom from want' and 'freedom from fear'. As a response, the Commission on Human Security (CHS) was established to propose a concrete programme of action to address critical and pervasive threats to human security, among others.

Conventionally, human security has been shaped by the physical threat to life mostly emanating from conflict or war; and states have sought arms to protect their citizen and the nation. This was especially true in the post-Second World War period when countries were still obsessed with the threat of war in a highly polarised world. With the Cold War obsession over, for most people today, a feeling of insecurity arises more from worries about daily life than from the threat of war or conflict. Food, shelter, employment, income, health, environment and freedom from crime are some of the emerging dimensions of human security all over the world. The genesis of this concept has emerged ever since the evolution of the United Nations and world leaders saying that the battle of peace has to be fought on two fronts: (i) the security front where victory implies freedom from fear and (ii) the economic and social front where victory means freedom from want. Only victory on both fronts can assure the world of an enduring peace; no provisions that can be written into the UN Charter will make the world secure from war if people have no security in their homes and their jobs.[4]

The absence of insecurity and threats to life could be taken as the simplest definition of human security. Life security incorporates freedom from 'fear' (of physical abuse, violence, persecution or death) and from 'want' (of gainful employment, food and health). The notion of human security therefore is to identify threats, avoid them when possible and mitigate their effects when they do occur. This ideal means preventing and mitigating widespread insecurity resulting from armed conflict, human rights violations and massive underdevelopment. This broadened concept of human security encompasses the notion of safety that goes beyond the concept of mere physical security in the traditional sense and states that people's livelihoods should be guaranteed through social policies against sudden disruptions to living a free and decent life. The Human Development Report 1994 (UNDP 1994), which treated human security as an extension of the human development paradigm, defines human security as encompassing economy, food, health, environment,

---

4 See The Report of State Secretary of The United States' Government on the outcome of the San Francisco Conference, June 1945.

security of persons, community security and freedom to engage in political activities.

The human security approach to human development thus is concerned, along with gross violations of human rights, armed conflicts and natural disasters with wide-ranging aspects of underdevelopment namely inequality, public health service deficits, international crime, population growth and environmental degradation. A high prevalence of disease and poor health in a country harms economic performance while higher life expectancy, a key indicator of health status, stimulates economic growth.[5]

3.2.3 MDGs: Integrating poverty and human security in development strategy

By the middle of the 1990s, people had started to realise that the structural adjustment policies of the Breton Woods institutions of the 1970s and 1980s, which were based on the trickle-down approach to development, failed to transform the economies as well as the social conditions in the global South. Rather, such policies increased income disparity between and within states. The human development approach which has evolved since the early 1990s attempted to address this challenge. Subsequently, human security entered the human development paradigm and it was recognised that the essence of human security was to respect human rights and fundamental freedoms. This was the building block for the UN Millennium Declaration of 2000[6] which

---

5 An analysis of 53 countries between 1953 and 1990 found that higher adult survival rates were responsible for about eight per cent of total economic growth.

6 Freedom: Men and women have the rights to live their lives and raise their children in dignity, free from hunger and from the fear of violence, oppression or injustice. Equality: No individual and no nation must be denied the opportunity to benefit from development; equal rights and opportunities of women and men must be assured. Solidarity: Global challenges must be managed in a way that distributes the costs and burdens fairly in accordance with basic principles of equity and social justice. Tolerance: Human beings must respect one other, in all their diversity of belief, culture and language. Respect for nature: Prudence must be shown in the management of all living species and natural

in turn formed the foundation for the Millennium Development Goals (MDGs). As such, the MDGs are drawn from the actions and targets contained in the Millennium Declaration that was adopted by 189 nations and signed by 147 head of states and governments during the UN Millennium Summit in September 2000. The MDGs encompass eight goals to be achieved by 2015 that respond to the world's main development challenges, including human insecurity. MDGs- based development strategy is well placed for linking poverty with human security. The eight MDGs which include eradicating extreme poverty and hunger, achieving universal primary education, promoting gender equality and empowering women, reducing child mortality, improving maternal health, combating HIV/AIDS, malaria and other diseases, ensuring environmental sustainability and developing a global partnership for development can be instrumental for promoting human security.

The MDGs synthesise, in a single package, many of the most important commitments made separately at the international conferences and summits of the 1990s; recognise explicitly the interdependence between growth, poverty reduction and sustainable development; acknowledge that development rests on the foundations of democratic governance, the rule of law, respect for human rights and peace and security; are based on time-bound and measurable targets accompanied by indicators for monitoring progress; and bring together the responsibilities of developing countries with those of developed countries.

Ever since Nepal became a signatory to the Millennium Declaration, the country has made efforts to integrate the MDGs into its national planning process, implement them and monitor the outcomes on a regular basis. The Tenth Plan of the country (NPC 2002), also known as Poverty Reduction Strategy Paper(PRSP), included the MDGs as key performance

---

resources, in accordance with the precepts of sustainable development. Shared responsibility: Responsibility for managing worldwide economic and social development, as well as threats to international peace and security, must be shared among the nations of the world and should be exercised multilaterally.

indicators. Subsequent plans have made the MDGs an integral part of the planning and budgeting process to address poverty and human security.

3.2.4 The interrelationship between poverty reduction and human security

In a broader sense, poverty reduction, human security and human development are interrelated and as they are ultimately related to human well-being. While human insecurity aggravates poverty or deprivation, it is also the poor who are the most vulnerable and constantly face the threat of insecurity in their lives. There, however, seems to be no unidirectional causation of this relationship and one factor triggers another, making the causation bi-directional. At times they can move concurrently in the same direction. In many countries including Nepal, poverty and human insecurity are strongly linked, with one issue exacerbating the other.

Economic growth can neither be achieved nor sustained without human security. Uneducated, unhealthy and insecure people cannot contribute to economic growth. Also, without broad-based, equitable and employment-intensive growth, poverty reduction cannot be achieved. Two schools of thought - economic growth and human development - are worthy of mention in this context. The economic growth school holds that economic growth is the engine of human development; that is, as societies become wealthier they make greater provision for basic social services like education and health which, in turn, builds human capital and promotes human development. The human development school holds that growth does not automatically trickle down; increases in income do not automatically bring about improvements in human lives. For these reasons, the human development school concentrates on the policies that best utilise the income growth that a country attains to be pro-poor, pro- women, pro-excluded and pro-environment. Such policies could be built on the four pillars of human development, namely productivity, equity, empowerment and sustainability (UNDP 2009). This means that efforts to expand economic activities towards higher growth (productivity) to reduce poverty must be accompanied by all citizens' access to opportunities and resources (equity), ability to make the choices they wish (empowerment) and protection of the economic, social and environmental rights and choices of future generations (sustainability).

Human development is concerned not only with widening people's choices for better living but also providing an environment in which they can exercise their choices freely and safely.[7] Human development therefore necessarily entails human security as its integral component. Security is one important dimension of safeguarding this exercise of choice. The Nepal Human Development Report 2009 mentions that violent conflict obstructs choice and thereby limits human development in at least four ways: (i) it curtails the possibility of living a long, healthy life by infecting, crippling and killing people; (ii) it restricts their options for obtaining knowledge and exercising their intelligence by substituting force for reason; (iii) it reduces their possibilities for attaining a decent life by destroying wealth of all kinds; and (iv) it shrinks their opportunities for collective decision-making because it inhibits and even prevents dialogue (UNDP 2009). Inclusive growth and poverty reduction cannot take place without the inclusion and encouragement of everyone who can potentially contribute to the nation and to society for their own development and for that of others.

As poverty is multi-dimensional and not limited to income, risks and vulnerability are also multi-dimensional. The relationship between poverty and human insecurity corresponds to the chronic and transient nature of numerous factors including income, education, health, nutrition and social life. Risks or vulnerability link both of these aspects. The focus of human security on downside risks thus means approaching poverty issues from the viewpoint of increasing risks or vulnerability.

Armed conflict, which also has a bi-directional relationship with poverty and human security, is triggered by grievances

---

7 This was the approach introduced by the global Human Development Report of 1994 and later enlarged by Human Development Report 2005 published by UNDP, New York.

against political, social, cultural and economic orders. Of the two key sources of armed conflict, namely 'greed' and 'grievance', the second is taken as the main cause of conflict in Nepal. Unequal distribution of not only income and wealth but also opportunities and resources has been one reason why people have revolted against the existing regime or raised arms. The sources of inequality emanate not only from social and economic policies, but also from the institutions and values governing the society. Some of the sources of inequality are: (i) weakening state power to redistribute income and opportunities and over-dependence on market forces, creating unequal economic power structures; (ii) unequal gender relations stemming from traditional socio-cultural structures that define the formal and informal rules for women's participation in relation to opportunity, decision- making, access to resources and control over them; (iii) caste differentials due to social stratification stipulated by long-standing social hierarchies and caste and ethnicity differences resulting from the norms and socially defined practices of dominant caste groups that define the degree and form of discriminatory practices towards disadvantaged groups; (iv) spatial exclusion resulting from the geographic isolation of some areas remote from the capital city and other urban centres, or from state- biased policies that affect the disadvantaged regions. In Nepal, inequality has undermined poverty reduction, inclusive development and human security.

3.3 Linking poverty and human security in Nepal

An overview of world history after the end of the Cold War shows that most conflicts are not contests between countries but rather internal disputes as disparities among their citizens (UNDP 2009). Nepal has been no exception to this global trend. Its people have fought for equal representation and participation in their state and society on several occasions, including the most recent conflict which culminated in the decade-long armed conflict. The popular mandate of the 2006 people's movement and uprising called for peace, democracy and justice, equality and prosperity by ending all kinds of political, economic and social discrimination through a restructuring of the state, polity, economy and society.

However, the focus of the state so far is on peace building and drafting a new constitution; not much work has been done to transform the economy and the society. Political freedom and expectations beyond the state's capacity to deliver, as well as deteriorating governance situation in the wake of prolonged transition, have created a huge gap in the delivery of basic security to most Nepali people. The result has been a deterioration of human security against an expectation of faster poverty reduction, higher human development and a better human security situation. Overlooking or further postponing the fulfillment of this demand for economic security may cause the country to relapse into conflict. Besides, with their increased consciousness of development beyond Nepal's borders, the Nepali people are looking not only to increase income, education and health, but also to claim a greater stake in their government and society, notably by exercising a greater voice in determining state policies along with ensuring human security.

Human insecurity aggravates poverty or deprivation and it is the poor who are the most vulnerable and constantly face the threat of falling into poverty. This calls for sufficient attention to the circular nature of poverty and human security linked through vulnerability. Although reduction of poverty in Nepal is noticeable (CBS 2011a), many people remain on the threshold of poverty, and are prone to fall into it with minor shocks.

Although measuring vulnerability has been a subject of wide discussion, broadly it has been broken down into the risk, options for managing the risk or the risk responses and outcome in terms of welfare loss (JICA 2006). Without addressing these dimensions of vulnerability, sustainable poverty reduction becomes a challenge. Therefore, a poverty reduction strategy based on a human security perspective has to include three dimensions of risk management: (i) preventative and mitigating measures against risks; (ii) protecting or coping measures when human security is threatened by increased risks; and (iii) promoting measures to enhance social opportunities or human capabilities of the poor to fight chronic poverty. Among the three, promoting measures to enhance social opportunities and human capabilities are taken as most effective towards the prevention of risks because these strengthen the ability of the vulnerable to resist risks of falling down into poverty (ibid).

3.3.1 Income poverty, vulnerability and human security

Income poverty is the subject of numerous theoretical and empirical studies. These studies categorise income poverty as either chronic poverty or transient poverty (JICA 2006).The latter concept is related to what is often referred to as poverty dynamics. It is important to reduce the risks faced by the poor so that they can cope with vulnerability (ibid). Three causal relationships exist between poverty and risk or vulnerability: static effect, where poverty is aggravated by fluctuating consumption; prolonged poverty effect, where expected income is sacrificed to avoid income fluctuation; and transforming effect, where transient poverty istransformed into chronic poverty when the poor sell off their meager assets to cope with decreasing income (ibid).

In the context of the human security framework for poverty reduction, these studies suggest that coping measures to reduce risks are necessary in order to avoid the transient poor falling into the category of the chronic poor and the chronic poor plummeting into destitution or death. It is true that chronic and transient poverties are different phenomena and policies aimed at stabilising living standards (social security policies) and improving living standards (poverty reduction policies) require different prescriptions. However, in real life, the two types of poverty cannot be considered separately or exclusively of each other. From the perspective of human security framework of poverty reduction, the focus of Nepali policy makers has to be on the low income poor facing the possibility of a future reduction in income.

Human security is best attained by progress in human development leading people away from deprivation, exclusion and abject poverty. The conventional measurement of human development - being able to acquire knowledge, live a longer and decent life and earn income to meet the basic daily necessities - serves as the basic foundation of human security. At the national and more so at the household level, people must have threshold income to support the minimum calorie, education, health and shelter requirements. Of course, states can deliver these goods and services through effective fiscal channels. In many developing countries, however, the state often fails to provide these services so that we end up with a situation of 'a richer nation and its poorer people'. There are at least three channels which would ensure income and security at the household level in Nepal to ensure 'freedom from want' irrespective of the state's presence for ensuring 'freedom of fear': agriculture, remittances and social transfers. In the following sections a brief discussion of three channels are presented.

a) Agriculture

For centuries and for some more decades to come, agriculture has remained and will remain the mainstay of the Nepali economy and will serve as a key strategy to reduce poverty and make people free from the basic wants of food and jobs. But as the following sections will deliberate, agriculture has been a vulnerable sector which has put the economic security of at least two thirds of Nepali households at risk. Food security is one important dimension of this dynamic.

Vulnerability to food insecurity is a function of the various risks to which one is exposed and of a person's ability to cope, which is highly dependent on his/her asset base. The households in Nepal most vulnerable to food insecurity have insufficient livelihood assets (human, social, natural, physical and financial) with which to produce enough food and/or earn sufficient income to purchase food and manage shocks. In addition to their meager portfolio of assets, these households usually have a high exposure to shocks and stresses that reduce their income or food production and require additional expenditures (FAO 2004).

As most poor are food insecure, food security is an important intervention to rescue people from absolute poverty and ensure human security. Although food security is not limited to the production of adequate food items but also to the ability of households to acquire enough food and utilise food items, in a country with several barriers to trade and transactions, local production makes a big difference in food security.

Food availability is governed by the level of local, national and international agricultural production and the ability to import, trade and transport essential food supplies from surplus to deficit areas. Judged from the availability perspective, since 2005 Nepal has transitioned from a food surplus country to a food deficit country (NPC 2010b). Although agricultural production has increased from 6.89 million Metric Tons in 2001 to 7.76 million Metric Tons in 2010, the same in per capita terms has declined from 297 kg per person in 2001 to 290 kg per person in 2010 (MoF 2011). This has happened at a time when the population demographic is shifting from dependent to working age groups who demands even more food items to consume.[8] Additionally, there is a geographical or regional variation in food production and availability. Of the 75 districts, 53 are food insecure; with mountainous regions being more food insecure than the Hills and the Tarai. There are also geographical and political barriers to trade. The geographical barriers are reflected in the lack of transport infrastructure to carry food items and political barriers can be seen in terms of export or import restrictions, tariffs and duties on trade and the administrative hassle associated with that trade. These physical, financial and social barriers govern the accessibility or ability of a household to acquire adequate food. These limitations can restrain home production, storage and purchase of food items resulting in either chronic hunger, migration or high household debts. Nepal's demographic health survey (MoHP et.al 2008) shows that two-thirds of children live in acute malnutrition, which is manifested in low weight to age ratios, low height to age ratios and other physical disabilities. The chronic hunger situation has the potential for the intergenerational transmission of poverty because physically disabled people may not be able to lead a healthy and able life, may lose opportunity

---

8 The NLSS (CBS 2011, p 4) shows that the daily per person calorie requirement has been increased from 2150 calories in 1995 to 2240 in 2010.

to seek better education and be talented and may not cope the risk and challenge in their livings.

The food utilisation aspect, which covers the quality of food, the intra- household distribution of food, the ability to absorb nutritious food and the gender dimension of food consumption, is an important aspect of food security in Nepal. A lack of knowledge about nutrition, sanitation, hygiene, gender equality and dietary requirements by age and reproductive stage means that many people remain food insecure. This implies that food security can only be ensured along with availability and affordability which takes into consideration the distribution and consumption patterns of food across regions, gender and age groups. As such, girls in Nepal are more often malnourished than boys, a fact which highlights the importance of looking at food security from a gender perspective.

Nepal's agriculture is highly vulnerable to weather conditions, natural disasters and market shocks.[9] As most farms are rain-fed, agricultural output is strongly correlated with rainfall conditions. Rainfall, however, has remained highly erratic, ranging between 2110 mm to 1456 mm over the last 15 years with coefficient of variation being as high as 11 per cent,[10] resulting in a high vulnerability of agricultural output. This is also the reason why agricultural production fluctuates heavily from year to year.[11] Besides, as there is no minimum support

---

[9] Rainfall uncertainty makes Nepal's agricultural production vulnerable. The problem is accentuated by the absence of crop insurance and minimum support price systems. Both self-employed people and wage earners in agriculture suffer from uncertainty; and income from agriculture has been a very irregular and uncertain source of household income. As agriculture is the main source of livelihood for two-thirds of Nepali households, such a vulnerable situation poses a threat to income protection, thus leading to human security risks.

[10] An analysis of rainfall data from 1995 to 2010 shows that the mean level of rainfall is 1746 mm, the standard deviation is 189 mm and the coefficient of variation is 11 per cent. Department of Hydrology and Meteorology, The Ministry of Environment, Government of Nepal.

[11] A statistical analysis of agricultural production data from 1997 to 2011 shows that paddy production varies between 4.5 million metric tons mean and 3.6 million metric tons, with coefficient variation at 7.3 per

price provision and as domestic prices are often influenced by the cross-border prices of agricultural products, there is high fluctuation in their market price. The coefficient of variation of key agricultural output prices for the last 15 years are 36.6 per cent for rice, 31.8 per cent for wheat, 25.7 per cent maize, 33.5 per cent for potato and 26 per cent for oilseeds.[12] The vulnerability of agricultural production and prices has been a serious threat to food security and ultimately to human security. The detailed discussion on the relationship between food security and human security is presented on chapter 5.

b) Remittances

Nearly 400,000 persons enter Nepal's labour market every year, yet the jobs created within the country equate to at most one third of this number. Underemployment is high, with at least 30 per cent of workdays being wasted (CBS 2008a). The distribution of job opportunities and wage rates are also uneven throughout the country. This causes working age people to migrate, both domestically and externally, in search of job opportunities. Migrant workers' remittance has been a major source of household income for the last 15 years or so. The number of households receiving remittances has increased from 23 per cent of all households in 1995/96 to 32 per cent in 2003/04 and further to 56 per cent in 2010/11 (CBS 2011b). Only 20 per cent of migrant workers are within the country; those working in India constitute 11 per cent of the total migrant worker population and the remaining 69 per cent are overseas workers. The percentage of third country migrant workers in the migrating labour force has trebled in the last 15 years (ibid).

---

cent. Maize production varies between 1.3 million MT an d 2.1 MT, with coefficient variation at 14 per cent. The coefficient variation for wheat, oilseeds and potato are also very high at 15.5 per cent, 11.4 per cent and 32.3 per cent respectively. Source: Statistical calculation by the author.

12 A statistical analysis of the wholesale prices of agricultural production data covering 1995-2010 shows that the standard deviation in the per kilogram prices are NPR 10 for rice, NPS 5 for wheat NPS 20 for oilseeds. Source: Statistical calculation by the author. Such a fluctuation poses a threat to agricultural producer income protection.

Income received from remittances constitutes nearly one third of the income of the recipient households. With 56 per cent of households getting remittances which equate to on average one-third of the household income, about 17 per cent of overall household income is estimated to stem from remittances. This is the second largest income after agriculture, which contributes about 35 per cent of household income (MoF 2011).

Analysis of the issues of migration for employment can be done from both the demand and supply sides; that is, through push and pull factors. The push factors include the threat of life because of prolonged armed conflict, poverty, hunger, food insecurity and lack of job security, particularly amongst youth who did not want to join the armed rebels. The pull factors include easy access to cross-border jobs, peer pressure and zest for modern amenities and higher income earning opportunities.

A study of Nepali migrant workers to India shows that the average age was about 30 years old; 70 per cent of the migrants were poor or very poor; and almost all migrants were male (WFP 2008). The impacts of such migration are manifold including exposure to hazardous and unsafe jobs, infection with Tuberculosis (TB) and HIV/AIDS and heightened insecurity at home.

Although migrant work has been a source of income for many households, there is a huge differential in access to such work and remittance amount across regions, social groups and gender. For instance, about two in three households in the Tarai receive remittances and the proportion for both the Hills and the Mountains regions are roughly one in two households. Similarly the per capita remittance received in the Tarai is about two and a half times what the households in the mountains receive on average. Additionally, more rural households receive remittances than urban households but the per capita remittance received is higher for urban areas than for rural areas (CBS 2011b). There is an astronomical difference between the per capita remittance received by an individual in the poorest and the richest consumption quintile. In per capita terms, the poorest consumption quintile receives one-twelfth of what the richest quintile receives (CBS 2011a). Poor and unskilled people are more exposed to riskier, dirtier and less remunerative jobs.

The amount of remittance received per household has increased from NPR 15,000 in 1995/96 to more than NPR 80,000 in 2010/11 (CBS 2011b).

Remittances have helped bring many households out of absolute poverty in the last 15 years. Although most remittance is utilised in consumption, it contributes to poverty reduction and increases human security because of the spending on food, clothing, shelter, education and health. Surveys show that the two most reported uses of remittance are for daily consumption and for repaying loans. About 79 per cent of the total remittance received by the households is used for daily consumption, while 7 per cent is used for loans repayment. Other uses are to acquire household property (5%) and for education (4%). Only a small percentage of the remittance (2%) is used for capital formation and the remaining (3%) is used for other purposes (CBS 2011a). This is evidence of the compulsion that has made people migrate for work.

The human security dimension of migrant workers is a serious concern, particularly for female workers and those workers exposed to dirty, dangerous and disgraceful jobs. Sexual harassment and exploitation are common in the case of female workers, particularly in the Gulf region. Accidents at work which result in loss of life or disability are common. Cultural and climatic shocks, stress and excessive workload have created inhuman situations for many migrant workers. Exposure to unsafe sexual relations and transmission of HIV/AIDS are common amongst many migrant workers, particularly amongst those in India (WFP 2008). Family breakdowns and betrayals due to prolonged absence from spouses are common. The informal social protection system has also broken down, with able family members away and unable to protect the family at times of threat. Different dimensions of migration remittance and their relationship with human security is analysed in detail in chapter 7.

c) Social transfers

State-led social security or social transfer is the third important source of household income which supports poverty reduction and protects human security. Social security provisions have expanded over the years to address elderly people and children. This is important while the country is observing a demographic transition.[13] This demographic transition is a key component of economic growth and political stability, particularly when youth and working age people tend to comprise the larger section of the population. The human security dimension is also important when a larger section of the population becomes dependent in terms of minors and/or elders. Although the dependency ratio has exhibited a decreasing trend over the same period, the increasing proportion of elderly people requires that additional social security provisions to be made for them, at the state, community or household levels. To address this, Nepal introduced an old age allowance in 1995 and a child grant scheme in 2010, along with piloting employment guarantee systems in some regions of the country. Besides, health insurance schemes are also widening and more formal sector employees are being covered with retirement benefits.

3.3.2 Inequality, conflict, poverty and human security

Empirical studies show that conflict in Nepal has its root in inequality, as 'grievance' rather than 'greed' is found to be the major cause of armed conflict (UNDP 2009). Although inequality in Nepal has political, economic, social and cultural dimensions, they are all linked with disempowerment and exclusion. Some of them are obviously related to growing income inequality triggered by the development model adopted by the country, particularly with the restoration of democracy in 1990. The adoption of market-based economic policies has of course

---

[13] Recent living standard surveys show that during the last 15 years, the proportion of the population aged 0-14 years has decreased from 42 to 37 per cent; whereas the 15-59 years age group has increased from 51 to 54 per cent. The group for people aged 60 years and over has increased from 7 to 9 per cent (CBS 2011, Nepal Living Standard Survey 2010/11, Volume 1, p 22).

created incentives and opportunities for more economic activities; it has in the meantime meant that some people have gained and some people have lost out. Those who could not compete in the market place have been excluded from the benefits of the economic system and their grievances resulted in the act of raising arms.

An analysis of household data provided by the last three living standard surveys of 1996, 2004 and 2010 show that income inequality in Nepal is one of the highest in the region. The Gini coefficient, a measure of income inequality, increased from 0.32 in 1996 to 0.41 in 2004. The recent trend shows some improvement but still the ratio is high at 0.33. As reflected in the Gini coefficient, the share of the lowest quintile in national consumption declined from 7.6 per cent in 1996 to 6.2 per cent in 2004 and improved slightly to 7.6 per cent in 2010. As the following sections will illustrate, inequality is not limited to income or wealth; it encompasses several dimensions of development (CBS 2011b).

Exclusion and inequality among regions, groups and even within particular groups, are reflected in poverty and human development outcomes. Although poverty has declined by more than one percentage point every year since 1995 to come down to 25 per cent in 2010, there is much variation in the poverty outcome by gender, location, region and ethnic group. The poverty rate in urban areas is much lower (15.5 per cent) than that in rural areas (27.4 per cent). There is a high variation in poverty rates amongst different geographical regions also. The urban Hill region (which encompasses Kathmandu) is the least poor region with a poverty incidence of 9 per cent. Within urban areas, poverty ranges from 9 per cent in the urban Hills to 22 per cent in the urban Tarai. Within the rural hills, poverty ranges from 16 per cent in the Eastern region to 37 per cent in the Mid- and Far-Western regions. Within the rural Tarai, poverty ranges from 21 per cent in the Eastern region to 31 per cent in the Mid- and Far-Western region (CBS 2011a).

Although female-headed households have slightly lower poverty rates, intra-household poverty is biased towards women and girl children. Also, the current state of better poverty outcome for female-headed households (CBS 2011a) is only a reflection that male family members are absent as migrant workers and send remittances to keep their family out of poverty.

The social dimension of poverty and human security is rather stark. Dalits[14] bear a much higher burden of poverty compared to non-Dalits. The percentage of poor among Dalits is 42 per cent compared to 23 per cent for the non-Dalits. Higher levels of education are negatively correlated with poverty. Poverty is substantially lower if the head of the house has received a decent education, favouring families of higher castes. Households with an illiterate head are more than 4.5 times more likely to be poor than households with a head that has completed 11 or higher (CBS 2011a). Similarly, households that have at least one women who completed primary education are much less likely to be poor than households in which the most educated female has lower than primary school education.

Poverty is also closely correlated with access to resources and opportunities. Surveys show that poverty falls drastically for households with more than 1 hectare of agricultural land (CBS 2011a). Poverty rate falls, both in rural and urban areas, with an increase in the size of arable land. In rural areas, households with more than 1 hectare of agricultural land have lower than average poverty rates. In urban areas, reduction in poverty appears even with smaller landholdings. Access to services is also an important correlate of poverty. Households that are closer to facilities are less likely to be poor than the national average. Having good access to higher secondary schools, public hospitals, paved roads, market centres, agricultural centres, cooperatives and banks have large effects on poverty.

Beside income, there is also inequality in education and health outcomes. Despite significant improvements in educational attainments over the last two decades, inequality persists in the literacy rates across all regions, castes and ethnic groups and

14 Dalits used to be considered as so called untouchable caste groups and one of the most marginalised population section of Nepal.

by gender. Surveys show that the caste dimension is prominent in the outcomes, even within the same region. For instance, among women aged 15-49 years, less than a quarter of Madhesi 'other caste' groups could read or write, whereas more than four-fifths of Madhesi Brahmin and Chhetri women were literate. By contrast, among Madhesi Brahmin, men's literacy rate was 94 per cent against only 83 per cent for women. The inequality is higher in the Tarai/Madhesi group than the Mountain/Hill group (MoHP 2007).

Surveys also find significant improvements in health outcomes despite the decade-long conflict. However, wide disparities persist in health outcome indicators across different caste and ethnic groups and by gender (MoHP 2007). For instance, while 95 out of 1,000 Dalit children do not survive to their fifth birthday, the corresponding figure for Newars is 43. Girls still have a higher mortality rate than boys. The under-five mortality rate of Tarai/Madhesi caste and ethnic groups is higher than that of the Hill/ Mountain groups (ibid). These figures indicate the severe caste, ethnic and geographical dimensions of human insecurity in Nepal. The human development outcome also has a gender, ethnicity and region bias. The Mountain region and Mid-Western Development region always remain at the bottom of the human development ladder. The hierarchical caste, ethnic and gender relations that structure the interactions of daily life at the family and community level among groups of Tarai-Madhes origin have always been more restrictive than those in the Hills. UNDP (2009) shows that against the national average Human Development Index of 0.509, the HDI level was the highest for the Madhesi Brahmins (0.625) whereas it was the lowest among the Madhesi Dalits of the Tarai (0.383) in 2006. Moreover, within a single caste group, there is inequality across regions: the Hill Brahmins and Chhetris have a HDI of 0.612 and 0.514, which are less than that of their Madhesi counterparts. On the other hand, among the Tarai Janajati, HDI falls below that of their counterparts in the Hill and Mountain regions (0.470 compared to 0.507). The vicious, self-reinforcing cycle of discrimination and inequality has been instrumental in provoking revolt and in turn threatening human security, as it is in the situation of conflict that basic human rights are violated, service delivery obstructed, rule of law weakened and human security undermined.

3.3.3 Achievements in human security

Human security can also be judged from the perspective of adequacy of income or consumption to meet basic human needs like food, shelter, clothing, education, health and other facilities. The latest living standard survey (CBS 2011b) shows that during the last 15 years, there has been an improvement in the adequacy of these things. Regarding food items, only 16 per cent of the respondents in 2010 said that their food consumption was less than adequate compared with 51 per cent in 1996. Similarly, the percentage of households reporting housing as inadequate has reduced to 22 per cent in 2010 compared with 64 per cent in 1996. Similar positive trends can be seen in clothing, education and health facilities. Compared to 58 per cent of the reporting households saying clothing was inadequate in 1996, only 17 per cent of the households reported such inadequacy in 2010. The proportion of households reporting inadequacy of education and health facilities also dropped from 45 per cent and 59 per cent respectively in 1996 to 16 per cent and 18 per cent in 2010 (ibid).

The above statistics reveal that Nepali households are gradually moving away from the insecurity of basic needs towards better security. But statistics always mask the inequality inherent in access to goods and services. This inequality has geographical, ethnic and gender dimensions. To highlight a few: against the national average of 17 per cent of households reporting food insecurity, 30 per cent of households in the mountains regions recorded this problem; and 35 per cent of the poorest quintile of households were reported food insecure. In terms of housing facilities too, about 36 per cent of households in the Mid-West reported inadequacy, against the national average of 22 per cent. The ethnic or caste dimensions of such inadequacy are even starker with upper caste people having better facilities that lower caste people.

Shelter is one important component of human security. Recent survey results show that during the last 15 years, the proportion of households residing in their own housing units has decreased from 94 per cent to 90 per cent and that the proportion of renters has increased from 2 to 8 per cent. The housing condition is rather poor, as only 26 per cent of households occupy housing units with cement-bonded outer walls and 18 per cent of households still live under thatched roofs. Nearly half of Nepal's households have no toilet/latrine facility in their own dwelling, although this is much improved compared with a quarter of the households having such facility 15 years before (CBS 2011b).

Accessibility to different facilities has improved almost universally during the last 15 years. By 2010, 95 per cent of households had primary schools within 30 minutes of travel time, compared with 88 per cent in 1995. Similarly, access to health centres has also improved during the same period. Access to education and health facilities is closely linked to poverty and to human security. Nepal's progress towards these goals is encouraging. The overall literacy rate of the population aged 6 years and above has increased by some 23 percentage points in 15 years. Gender-wise, the progress is more encouraging as this increase is higher for females (27 points) compared with males (19 points). Adult literacy rate has increased significantly during the same period from 36 per cent in 1995/96 to 57 per cent in 2010/11. Female adult literacy increased by some 25 percentage points during this period. In the last 15 years, the proportion of fully immunised children has increased remarkably. The proportion of married couples using some form of family planning method has increased from 15 to 39 per cent in the last 15 years. The proportion of women receiving prenatal care is 78 per cent and receiving post-natal care is 20 per cent in 2010/11 (CBS 2011b). All these issues have important positive implications for the human security situation in the country.

3.4 Environment: A link between human security and poverty

The environment-poverty nexus is a two-way relationship

(Jehan and Umana 2003). The environment affects poverty situations by (i) providing sources of livelihood to poor people, (ii) affecting their health and (iii) influencing their vulnerability. Poverty also affects the environment by (i) forcing poor people to degrade the environment, (ii) encouraging countries to promote economic growth at the expense of the environment and (iii) inducing societies to downgrade environmental concerns. As such, the environment is very important to poor people. Their wellbeing is strongly related to the environment in terms of, among other things, health, earning capacity, security, physical surroundings, energy services and decent housing. In rural areas, poor people may be particularly concerned with their access to and control over natural resources, especially in relation to food security. For poor people in urban areas, access to clean water and environment may be a priority.

Nepal's fragile topography and habitation result in many natural and man- made disasters. There were 3,408 floods and landslides between 1988 and 1997, and 2,110 such cases between 1998 and 2007. There were

11,620 epidemics between 1988 and 1997, and 5,183 cases between 1998 and 2007 (CBS 2008b). These disasters have made many people fall into poverty and vulnerability over the last decade.

The impact of environmental degradation is higher for the poor than for the rich. The overwhelming majority of those who die each year from natural or man-made disasters are poor people. All over the world, it is poor people who generally live in ecologically fragile lands, nearest to flooding rivers or dirty factories, busy roads and dangerous waste dumps. It is most often the most vulnerable segments of society, those people already in poverty, with little education and access to political power, who experience the brunt of environmental change. Within Nepal, a country in which 25 per cent of the population lives below the national poverty line and over 70 per cent depend on the land for their sustenance (CBS 2011a), environmental vulnerability carries a critical dimension of poverty and human security. The detailed discussion on relationship environmental, energy security and human security is presented in chapter 9.

3.5 The regional and global contexts for linking poverty and human security

Currently, the global economy is at a critical juncture as activity has weakened and downside risks are growing. Against a backdrop of unresolved structural fragilities, a series of shocks have struck the international economy in recent years. The structural problems facing the crisis-hit advanced economies have proven even more intractable than expected and the process of employment-focused growth even more intricate. Due to these adverse repercussions, the prospects for the rapid reduction of global poverty have become uncertain again.

Inflationary pressures driven by high and volatile food and energy prices have serious implications on poverty and human security. Such pressures pose a challenge to credible economic management in terms of needing to spend higher amounts to create safety nets to protect the poor from the impact of high food and energy prices. Along with higher real wages, rising energy prices have raised the cost of food items through higher irrigation, storage, processing and transportation costs. The neglect of agriculture by the donors as well as national governments for decades has also been instrumental in this regard. The financialisation of commodity markets is equally important to explain the increase in commodity prices. The speculative flow of money into commodity derivatives has increased dramatically in recent times, which has also distorted the market. This is reflected in the large correlations of commodity prices with both equity prices and currency prices. Globally, food inventories are very low, and are creating an incentive for speculation, whereas agricultural supply has not kept pace with demand as a result of the neglect of agriculture by national governments as well as donors. Against the backdrop of sluggish global economic recovery and unstable global financial markets, building stability would require, among other issues, ensuring food security. Natural disasters - also caused by climate change, population increase, changing consumption patterns to high protein food and beverages, alternative use of food items to animal feed and bio-fuel and adverse terms of agriculture- have been instrumental in depleting the per capita availability of food grains and their inventory. In this context, recent regional initiatives such as the South Asian Association for Regional Cooperation (SAARC)

Food Bank and Association of Southeast Asian Nations (ASEAN) plus three countries (China, Japan and South Korea) emergency rice reserve agreement for dealing with natural disasters, balancing food demand and supply and strengthening food information sharing is a big step forward in the building of a food security cooperation mechanism.

For the last decades, investment in agriculture has reduced. Multilateral financial institutions as well as national governments have put a low priority on agriculture which otherwise could ensure broad-based growth with better income distribution. The Asian agenda for food security, rural employment, poverty reduction and egalitarian growth must revolve around the promotion of agriculture through higher investment.

Poverty and human security are not confined within any particular territory; they are also cross-border issues. As such, poverty anywhere is a threat to human civilization everywhere. So is human security. In a highly integrated world, threats to human security can emanate from political, economic, social or environmental shocks from outside national borders. As Nepal resides between the world's two most populous countries which are also emerging economic powerhouses, it will have to face threats to human security from the events in the neighbourhood; particularly from India. The threats to or prospects of human security in Nepal are guided by how its neighbours are moving ahead in development.

We live in an unequal world[15] and also in an unequal society.

---

15 The overall gap between rich and poor, globally and within countries, has been growing. The difference in per capita income between the world's wealthiest 20 per cent and the poorest 20 per cent grew from 30:1 in 1960 to 78:1 in 1994. It fell slightly to 74:1 in 1999. For detail see World Bank, (1996). Poverty Reduction and the World Bank: Progress and Challenges in the 1990s. Washington, D.C: WB and

Inequality in the distribution of resources and opportunities and has been one of the major reasons for global and domestic conflicts. When only a small number of countries or people monopolise available resources and opportunities exercise exclusionary development policies and programs, it is likely to inculcate grievances leading to serious conflict. The current global tensions and domestic conflicts in many countries could be seen from this perspective. The progress in poverty reduction would have been much faster had we been able to reduce inequality. If we have to fight poverty, development processes must be focused on inclusion and social justice, as profit-driven capitalist markets do not necessarily help poverty reduction. It is for this reason that the overly market-centric policies of Multilateral Institutions are often criticised for failing to improve the lives of half the population of the world. As such, the market harnesses self-interest in a helpful and sustainable way but only for those who can pay or who have the ability to benefit from it, leaving the rest feeling cheated. The resentment seen in the Capture Wall Street movement subsequent to the financial crisis of 2008 is only a minor manifestation of this sentiment. We have seen from experience that the right kind of global institutions are necessary for a new world economic order and also to ensure that globalisation works to benefit all. While there should be no barriers to global trade and investment, everyone should have access to global knowledge as the 'global common goods'. People who have been responsible for the over-consumption of global environmental resources causing climate change and adversely affecting the livelihood of millions of people must contribute more to compensate for the loss.

3.6 Conclusion

Poverty is a threat to human security. Reducing poverty depends upon improving personal capacities and increasing access to resources, institutions and support. Poor health, illiteracy,

---

United Nations (1997). Critical Trends: Global Change and Sustainable Development. New York: UN.

inadequate schooling, social exclusion, powerlessness and gender discrimination contribute to poverty. Nepal's poverty assessment clearly manifests this truism and poverty has exposed people to vulnerability and human insecurity.

Despite a progress in poverty reduction after the restoration of democracy in Nepal in 1990, the outcome has been highly unequal across regions and social groups. There is a vast difference in the living standards of people from rural and urban areas, different geographical regions and social groups. As political, economic and social power continues to be concentrated in the hands of the urban elite and given the patriarchic and caste-based society, the majorities of the population including people residing in remote areas, women and disadvantaged minorities - have continuously been marginalised from their share of development benefits and continue to face human insecurity.

Development with the participation and inclusion of all stakeholders is central to poverty reduction and the promotion of human security. Inclusion is a necessary condition for egalitarian development but it must be followed by equity. Inclusion does not necessarily ensure equity and justice; it can often end up being symbolic. So efforts must be made to ensure that inclusion is meaningful, effective and sufficient enough to distribute development outcomes in a more egalitarian way. Inclusion must promote economic empowerment, ensure human security and reduce disparity.

Economic disparity is a global concern that frequently fuels hatred, violence and terror elements which undermine human security. Greater economic differences between nations, socio-economic classes, members within the same class and within a family cause unequal access to resources which lead to feelings of inferiority, humiliation and frustration. Experiences from Nepal demonstrate that people can turn violent and resort to terror as a last resort to acquire their rights and resources.

Human security is a cross-border issue and global economic disparity is fundamentally incompatible with global security and poverty. Global institutions must work together to use global resources for the kind of development which negates the demand for arms for security. Along with national efforts, regional and global cooperation is necessary if sustainable poverty reduction and human security outcomes are to be achieved. National, regional and global institutions working in these areas need to be reengineered accordingly.

Policy makers in Nepal have to incorporate human security into poverty reduction strategies so as to identify risk and vulnerability factors and integrate them into poverty analysis.

References

Alkira S, Santos ME. 2010. *Acute Multidimensional Poverty: A New Index for Developing Countries*. OPHI Working Paper 38. Oxford:University of Oxford.

CBS [Central Bureau of Statistics]. 2008a. *National Labour Force Survey*. Kathmandu: Central Bureau of Statistics, National Planning Commission, Government of Nepal.

CBS [Central Bureau of Statistics]. 2008b. *Environmental Statistics of Nepal*. Kathmandu: Central Bureau of Statistics, National Planning Commission, Government of Nepal.

CBS [Central Bureau of Statistics]. 2011a. *Poverty in Nepal*. Kathmandu: Central Bureau of Statistics, National Planning Commission, Government of Nepal.

CBS [Central Bureau of Statistics]. 2011b. *Nepal Living Standard Survey, Volume I and II*. Kathmandu: Central Bureau of Statistics, National Planning Commission, Government of Nepal.

CHS [Commission on Human Security]. 2003. *Human Security Now*. New York: United Nations.

FAO [Food and Agriculture Organisation]. 2004. Food *Insecurity and Vulnerability in Nepal: Profiles of Seven Vulnerable Groups*. ESA Working Paper No. 04-10. Rome: Food Security and Agricultural Projects Analysis Service (ESAF), Food and Agriculture Organisation.

Jahan S, Umana A. 2003. The environment-poverty nexus. *Development Policy Journal* 3: 53-70.

JICA [Japan International Cooperation Agency]. 2006. *Poverty Reduction and Human Security*. Tokyo: JICA.

MoF [Ministry of Finance]. 2011. *Economic Survey 2010/2011*. Kathmandu: Ministry of Finance, Government of Nepal.

MoHP [Ministry of Health and Population]. 2007. *Nepal Demographic Health Survey 2006*. Kathmandu: Ministry of Health and Population,

New Era and Macro International.

MoHP [Ministry of Health and Population], New Era , Macro International. 2008. *Nepal Demographic Health Survey 2007.* Kathmandu: Ministry of Health and Population, New Era and Macro International.

NPC [National Planning Commission]. 2002. *The 10th Plan.* Kathmandu: National Planning Commission, Government of Nepal.

NPC [National Planning Commission]. 2010a. *MDGs Progress Report 2010.* Kathmandu: National Planning Commission, Government of Nepal.

NPC [National Planning Commission]. 2010b. *The Food security Atlas of Nepal.* Kathmandu: National Planning Commission, Government of Nepal.

UN [United Nations]. 1998. *UN Statement - signed by the heads of all UN agencies.* New York: United Nations.

UNDP [United Nations Development Programme]. 2009. *Nepal Human Development Report 2009.* Kathmandu: United Nations Development Programme.

UNDP [United Nations Development Progrmme]. 1994. *Human Development Report.* New York: United Nations Development Programme

UNDP [United Nations Development Programme]. 2005. *Human Development Report.* New York: United Nations Development Programme

WB [World Bank]. 2000. *Ending Poverty.* Washington, DC: World Bank.

WFP [World Food Programme]. 2008. *Passage to India, Migration as a Coping Strategy in Times of Crisis in Nepal.* Kathmandu: World Food Programme, Nepal Development Research Institute.

WSSD [World Summit for Social Development]. 1996. *World Summit for Social Development.* Copenhagen: United Nations

****

Chapter 4

Social protection for human security[1]

Sony KC Bishnu Raj Upreti, PhD

4.1 Introduction

"Everyone, as a member of society, has the right to social security".

The statement above became an axiomatic fact after being embedded in Article 22 of the Universal Declaration of Human Rights of 1948 and highlights the importance of making each member of society more secure. The extent to which people have achieved their rights to social security could be immeasurable, as it might vary from country to country and region to region, or even within a society. However, it can be understood that the human need for security is something that was addressed in the past by various organisations.

This chapter will focus on understanding social protection, of which social security is an element, its importance and those responsible for framing and putting it into practice for people's welfare. The chapter will address why and how social protection is a human security issue and will explain the links between

1 This chapter is the part of outcomes of the Security Livelihood Research Consortium (SLRC) research project implemented in Nepal. The authors would like to sincerely thank the Secure Livelihoods Research Consortium and its Management team for providing the opportunity to research this important issue. The opinions expressed in this chapter are the authors' and do not necessarily reflect the official view of SLRC or the South Asia Office of NCCR North-South.

social protection and human security. Various practices and examples of Nepal will be cited in order to provide a scenario of the existing social protection mechanisms, particularly focusing on their fragile condition. In today's world, social protection is a much needed and required element, without which poverty and extreme vulnerabilities cannot be reduced. Though various organisations have been focused towards reducing poverty and related problems (for example, in pursuit of the Millennium Development Goals), the change in trend suggests that social protection could positively contribute to the reduction of poverty and other goals that are aimed to reduce risks and insecurity.

4.2 Understanding the concepts: Social protection and human security

a. Social protection

The International Labour Organisation (ILO 2000) defines social protection as the action taken by society to fulfill its member's demands arising from economic and social vulnerabilities and risks which places them in a situation of suffering. This suffering can be triggered by factors such as a lack of income-generating paths, a lack of health care services and other forms of remuneration. Similarly, according to the Asian Development Bank (ADB), social protection is the set of policies and programmes that are designed to reduce poverty and vulnerability by promoting efficient labour markets, diminishing people's exposure to risks and enhancing their capacity to protect themselves against hazards and the interruptions/ loss of life. Likewise, the United Kingdom's Department for International Development (DFID) defines social protection as a sub-set of public actions that help to address risk, vulnerability and chronic poverty (Scott 2012).

In general, the concept or understanding of social protection varies among people, institutions or organisations working on social protection issues. This variation occurs because the issues of protection rely on the situation of a society, country, region or even the individual needing it. However, these various institutional definitions do not fail to identify social protection as the fundamental element of policies aiming to condense poverty and address risk and vulnerability.

Norton et al. (2001, p 7) reveals social protection as the element that focuses on providing support to the most deprived and vulnerable of the poor and also providing security to those that are not poor but are in need when they encounter "shocks and life-cycle events". Hence, the basic notion of inventing and applying social protection is any form of security service which caters to both the poor and the non-poor. The interventions can be based on age, gender, job and health status of people, the condition of the area (country, region, society) and whether it is undergoing conflict, natural hazards or other such calamities. Hence, social protection can denote one meaning but incorporate various forms and practices. For example, Harvey and Holmes (2007) reveal social protection as a crucial basic service alongside health, water and education, especially if a country is affected by conflict. This definition highlights the fact that fragile states are more in need of security where social protection functions as the core basic service.

Social Protection covers unexpected events including "risks, vulnerability and chronic poverty" (Holmes 2010, p 1). When people are in need, whether due to poverty or other unexpected events, introducing protection mechanisms play a crucial role in securing them by addressing their demands. Defining social protection in a simple sentence would be almost impossible as it covers many issues and individuals with different needs under different circumstances; however, holistically, it needs to be inclusive, realistic and a fundamental right as a mechanism for rehabilitation. The idea of social protection can vary according to the practices and needs of the country, area or region. It is not only an approach to address people's immediate needs but also something that can be practiced over a long period of time. Harvey (2009) depicts it as the suitable and reasonable form of service mechanism which helps tackle poverty and susceptibility that has been embedded in a society for a long time. This idea suggests that social protection mechanisms should not only provide immediate and quick relief but should also serve and flourish in the long run. Its major aim is to build mechanisms to reduce poverty and act as a shield against vulnerable situations. Social Protection interventions can range from a quick response to long-term support, through policy dimensions for effective and improved results. In simple terms, social protection manages people's lives when they are on the verge of vulnerability.

It is also very important to consider that social protection links to other issues like "poverty and vulnerability, pro-poor growth, agricultural development, humanitarian to development transitions, rights, exclusion and voicelessness and the capacity of developing country states to fulfill essential functions" (Scott 2012, p 5). For example, in Nepal the introduction of an 'Old Age Allowance' on 26 December 1994 by the Communist Party of Nepal-Unified Marxist-Leninist (CPN-UML), remains popular, providing many vulnerable elderly people with cash support (Rajan 2003). The Old Age Allowance was initially a universal flat allowance of NPR 100 (USD 1.13)[2] per month for each citizen above 75 years old. Over the course of time, such initiatives allowed the government to expand their programmes and now elderly people are provided with NPR 500 (USD 5.68) per month and the age has been reduced to 70 years.

b. Human security

The concept of human security evolved after the realisation that human beings need some form of protection against the uncertainty that their belongings or their state of living could be seized (Dahl-Eriksen 2007). In the past, security was regarded as something to do with region or in association with war and destruction. It was more inclined towards securing land or territory from being captivated or taken over by others; for example, colonial rule was about expanding territory. Over the period of time, the understanding has been broadened that human beings also need protection of other forms, for example, security of language and culture, property and land, gave rise to

---

2 USD 1=NPR 88 as per the conversion rate of 24 August 2012, available from web site of Nepal Rastra Bank; http://www.nrb.org.np/.

the term 'human security'. Dahl- Eriksen (2007, p 18), states that being secure is being protected from harmful situations and asserts that one cannot attain "total security". He also states that the coining of the term 'human security', though difficult to explain, also contributed to the evolution of the issue of human rights. Today, human security in the form of social protection can be tallied with human rights (particularly of the poor). Human security can be taken not only as a physical security demand but also emotional, psychological, social, financial or others.

4.3 Scope of social protection

The 1995 World Summit on Social Development, held in Copenhagen, took social protection as an essential subject matter and stated that governments must develop and implement policies to ensure that all people have adequate economic and social protection during unemployment, ill health, maternity, child rearing, widowhood, disability and old age (Singh 2007). Hence, it is important to realise that social protection is necessary to address human needs and that its implementation can secure people by addressing their needs. This idea also demonstrates how social protection issues as an important tool for human security. In other words, human beings feel guarded in some form through social support of various forms. Haan (2011, p 351) reveals that with the financial crisis which shook East Asia in 1997, the importance of social protection became much more central to 'international development research and debate'. This shows the rise in trend and demand for social protection in risky situations and financial crises. He further reveals that social protection is a 'magic bullet for poverty alleviation' (ibid, p 354). This can take us back to the ongoing Millennium Development Goal 1 (also see Table 4.7) that calls for 'eradicating extreme poverty and hunger' to which the addition of social protection can be a positive catalyst, given the condition that the set social protection mechanism is effective on a long term basis.

During the twentieth century, social protection for human security has been a major social attainment. Its introduction and practice have created advancement in societies by protecting citizen from a state of helplessness and assisting them towards a secured living (Garcia and Gruat 2003). Hence, it is an essential component which when introduced and implemented acts as a shield that prevents people from social and economic insecurity.

In light of the universal declaration that every citizen has the right to security, the importance of social protection remains high in conflict affected areas. This truism stems from the fact that the consequences of conflicts often leave people vulnerable, homeless and with no livelihood options. In such situations people are inclined to seek some sort of support which can be termed as social protection. In fragile states, it is thus particularly crucial in providing basic services. For example, due to a decade-long conflict, the people of Nepal lived through a severe situation for which they needed emergency as well as long -term support. Many conflict-affected people in Nepal, among which were 250,000 internally displaced persons (Ghimire and Upreti 2008), are still lacking a proper protection package from the government, and are still longing for better living options. Among the affected are women, children, disabled and elderly striving for psychological, social and emotional support along with financial support. Hence, social protection is a required basic service for those in a fragile condition due to fragile states.

However, the question of every individual being a member of society is debatable in today's context. For example, there are street children, children of slum dwellers, refugees and others without citizenship in Nepal. Not having a citizenship is one of the biggest disadvantages as it prevents people from acquiring any benefits given by the state. As these people are not officially members of society, they are prone to risk and vulnerability. For them, forms of social protection (either support to attain citizenship or other forms such as rescue from the street and food) plays a major role. However, the approach in dealing with these various groups and making secure with some form of social protection has to be different.

Harvey (2009) points out that social protection embodies two objectives, one of tackling economic threat and susceptibility and the other of tackling social threat. For example, as aforementioned, Nepal's decade- long insurgency left many people in a vulnerable situation. Many are still jobless and searching for livelihood options. Had there been a well designed social protection framework and implementing mechanism during the conflict, the situation for affected people would not have been as dire as it is today. Without any protection mechanism for the conflict- affected people, the situation in Nepal has posed both economic and social threats. In such a situation, generating just one form of protection would have been inadequate. Many people needed emotional support while others needed support in income generation. These people hailed from diverse ethnic groups, ages and education levels. The need and scope of protection remains high in fragile states as human security becomes powerless and people's lives are in turmoil.

However, certain critics believe that social protection is not a valid instrument as its expense can actually reduce public funds and put a hold on other investment areas. Additionally, there are critics who believe that such policies could actually increase dependency in people who would neglect work, thus creating an adverse impact on the economic and social pattern (Garcia and Gruat 2003). For example, Brieger (2010) reveals that the nets distributed to abate malaria in African countries were used for other reasons such as fishing, drying fish, making wedding veils and setting ant traps. Although these arguments are valid, the essence of needing social protection for human security and making it work by creating a framework which will reduce people's dependency or misuse of it, can be sorted out. In addition, some assistance is intended for dependants such as the elderly, children and disabled people who cannot actually work and feed themselves. For such people, arguments of dependency or misuse of support cannot be generated. This idea indicates that the need for social protection is based on age or even dependency.

Apart from the issues of social protection and human security, because people depend upon the state for some form of protection mechanisms to attain human security it is important to consider the state and its delivery mechanism. Harvey (2009) suggests that social protection is a scheme which can help to build up the state's legitimacy by allowing the state to guarantee the citizens' rights to security and prevent political vulnerability and risks that may arise unexpectedly. This idea leads us to the notion that it is an important means that can help measure the state's legitimacy and also see how a state is functioning. Social protection also functions as a protective element to those who experience a vacuum in their lives due to shocks and unexpected events. The relationship between people and state is intact like the relationship between people and the forms of protection given to them. People determine the state's ability based on the type and effectiveness of its service delivery mechanism.

Moreover, Garcia and Gruat (2003) have clearly mentioned two types of shocks that would encourage people to seek out security: 'idiosyncratic and covariate' shocks (p 2). The first one denotes shocks caused at a personal level where an individual experiences vulnerability due to factors such as "disability, old age, death or social shocks such as crime and domestic violence" (ibid, p 2). The second one denotes shocks which affects a larger audience (country, region or state) and is caused either due to natural circumstances (for example tornadoes or floods) or human follies (conflicts and war). Hence, it can be inferred that social protection is an important element that addresses the needs of people during shocks that are unexpected yet devastating.

Though it is clear that social protection is fundamental, it is crucial to consider what the critics have to say. The fact that it is an expensive action means that, while framing the protection mechanisms, it is important to consider peoples' most pressing and urgent demands. Of course, government and non-government organisations, donors, informal and business sectors cannot provide support in all the areas (such as elderly, children, disabled, widows). Hence, people who demand some forms of protection also have to consider whether their demands are urgent and important in comparison to people more vulnerable than them. For example, there might be confusion if people demand pension schemes despite having a job versus an earthquake that calls for a quick rescue. In such instances, support mechanisms might be in turmoil as it is impossible to use public or private funds to cover all instances. Hence, issues of importance and urgency must be considered when framing social protection mechanisms.

4.4 Who should provide social protection?

According to the ILO definition of social protection, it is the society that takes care of its members. However with variations in understandings of the term, it is not only society but also the state and the government that are responsible for generating social protection mechanisms. There is also a growing recognition of the importance of social protection within both formal and informal sectors. Norton et al. (2001) reveal that people are provided with some form of protection by the government, the non- government sector or an amalgamation of various organisations. Hence, based on the practice and norms of society along with the degree of need, social protection interventions are provided for human security to vulnerable people (or people in general).

In Nepal, existing social protection packages are handled by both formal and informal sectors. For example, systems like dharma bhakari[3] and guthi[4] provide community-run, informal support to people. There are also packages like the old age allowance, the widow allowance, food for work, cash incentives, maternal and child care incentives and others (see section 4.7) that are run by state or private sectors in Nepal, making it a formal practice.

Devereux and Sabates-Wheeler (2004) also link social protection to vulnerability, stating that it is the joint effort of the public and private institutions to support the needy through

---

3 A system of collecting and storing grains by local communities in grain reservoirs so that it can be used for the needy when there are unexpected events such as natural calamities.

4 A cooperative system practiced by some group of people thus supporting the community when in need.

various approaches like income, livelihood support, social status maintenance and human rights assistance. Harvey (2009) also reveals that the concern of international and national institutions and donors has been increasing towards building safety nets. This further leads us to the understanding that it is not only the government or the state they can help create such mechanism but also international organisations are involved.

Moreover, Garcia and Gruat (2003, p 13) revealed that the international community has come together to help eradicate poverty using social protection as a fundamental mechanism. Some of the international communities that have been mentioned here are: The World Summit of Children 1990; The United Nations Conference on Environment and Development 1992; The World Conference on Human Rights 1993; The International Conference on Population and Development 1994; The Fourth World Conference on Women 1995; The Second United Nations Conference on Human Settlements (Habitat II) 1996; The World Food Summit 1996; The United Nations Millennium Declaration 2000 adopted by the General Assembly; The United Nations World Conference Against Racism 2001 and the Second World Assembly on Ageing 2002. This list demonstrates that there are many international communities active in supporting human security. Hence, with an understanding that social protection can be provided by any sector or group that is inclined towards ensuring human security, it is also to be understood that the state is the sole actor on which most people depend.

4.5 Different categories

In addition to its various definitions, social protection also has many different types. Scott (2012) identifies social protection as incorporating social assistance, social insurance, labour market interventions, community-based or informal social protection. Social assistance includes conditional[5] and unconditional[6] forms

[5] In conditional transfers, suppliers often expect something in return (for example, the food for work program that gave food to children and in return they had to attend school).

[6] Unconditional transfers are often those that are given to people and the supplier does not expect anything in return (such as pensions).

of support such as cash and resource transfers. Social insurance is inclined towards preventing the risks that might occur, for example through employment security and benefits like provident funds. Labour market interventions are more inclined towards those workers who are paid minimum wages, thus acting as a protection mechanism for them. Finally, community-based or informal social protection is mostly dealt with at the community level. The Asian Development Bank (ADB), the International Labour Organisation (ILO) and other such organisations also have their own categories of social protection.

It might be difficult to look into the aspects of different social protection categories all at once. Slater has clarified that social protection can be viewed from two different angles which in fact avoid confusion:

Table 4.1 Two discernable patterns of social protection

Two views	SP as part of services	SP as part of livelihoods
The services	Social Security	Social Safety Nets
	• Chronic poverty • Life cycles • Long term programmes • Consumption focused • Transfers • Link to basic services e.g. health	• Vulnerability • Systemic shocks • Fixed-term programmes • Asset/production focused • Transfers/insurance • Link to agriculture and employment

Source: Secure Livelihoods Research Consortium Training by Rachel Slater in 2012 in Colombo, Sri Lanka

Table 4.1 shows how different forms of social protection can be perceived in a simple way. The two noticeable patterns that are juxtaposed in the table are common. When considering social protection as part of services, Slater makes it clear that social security becomes a component under which fall forms of security that help reduce vulnerability such as old age allowances and health benefits. Alternatively, considering it as part of livelihoods is linked to creating safety nets for people who are working.

Such supports include emergency relief (earthquake, floods, etc.) or introducing and immaculately implementing the livelihood generation programmes that are long-term focused. The table can also be used to identify who is liable for social security, social protection or safety net and based on people's situations; various protection interventions can be built and carried out.

4.6 Social protection approaches and framework

By generating an understanding that social protection was rebuked for being expensive and harmful to development activity, the World Bank (WB) came up with a new design to address and understand it. It is impossible to have social protection for developing countries as it is equally impossible to meet the variety of demands of every individual through the protection mechanisms. Hence, the World Bank focused more on developing an approach to social protection through the Social Risk Management (SRM) tool, which resulted in creation of the SRM framework.

Table 4.2 Why social risk management framework for social protection

S.N.	Important assessment of SRM	Important consequences of the assessment
1	The poor are typically most exposed to diverse risks. These risks range from natural (such as earthquake and flooding) to manmade (such as war and inflation) to health (such as illness) to political (such as discrimination).	The poor are the most vulnerable in society as shocks are likely to have the strongest welfare consequences for them. For welfare reasons, therefore, they should have increased access to SRM instruments.
2	The poor have the fewest instruments to deal with these risks (such as access to government provided income support and market-based instruments like insurance).	The high vulnerability of the poor makes them risk-averse and thus unable or unwilling to engage in higher risk/higher return activities.

Source: Holzmann et al. (2003)

Based on Table 4.2 and the World Bank's changing designs to address social protection, it can be inferred that the poor have been the central figures needing the most support. This takes us back to the debatable issue that social protection can actually help poverty reduction. Managing the risks that are tangible or intangible, idiosyncratic or covariate can actually be a means to human security (Garcia and Gruat 2003). Holzmann and Jorgensen (1999 and 2001) and Holzmann (2003) as cited in Holzmann et al. (2003, p 5) reveal that making individuals aware by making the risk management tools accessible, especially to the poor "is both an end as well as a means to development". If poverty reduction is an aim then risk management, a tool of social protection, is a positive booster to eradicating poverty.

Risks can be both predictable and unpredictable. Predictable risks, for example, weather risks, can be dealt with before their arrival. Moreover, people can to some extent save themselves from insecurity by trying to reduce the risk or planning to prevent them before the event occurs. However, risks that are unpredictable, such as floods, cannot be dealt with instantly. In such situations, coping mechanisms are helpful to prevent vulnerability.

It is also important that every human being knows how to reduce risks or cope when an event occurs. In order to assist people in achieving this state of awareness, the supplier side needs to take responsibility to create programmes such as earthquake and fire drills.

Additionally, the people (demanders) here have a responsibility to become aware by attending the programmes and improving their own knowledge and that of their family members.

Table 4.3 Understanding social risk management framework

S.N	Type	Implication
1	Risk reduction	Can be planned before risky events occur; lessening the risk that might occur can help people feel secure, thus increasing their expected income and welfare; reducing risks are those that fall outside of SP tools such as environmental policies, investments in education, etc. SP interventions for risk reduction include strategies designed to reduce the risk of unemployment or low wages through alternate trainings, labour markets, etc.
2	Risk mitigation	Aims to address the risk before it occurs; supports individuals to reduce the impact of potentially damaging risks (to assets, people, etc.) For example, two different types of crops that can be harvested in different seasons which can then mitigate the risk of not having income for six months in a year.
3	Risk coping	Aims to address the risk after the event has occurred; coping can be seen in the form of borrowing, seeking public or private assistance or even the government.

Source: Holzmann et. al (2003: 6-7)

Table 4.3 reveals that the SRM framework can help people to be strategically aware of the risks and prepare for the best. By adapting to the three elements of risk management, people are more likely to avoid falling into poverty or even the poor have more capability to save themselves. Though the framework is more inclined towards the poor, any individual can benefit by adapting to the mitigating methods through knowledge transfer and sharing. Hence, managing risk, whether through reduction, prevention or the formation of coping mechanisms, can be one of the best social protection mechanisms for human security. Also, it is important to notice that the SRM framework connects to social protection as part of services as well as livelihoods.

In addition to the Social Risk Management framework, another approach to social protection is through the effective use of the '3Ps' (prevention, promotion and protection), also introduced by the World Bank, along with the addition of a 'T' (transformative) by Devereux and Sebates-Wheeler. The main focus of the 3P approach was on resilience and opportunity thus reiterating the role of social protection.

Figure 4.1 The 3P framework: Functions of the institution and resilience opportunity

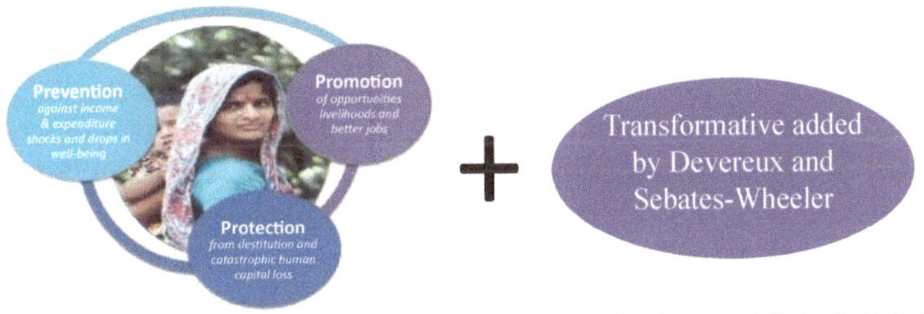

Source: Compiled by the authors from WB (2012) and Devereux and Sebates-Wheeler (2004)

After adding the T to the 3Ps, the framework is shaped into a much more logical and sensible pattern. The 3Ps framework exaggerates the fact that social protection cannot only be inclined towards protection; instead, it should also have promotion- and prevention-aspects to remain more effective. Prevention is more focused on assisting people to get away from risks that can be achieved through "social insurance programmes such as unemployment and disability insurance, old age pensions and complementary programmes like crop and weather insurance, health insurance" (WB 2006 as cited in WB 2012, p 2). Such supports help people cope with shocks and feel a sense of security. Protection, alternatively, refer to a defence from hardships and disastrous loss of human capital. In order to cope with the loss, assistance in the form of "cash transfers, subsidies, education and health for children and households" can be useful (ibid, p 2). Such social protection mechanisms can help lessen inequality that could occur as people go through distress due to loss of belongings and property. Promotion is essential in order to make protection mechanisms effective and long-term. Informing people about better opportunities and livelihoods can help them become secure as they can apply for vacant positions. Social protection, therefore, can build into the protection, prevention and promotion activities in which missing one 'P' could create chaos and undermine human security.

Social protection measures seem to be developing with time. Devereux and Sebates-Wheeler (2004) came up with a new term - 'transformative approach' - which adds to the World Bank's 3Ps. The authors reveal that the approaches for dealing with risks and vulnerable situations in society need a "transformative element" (ibid, p 9). The term 'transformative' refers to various policies which explain the power inequality which induces and provokes vulnerabilities. Devereux and Sebates-Wheeler illustrate that providing support to the business sectors could help marginalised people raise their voice and attain their rights, for example through awareness-raising campaigns to transform public perception and changing the regulatory framework that can protect the marginalised people. Hence, along with protection, promotion and prevention, transformation becomes an important aspect of social protection.

Moreover, Devereux and Sebates-Wheeler (2004) argue that some social protection mechanisms can fulfill both the promotive and transformative actions while some do not. For example, microfinance schemes are meant to help people with social insurance and economic opportunity, which is an action of promotion, but they can also be transformative by making the public aware and changing their perceptions. All these elements are interlinked, and are a sound and reasonable approach to social protection.

Scott (2012) reveals that there are other factors that are to be taken into consideration while framing or dealing with the issues of social protection, with which Garcia and Gruat (2003) also agree. While Scott (2012) mentions the need of issues like pro-poor growth and exclusion, Garcia and Gruat suggest elements that show equivalent treatment such as "gender equality" being the most important.

It is also very important to understand the impacts created by implementing social protection. For example, at a recent Secure Livelihood Research Consortium (SLRC) training, Slater (2012) exemplified an effective impact of social transfers, a form of social protection and its direct and indirect benefits on recipients and non-recipients.

Table 4.4 Impacts of social transfers

	Direct beneficiaries	**Indirect beneficiaries**
Direct impact	Cash transfers raise household incomes and reduce poverty South Africa: Social grants = poverty gap reduced by 47%.	Cash transfers are spent on secondary beneficiaries, not just recipients Namibia: Pension cash is spent on relatives: grandchildren = 55%; adult children = 25%.
Indirect impact	Cash transfers are not only consumed but invested. All countries: cash spent on seed, education and such	Cash transfers generate income multipliers and economic growth, Zambia: cash-for-work: workers hired farm labours

Source: Secure Livelihoods Research Consortium Training by Rachel Slater in 2012 at Colombo, Sri Lanka

Table 4.4 clearly depicts that providing a form of protection (social transfer in this case) does not only benefit the targeted population but also has positive side effects on others. For example, the first quadrant reveals a case of South Africa where the provision of cash transfer helped raise household income. The provision of social grants led to a reduction in the poverty gap. In addition, the provision of cash transfers such as pensions are also spent on grandchildren or others who, while not the intended beneficiaries, benefit indirectly. Instruments designed for human security can benefit people through having a direct or indirect impact on their lives. These forms of grants seem beneficial as they do not sacrifice a long- term provision for short-term contentment.

4.7 Existing social protection provisions in Nepal and the downfalls

World Bank (WB 2011) report on Social Safety Nets in Nepal, conducted a social protection survey in 2009 using nine districts[7],

[7] The nine districts were Khotang, Palpa, Surkhet and Doti in the Hills, Sankhuwasabha and Mugu in the Mountains and Siraha, Sarlahi and Bardiya in the Tarai region of Nepal.

1,680 respondents, as their major focus. The Nepal Safety Nets Survey examined through their survey the 29 different types of protection and programmes for Nepal (ibid, p 18) which already denotes that there are many existing programmes on social protection. The 29 programmes mentioned are:

Table 4.5 Various social protection programmes

1. Old age allowance	2. Widow allowance	3. Disability allowance
4. Any maternal incentive scheme	5. Education scholarship (Dalits)	6. Education scholarship (Girls)
7. Disability scholarships	8. Education scholarship (general)	9. Martyr's family benefits
10. People's movement victims benefits	11. Compensation for road accident	12. Compensation for floods or natural calamities
13. Micro finance	14. Insurance for health	15. Insurance for livestock
16. Public food distribution system	17. School meal programme	18. Nutritional supplement programme for children
19. Nutritional supplement programme for pregnant women	20. Food for Work	21. Cash for Work
22. Rural Community Infrastructure Works (RCIW)	23. Subsidised fertilizer	24. Subsidised seeds
25. Subsidised credit	26. Youth self employment programmes	27. Technical and vocational training
28. Natural disaster rescue and rehabilitation	29. Bonded labor rehabilitation	

Source: WB (2011)

Among these, the World Bank based on the safety Nets Survey reveals major safety nets programmes as the following (ibid, p 58):

A. Cash based transfers: old age allowance, poor widow or single women allowance, disability allowance

B. Conditional cash transfers: scholarship programmes, maternity incentive schemes

C. Food based transfers: Public food distribution programme, food for education, maternal child nutrition

D. Public work programmes: Rural Community Infrastructure Works, The Nepal Food Crises Response Programme, The Karnali Employment Programme, Other labor intensive infrastructure programmes such as Employment Intensive Investment Programme (EIIP), The Employment Creation and Peace Building based on Local Economic Development (EmpLED) project

E. Programmes for conflict affected persons: Cash transfers, other social funds such as funds for construction of damaged infrastructure

Besides, in the context of Nepal, are the civil service pensions such as provident fund, social funds or other social care services (informal) as guthi, bhakari systems.

So far the most visible, highlighted and talked about forms of social protection are the old age allowance, the widow allowances, the Karnali Employment programmes and scholarships to promote education. The old age allowance (see section 4.2 a) and single women's allowances are universal (includes every individual that fall in this category), and are the two largest programmes in Nepal. There are two categories of senior citizens who receive benefits: elderly people aged 70 and above Dalits and those from the Karnali area who qualify for the allowance when they cross the age of 60. The Economic Survey 2009/2010 reveals that a total of 640,119 senior citizens across the country benefited from the old age allowance in 2009. Among them, 532,634 were senior citizens aged above 70, 93,377 were Dalit senior citizens aged 60 and above 14,108 were senior citizens from the Karnali area aged over 60 (MoF 2010).

The single widow allowance has increased to NPR 500 per month from NPR 150. Single women or widows above 60 years of age without proper livelihood options qualify for this grant (WB 2011). This grant was founded in 1996-97 by the Nepali Congress (NC) and is considered one of the most effective. The disability allowance introduced in 1996-96 targeting people aged above 16 years with enduring disabilities (completely blind, handicapped or totally dependent on others due to lack of ability to take care of self) were provided NPR 100, which in 2008/2009 the government raised to NPR 1000 for those permanently disabled and NPR 300 to those with partial disabilities (ibid, p 54).

The Karnali Employment Programme, targeted towards five poor districts (Dolpa, Humla, Kalikot, Jumla, Mugu) in the Karnali Zone of Nepal began in 2006/07 when the Ministry of Local Development (MoLD) introduced work schemes for poor people and in turn provided cash.

Table 4.6 Karnali employment programme: Progress report from five districts (2009/10)

No.	District	No. of Programmes Competed	Average no. of employment days	Average Progress (%)	Budget approved and spent (US $)
1	Mugu	133	15	97.42	425,700
2	Dolpa	135	12	98.46	307,412
3	Humla	106	11	98.46	362,064
4	Jumla	87	10	97.61	821,219
5	Kalikot	153	13.50	97.80	98,315

Source: WB (2011)

Table 4.6 reveals that poor people from the poorest districts of Nepal have been provided with some form of livelihood security through the Karnali Employment Programme (KEP). Huge amounts of money have been spent, with numerous successful programmes and decent progress. Such incentives and offers from the government side is an example of better protection mechanisms for human security in relation to fighting poverty. However, Regmi and Ghimire (2010) reveal that the programme, though intends to fight poverty is not pro-young. Their study about the KEP in Jumla, Humla and Kalikot shows that youths were not motivated to adopt such an employment programme as it was temporary. Also, since the programme intends to benefit one person per family, older people joined the jobs thus restricting the youths. Additionally, the participation of women also remained low due to the restriction (ibid, p 56). This means that implementation of certain programmes, though successful, was negated by restricting others who might be more in need of jobs. This could be one factor why migration among youths takes place due to lack of jobs for them in home country.

In terms of education, various forms of scholarships have been provided to children promoting the "Education for All" slogan across the country. Food-for-Education is one of the most highlighted forms of protection in terms of supporting education. It holds an aim of increasing enrollment rates, especially of girls and provides them food as incentive so that girls that are hungry can go to school by relieving short-term hunger. This programme is a joint venture of partnership between the Ministry of Education, World Food Programme (WFP) and United Nations Children's Fund (UNICEF). So far the programme has reached 450,000 school children in 4000 schools covering 21 districts (WB 2011, p 58).

4.7.1 Loopholes in the mechanisms, evidence

Despite these mechanisms, there are still some loopholes in the social protection arena which has failed to address longevity in terms of its existence and functioning. Though the schemes mentioned above show progress and growth, the balance between many schemes and programmes to its effective implementation is still a question for Nepal. For example, in the Food for Education Programme, 2009/2010 records show that 182,000 children were targeted for the daily meal planwhile the coverage was 154,359 (WB 2011). The imbalance between targets and coverage denotes various questions and thoughts about the insecurity of the remaining 27,641 children who fell into the target. The lack of proper implementation and monitoring of the programmes could actually affect an individual's right to human security.

A report by Powell-Jackson (2008) on "Evaluation of Safe Delivery Incentive Programme" points out information on the Maternity Incentive Scheme (MIS), now known as the Safe Delivery Incentive Programme (SDIP). In order to promote safe motherhood, women are given incentives for delivering their babies in public health facilities. The numbers of children that can be delivered are two. This programme is run in 75 districts and women are provided NPR 500 in the Tarai, NPR 1000 in the Hills and NPR 1500 in the mountains. In the districts where there is a low HDI rating, delivery is done for free and trained health workers are also given NPR 300 for deliveries. It has been reported that SDIP has created a positive impact in the use of government services, especially in the Tarai and mountain regions of Nepal. However, it is also clear that only 27 per cent of women were aware about the SDIP when they were pregnant. Additionally, women who were educated, those who fell in a higher caste category, were the ones seeking benefits. This creates an ambiguous aftermath since it excludes women who fall in the lower caste category, who are uneducated and marginalised. Not knowing that a child could be delivered safely restrains pregnant women, thus shunning their human security issue. If promoting safe motherhood is the major focus of the programme, it has to ensure that every single woman, from poor to well off, from illiterate to literate, marginalised to less marginalised, is aware of the programme.

Simply providing and formulating various programmes (Table 4.5) does not answer the human security issue. A complete cycle which includes supply and demand with a sustainable approach and monitoring can help address human security. For example, (see Fig 4.2) the old age allowance being a universal package still shows loop holes. Their major complaints so far have been distance, time and respect. An article, 'No country for old men' by KC (2011), reveals the plight of four elderly people who came home empty handed despite their travel to the office that distributed allowance. While elderly people have to travel far to get their benefit, the support of NPR 500, that still does not make them secure.

Figure 4.2 Factors that makes human security when linked to social protection

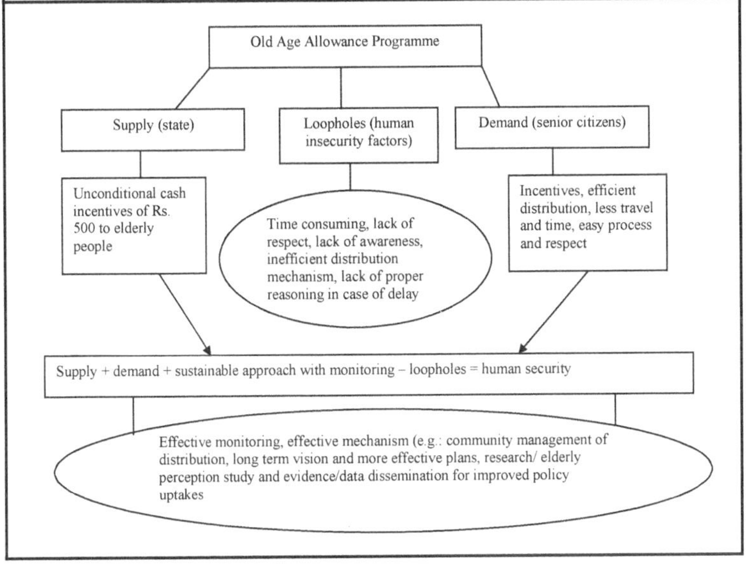

Source: Designed by the authors

The ideology here is that the state has not failed to care for elderly people but they have failed to address the essence of holistic human security. Simply answering demands can never be accomplished unless there is a proper mechanism of monitoring and evaluation along with a long-term fulfillment of the demands. Children, senior citizens, disabled and other such categories need long-term security. From Figure 4.2 it is clear that the state is defining its own illegitimacy by creating loop holes. Loopholes can take away the demander's security as well as the supplier's. The Figure is just an example; other such programmes such as the safe motherhood programme, nutrition and maternity care also require similar mechanism to address human security.

Another striking fact is that most of the social protection programmes either appear as "come and go" phenomenon or do not last long due to implementation failure. Also there are hardly any programmes that address human security in the form of psychological, emotional, or other forms of support besides financial. From such a perspective, most forms of protection mechanisms are nullified as they do not cover the holistic pattern of human security. For example, the Martyr's family benefits provides allowances for children's education, NPR 1000 per month for children in kindergarten and grade 1 to 5, NPR 1500 per month for those in grade 6-10 and NPR 2000 per month for those in higher secondary and higher education (WB 2011). However, there are no provisions of psychological support for children and families of martyrs, which conceals the holistic human security aspects in relation to social protection.

4.8 Why is social protection a human security issue?

After understanding the essence of social protection, including current research and existing frameworks, it is very important to understand that it is a human security issue. It helps to reduce risks, prepares people to prevent or cope with risk and saves people from vulnerable conditions. Social protection, on the one hand, answers people's needs and on the other, keeps them content as they are assured that if anything happens and if they fall into a helpless situation, they have security mechanisms to rely on.

During the UN's World Summit for Social Development in Denmark in 1995, the then Brazilian Ambassador opined that "state security depends on human security and human security is linked to a set of moral issues such as the limits to human suffering that must be addressed" (Timothy 2004, p 20). In his opinion, the importance of human security is highlighted more in comparison to state security. To put it simply, when humans are secured, the state then becomes secured as people's judgment determines state's legitimacy. Moreover, like various institutional definitions of social protection, the ambassador's statement makes clear the need for addressing issues of human suffering (or vulnerabilities). This takes us to the level of understanding that human security is an important and urgent need which eventually leads to state security. Human security can be fulfilled by rescuing human beings from suffering such as poverty, lack of better livelihoods and health facilities.

By looking at human security and social protection, it can be assumed that the latter can be a component of human security. More than half the world's population has been striving to get out of poverty. Though it is difficult to fight poverty, with the introduction of the Millennium Development Goals (MDGs) the world's aim to fight poverty has not proved to be a failure. Social protection is therefore a human security issue because it helps human beings create a secure space when they are exposed to vulnerability.

Social protection can help provide human beings with basic needs for survival, as well as encouragement and hope. However, if there is no protection mechanism in place (established by responsible people and governments), things can go wrong. There are many forms of social protection that could be taken as a human security issue. For example, the suicides by 25000 farmers in India since 1997 demonstrate that it is needed for human security (Shiva 2004). With globalisation and new technologies, these farmers lost their jobs, racked up enormous debt and became vulnerable. With no help from the state and a lack of protection mechanisms, the farmers who had lived their lives farming and contributing to India's economy took their own lives. Had there been an effective social protection mechanism in place, or the denial of adopting new technology that would hamper these people's lives (which, as a risk reduction mechanism, is also a form of social protection), or a benefits mechanism to help these farmers cope with the risk, their lives would not have ended in such misery.

In most countries where the majority of people earn less than one dollar per day, social protection serves as a system designed for their protec- tion. In this instance, the form of protection would be referred to as social security to tackle chronic poverty (also see Table 4.1). Alternatively, for individual who can make a living through a high income but who still be victims of unknown situations such as natural calamities, social protection takes the form of social safety nets and risk management. In this way, every human being is entitled to some form of security, be it financial or technical.

Social protection is a human security issue; examples and researchers show that it helps reduce poverty when implemented successfully. In the European Union, social protection played a major role in reducing poverty by 50 per cent (Fig 4.3). Such evidence makes the various forms of protections and its implementation a successful story.

Figure 4.3 European Union, Social Protection Reduces Poverty by 50 per cent

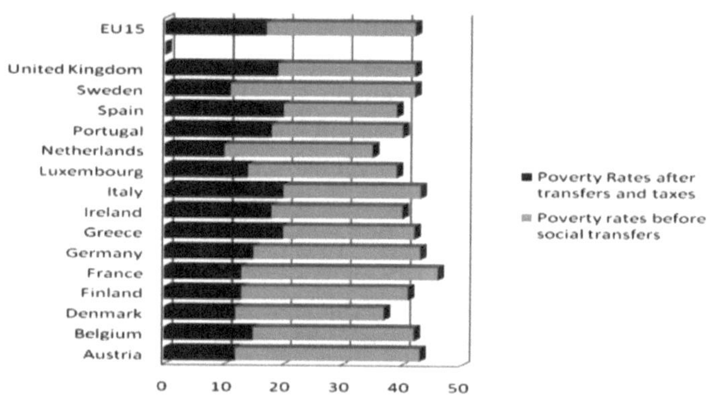

Source: Ortiz and Yablonski (2010) as cited in Ortiz (2010)

From Figure 4.3, the presence of social protection in one of the MDGs goals, poverty reduction, is evident. Most of the countries listed in the figure are tagged as developed nations and the picture of their poverty line reduced to 50 per cent seems tangible. However, for developing countries such as Nepal, the problems might be political barriers or even the sole understanding of social protection and its long run benefits. It was not a well-observed phenomenon and consequently, it remains inconsistent and unclear. Every human wish to be free from poverty. Figure (4.3) proves that if policies are well set, implemented, monitored and studied, social protection can help to reduce poverty.

One aspect of scrutinising and understanding the fact that social protection is a human security issue. A strenuous effort has been made by many countries to attain the set goals. The eight MDGs cover issues and components of human security by addressing the concerns of poverty, gender, children, education and health issues. With the introduction and implementation of social protection to meet the MDGs, it seems like achieving the targets has become easier. Table 4.7 shows how the MDGs have been successfully achieved through the introduction of social protection and also how social protection could be a human security issue.

For example, poverty being one of the sole causes of human insecurity, has been addressed by providing pension programmes, cash transfer programmes, social funds, health insurance, gender-sensitive policies and jobs markets for youth so that they will not face unemployment crises. All these elements are a form of protection, which takes us back to the thought that social protection in fact answers the needs of human beings and creates for them a web of protection and security. Providing benefits such as allowance to the elderly can actually rescue people who cannot make their own living or are helpless. Moreover, the world has been striving to eradicate poverty and help human beings escape from vulnerability. The MDGs came as a package but what positively altered its achievement were the social protection interventions.

If we make an attempt to eliminate the social protection interventions column from Table 4.7 and think about the MDGs results, we can make an assumption that it would definitely take much longer than the set time to achieve the goals. Also, given the fact that the 2015 deadline is approaching, without social protection as an enhancer, the MDGs would not have answered the human security issues (Table 4.7). It is clear and evident that introducing social protection can actually help attain human security issues.

Table 4.7 Social protection as a human security issue in relation to the MDGs

Human security issue	MDGs	Social Protection interventions, examples by World Bank
Fight poverty	1	The provision of pensions reduces poverty among the old and disabled; safety nets smooth/raise income, thereby directly affecting poverty; fee waivers for health and education allow families to obtain services without impoverishing themselves; transfers targeted to children or youth can help reduce current as well as intergenerational transmission of poverty; social funds empower the extreme poor; etc.
Education	2	Social insurance smoothes household income (protects from shocks) and thereby increases children's school enrollment and lowers child labor; benefits (cash/food) conditioned on school enrollments create incentives for families to send children (especially girls) to school; increased incomes can reduce child labor and increase school enrollment; etc.
Gender balance	3	Girls' enrollment may be especially sensitive to income or price and safety net interventions can address both; social funds contribute to access of girls to schools through attention to appropriate sanitation, security, etc. in the construction of buildings; maternity (and paternity) leave encourages more women to enter and stay in the workforce; etc.
Health and benefits	4/5/6	Income smoothing helps protect health status in times of stress; health insurance makes medical treatment more accessible; adequate maternity leave improves maternal health; cash/food transfer programmes can reward the use of preventive health care; income support increases access to health care; safety nets for orphans and vulnerable children can help cope with impacts of diseases and protect them from HIV; etc.
Securing environment for better life, eventually leads to human security	7	Lower transient poverty may reduce household's need to unsustainably exploit natural resources; assessments built into social funds are important for continued environmental sustainability; etc.
Secured for being a youth	8	Well-structured labor market programmes help to secure access of youth to job market; youth leaders can be promoted though social funds; etc.

Source: Adapted by the authors from WB (2003)

UNICEF (2010) also provides some evidence that social protection acts as an accelerator of the MDGs, particularly in reducing poverty, the main cause of human insecurity in most countries. UNICEF reveals that with the provision of social pension and transfers, the poverty gap in Senegal and Tanzania could be reduced by 35 per cent to 40 per cent (Gassmann et al. 2006 as cited in UNICEF 2010). Also in Mexico the programme called 'Oportunidades' managed to reduce the poverty gap by 30 per cent (Skoufias and Parker 2001 as cited in UNICEF 2010, p 2). The aforementioned examples support an understanding of why social protection remains a human security issue and what factors are held accountable for this assumption.

4.9 Conclusion

Social protection is one of the most important assets that human beings can ever possess. While some countries today still face large-scale poverty and have few solutions to address it, other countries possess social protection mechanisms but with varying degrees of effectiveness. For example, while South Africa has through cash transfers been able to fight poverty, some countries in Africa which have been provided nets to combat malaria are misusing the given support. Such practices lead skeptics to wonder whether social protection, a must-have for every human, can be only fulfilled from the supply side while receivers do not cope with it well. It seems as if the supply side (government, research institutions, donors, organisations working for social protection) have been putting in strenuous effort to answer people's demands.

It is crucial to consider that, despite understanding that all human beings are sole owners of security, social protection is an expensive tool and that prior to introducing it and taking it to the next level, beneficiaries must be mapped based on their urgent and emergency needs and their vulnerability. For example, the poor and disadvantaged[8] automatically fall on

8 Disadvantaged here can be understood as people with disabilities; minority caste/class groups (in case of Nepal), women and children of poor households who cannot afford to send children to school or fulfill basic needs.

this category. Social protection based on collaboration between suppliers and demanders seems to function well as providing support and grants and expecting something in return (except for urgent cases such as occurrence of covariate risks) proves effective. If the social protection mechanism is introduced and but does not prove effective, the huge budget, time and even human condition will be negatively impacted.

Should social protection be focused firstly on the poor and then the rest of the citizen? In general this should be a rule of thumb. In other words, every human being needs social protection but it is necessary to understand the categorisation and put the poor and disadvantaged in the first place. For example, in Nepal the large gap between poor and rich makes the poor much more needy of some form of social protection mechanism, particularly of livelihood and income generation support to fulfill their basic needs. Some protection mechanisms such as cash transfers in Nepal are pro-poor and have benefited this group of people. Social protection therefore is a human security issue because it addresses the needs of the needy. Uncertainty is fundamental to all people but especially to the poor who face "chronic rather than stochastic insecurity" (Wood 2003, p 455). Their situation is unpredictable as they are already shunned in society, and are highly prone to risks, as opposed to people who are better off. In general, if a natural calamity takes place and affects a rich landlord's house along with a small shack owned by a poor person, it is more likely that the landlord, knowing many people around, will be able to seek immediate support as opposed to the poor. This is natural, at least in the case of Nepal, where politics, hospital facilities and anything one could name ironically favour the rich rather than the poor. Hence, the poor are always vulnerable and eschewed.

In conclusion, social protection is an important human security issue, most focused on those that are unable to compete in society to sustain their lives. And if every human deserves or is entitled to security, there are many ways human beings themselves can address this issue through environment conservation to reduce the risk of natural calamity, self-awareness about various risk factors or even creating their own informal mechanisms in the area they live, so as not to depend on the government, state or others for important yet not urgent needs. Of course, they are entitled to securities such as those from theft, murder and such provided by their government.

However, it is also important to note what framework of social protection can be useful based on the country's context. If it is a fragile state, like Nepal, Sri Lanka or countries emerging from conflict, the social protection intervention no doubt requires different and unique features. However, whether the comfort or security is psychological, financial or both, needs must be identified before allocating budgets or reaching out to the needy with inadequate preparation.

Several factors such as affordability, vulnerable groups and their demands (categorised as urgent and important needs; urgent but unimportant; not urgent and unimportant; not urgent but important), suppliers' ability (their funding mechanism) and demanders' ability to adapt to the given interventions should be considered to make proper use of social protection. This consideration is necessary because sometimes the general public fails to perceive what the supply side has to deal with while framing social protection interventions and support mechanisms to provide them with security. For example, the old age allowance for Nepal is NPR 500 (USD 5.60) per month per person which is perceived by the general public as a very low amount. However, when looking into it from the government's side and the state funds, it is a huge amount being invested in social protection as there are many elderly people in the country. In 2001, there were 1.6 million elderly inhabitants which at the time constituted 7.46 per cent of the total population. The rate has been increasing at 3.39 per cent per year (Dahal 2007). Also WB (2011) report based on a Social Safety Nets Survey (2009) reports that less than one per cent of respondent who faced shocks in 2008 mentioned about receiving assistance from the government. Many were supported through families, social and other forms of networks. The coping mechanisms also vary based on geographical area, diverse ethnicity people have, their livelihoods patterns and wealth. Additionally, providing emotional and psychological support during and after shocks are important factors to consider when it comes to human security and social protection. Hence, interventions can be conducted with transparency so that the suppliers and demanders are both content in what they give and take.

Human security is an important phenomenon which has been on the world's agenda for a long time. Over the years, much has changed in fulfilling the essence of human needs in relation to securing their lives and putting mankind in risk-free situations. However, nothing can be achieved in a single try and sometimes trial and error seems like the only option. Many social protection options have evolved over the time. While some have worked very well, some have faded out. Hence, human security is not a means that is to be obtained or provided by a 'hook or crook' approach but it is something that needs a systematic approach. Human security and social protection are interlinked phenomenon and without the latter it would be difficult to aim for the former. Both the supply side and the demand side need to understand that social protection does not always have to be something in the form of financial investment; it could also be in the form of technical support such as earthquake drills to reduce risk and promote security. Security is our basic human need and social protection is the key to open it. If everyone as a member of society has the right to social security, as defined in the Universal Declaration of Human Rights, their responsibility, after attaining the right, is to use it dutifully and not misuse it.

References

Brieger W. 2010. Millions of nets – but are they being used?. *Africa Health.* Also available at: www.africa-health.com/articles/july_2010/Malaria.pdf; accessed on 20 August 2012.

Dahal V. 2007. *Elderly People in Nepal: What happened after MIPPA, 2002?* High-level Meeting on the Regional Review of the Madrid International Plan of Action on Ageing (MIPAA) 9-11 October 2007. Macao: Madrid International Plan of Action on Ageing.

Dahl-Eriksen T. 2007. Human Security: A New Concept which Adds New Dimensions to Human Rights Discussions?. *Human Security Journal* 5:16-27.

Devereux S, Sabates-Wheeler R. 2004. *Transformative Social Protection.* Brighton: Institute of Development Studies (IDS).

Garcia BA, Gruat JV. 2003. *Social Protection: A Life Cycle Continuum Investment for Social Justice, Poverty Reduction and Sustainable Development.* A Conference Report. Geneva: International Labor Organisation (ILO), pp 1-64.

Ghimire AB, Upreti BR. 2008. Conflict Induced Displacement: An Emerging Phe- nomenon of Internal Migration in Nepal. *In:* Pyakuryal KN, Upreti BR, Sharma SR, editors. *Nepal: Transition to Transformation.* Kathmandu: Human and Natural Resource Studies Centre (HNRSC), South Asia Re- gional Coordination Office of the Swiss National Centre of Competence in Research (NCCR North- South), pp 101-139.

Haan de A. 2011. Social protection in international development: Editor's introduction to the special issue. *Canadian Journal of Development Studies* 32(4): 351-356.

Harvey P, Holmes R. 2007. *The potential for joint programmes for long-term cash transfers in unstable situations.* A report commissioned by the Fragile States Team and the Equity and Rights Team of the UK Department for International Development. London: Humanitarian Policy Group, Overseas Development Institute.

Harvey P. 2009. *Social Protection in Fragile States: Lessons Learned.* Promoting Pro-poor Growth. London: Overseas Development Institute.

Holmes R. 2010. *The Role of Social Protection Programmes in Supporting Edu- cation in Conflict-Affected Situations.* Background paper prepared for the Education for All Global Monitoring Report 201., The hidden crisis: Armed conflict and education. London: Overseas Development Institute.

Holzmann R, Jorgensen S. 1999. Social Protection as Social Risk Management: Conceptual Underpinnings for the Social Protection Sector Strategy Paper. *Journal of International Development* 11(7):1005-1027.

Holzmann R, Jorgensen S. 2001. Social Risk Management: A New Conceptual Framework for Social Protection, and Beyond. *International Tax and Public Finance* 8(4):529-556.

Holzmann R, Sherburne-Benz L, Tesliuc E. 2003. *Social Risk Management: The World Bank's Approach to Social Protection in a Globalising World.* Washington, D.C.: World Bank.

ILO [International Labour Organisation]. 2000. *World Labour Report: Income security and social protection in a changing world.* Geneva: International Labour Organisation..

KC S. 2011. No country For Old Men. *The Kathmandu Post Vol xix No. 236.*Kathmandu: Kantipur Publication

MoF [Ministry of Finance]. 2010. Economic Survey Fiscal year 2009/2010. Kathmandu: Ministry of Finance, Government of Nepal.

Norton A, Conway T, Foster M. 2001. *Social Protection Concepts and Approaches: Implications for Policy and Practice in International Development.* London: Center for Aid and Public Expenditure, Overseas Development Institute.

Ortiz I. 2010. *A Social Protection Floor as Development Policy.* Key note Speech. Bangkok, 27 October 2010.

Powell-Jackson T, Neupane BD, Tiwari S, Morrison J, Costello A. 2008. *Evaluation of the Safe Delivery Incentive Programme.* Final Report of Evaluation. Kathmandu: Support to the Safe Motherhood Programme-Nepal, Government of Nepal.

Rajan SI. 2003. Old age Allowance Programme in Nepal. Trivandrum: Centre for Development Studies.

Scott Z. 2012. *Topic Guide on Social Protection.* Birmingham: The Governance and Social Development Resource Centre (GSDRC), University of Birmingham.

Shiva V. 2004. *The Suicide Economy of Corporate Globalisation. Counter Currents. ORG* www.countercurrents.org/glo-shiva050404.htm; accessed on 26 April 2012.

Singh P. 2007. *Social Protection in ASEAN: Issues and Challenges for ASEAN and its Member Countries* (ASEAN GO-NGO Forum, 2007).

Timothy K. 2004. Human Security Discourse at the United Nations. *Peace Review* 16 (1):19-24.

UNICEF [United Nations International Children's Fund]. 2010. *Social Protection: Accelerating the MDGs with Equity.* Social and Economic Policy Working Brief. New York: United Nations International Children's Emergency Fund.

WB [World Bank]. 2003. *The Contribution of Social Protection to Millennium Development Goals.* Washington, D.C.: World Bank.

WB [World Bank]. 2006. *World Development Report: Equity and Development.* Washington, D.C.: World Bank.

WB [World Bank]. 2011. *Social Safety Nets in Nepal.* Kathmandu: South Asia Social Protection, Nepal and World Bank.

WB [World Bank]. 2012. *Building Resilience and Opportunity. The World Bank's Social Protection and Labour Strategy 2012-2022.* Concept Note. Washington, D.C.: World Bank.

Wood G. 2003. Staying Secure, Staying Poor: The Faustian Bargain. *World Development* 31(3):455-471.

****

Chapter 5

Food security: A fundamental basis for human security

Yamuna Ghale Nirmal Kumar Bishokarma

5.1 Adequate food is a major factor of human security

Human security is broadly defined by the Human Development Report 1994 as keeping economic, health, environment, personal and political aspects within a common framework. However, the concept is criticised by many actors, as human security comprises many domestic issues that are very contextual. Thus security defined within the narrow framework, is constantly being challenged. Though the concept is continually revisited, no agreed framework exists so far. After the end of the two World Wars (1918-1945) and the Cold War (1945-1990), the concept of security changed from a state-centric, traditional view to a community- and individual-centric approach (Spring 2009). Traditionally, security concerns were considered as external threats and the objectives of security policy were to protect state territory and national sovereignty (Kumar 2012). Insecurity was considered as a military threat and the means of addressing such threats was through military force (Quilop 2007). In this regard, during the World Wars security was determined by the size of the army and the number of weapons and warfare animals like horses. During the Cold War, it was perceived that threats from nuclear weapons could only be countered through international cooperation and military organisation (McDonald 2010), which led to the critical polarisation between the nations of the North Atlantic Treaty Organization (NATO) and the Warsaw Pact. Since the end of the Cold War, the landscape of national and international security threats has shifted to new mode of security known as human security, encompassing the concept of health, environmental degradation and food security. The experience of the World Wars clearly demonstrated that a lack of basic necessities such as food in one nation could become a problem or a threat for all other nations (Barrett and Maxwell 2005). In this context, food is a major component of non-traditional security challenges (Upreti 2012). It has tremendously disturbed the international trade, transportation and cooperation of food, causing food shortages in many countries (Defra 2006). In addition, food has caused labour and resource shortages and price hikes beyond the borders of countries.

According to the UNDP Human Development Report 1994, human security has two main components: safety from chronic threats such as hunger, disease and repression; and protection from sudden and harmful disruptions in the pattern of daily life (UNDP 1994, p 23). The Report categorised seven types of threat to human security: economic, food, health, environmental, personal, community and political security. So the definition of human security emphasises the provision for and freedom to lead a full life, including secure access to food (McDonald 2010). The concept of human security states that individuals are equal with the state and that state security is meant for individual and community security, not as an end in itself (Bhattarai 2010). Human security focuses on personal safety, well-being and individual freedom; in other words, physical safety and the provision of basic needs, human rights and, more importantly, economic and social rights (UNDP 1994). Amongst these concerns, food security is a key and critical dimension of human security, firstly because it is one of the most important basic needs and secondly because achieving food security is a fundamental right of every individual and community (Hastings 2010).

Political ecology theories state that resource scarcity in general and food insecurity specifically are major causes for conflicts and warfare. There is extensive writing on the impacts of conflict and insecurity on food security and vice-versa. Homer-Dixon (1994) holds the hypothesis that resource scarcity is a decisive factor in many violent conflicts causing human security. Livelihood and food insecurity also determine who participates in warfare. The civil unrest (protests, marches and often violent uprisings) which erupted around the world in 2008 in response to rising food prices demonstrated the importance of food security as integral part of human security (Gasper 2005). The stunningly violent food riots in 2011 in Tunisia and Algeria resulted in the deaths of hundreds of people. The decade-long armed conflict in Nepal (1996 to 2006) has shown that the main target of the insurgents were the poor and food-insecure rural people (Bishokarma 2010). Since food security and hunger undermine a person's dignity and wellbeing, they can become major factors in making hard decisions like joining armed conflict. Likewise, a country's ability or inability to produce and procure enough food for its people to avoid hunger and malnutrition is a critical aspect of human security (Boonchai and Sedsirot 2007). Wall (2005), in a study of the Darfur famine in 1983 and 1984, concludes that famine not only causes death, but also constitutes the reason for destitution and social breakdown.

5.2 International instruments on food and human insecurity

5.2.1 Basic concepts of international instruments

Human security is a multidimensional concept. It emphasises the individual and highlights the fact that security should be viewed not from the perspective of anything or anyone else but the individual (Quilop 2007). The concept of human and food security evolved from the end of the First and Second World Wars and was subsequently developed and refined during different periods (Table 5.1).

Table 5.1 Evolution of international instruments

Instruments	Basic concepts	Founder/Anchoring organisation
First World Food Conference 1943	Economic understanding of security	Franklin D. Roosevelt
Universal Declaration of Human Rights (UDHR)1948	Food: a basic human rights	United Nations (UN)
Second UN Conference on Food and Agriculture 1974	Food: a security issue	Food and Agriculture Organisation (FAO)
International Covenant on Economic, Cultural and Social Rights 1976	Food: a basic human right	UN
Voluntary guidelines on Right to Food (RtF)	Focus on three pillars of rights to adequate food: respect, fulfill and protect	FAO
Human Development Report (HDR) 1994	Food: as part of Freedom from Want	United Nations Development Programme (UNDP)
The International Commission on Intervention and State Sovereignty 2001	Focus on human needs of those seeking and protection and assistance	World Bank

Source: Compiled by the authors from various sources

5.2.2 Evolution of the concept of the political economy of food

The food security dimension of human security evolved at the end of the First and Second World Wars. Franklin D. Roosevelt stated at the 1943 United Nations Conference on Food and Agriculture that there are four freedoms for human beings (Spring 2009). One of his four freedoms was freedom from want, which incorporates an economic understanding of security instead of a traditional weapons-based security. The conference recognised that freedom from want means a secure, adequate and suitable supply of food. Recognising the importance of food in regard to human security, the FAO (Food and Agriculture Organisation) was established under the United Nations in 1945. It has been defining and leading food security concerns globally. The first Director General of the FAO, Sir John Boyd Orr, stated that feeding the world's poor would not only create a safer world, but would also avoid catastrophes such as the First and Second World Wars which were critical questions for human security (Schanbacher 2010). The conceptualisation and importance of food as a security issue gained global recognition during the 1974 World Food Conference (Heukelom 2010). The conference highlighted the fact that an unsatisfied need for food poses one of the most fundamental threats to human security (Spring 2009). It concentrates on the human dimension of food in terms of community and individual access to food, which embodies the core challenge to achieving global food security (Heukelom 2010). The first conference focused on the production side while the later concentrated on the supply and distribution of food.

Since the late 1990s, two different concepts of human security have emerged in the political realm. The Governments of Canada, Norway and European members of human security networks have preferred a narrow concept of human security focusing on freedom from fear that deals with humanitarian initiatives and human rights (Bhattarai 2010). Alternatively, the governments of Japan and other likeminded countries have opted for a wider concept that considers the concept of freedom from want as the human development agenda (Gasper 2005). As food is a very important aspect of freedom from want (Hastings 2010), it is an important dimension of human security.

The definition of food security which resulted from the FAO conferences is the most common: food security exists when all people, at all times, have physical and economic access to enough safe and nutritious food to meet their dietary needs and food preferences for an active and healthy lifestyle (World Food Summit 1996). At its fiftieth anniversary symposium in 1995, the FAO stated that the goal of food security is to ensure an adequate quantity and quality of food for every individual at all times (FAO 1995). To ensure food security, natural resource management and market and technological know-how are required (Lang 2002). Food security was considered as the adequate and stable supply of farm products and food for domestic use (OECD 1981). In this scenario, the International

Fund for Agricultural Development (IFAD) was established in 1974 to finance agricultural development, knowing that food insecurity is not only a problem of production but also the structural cause of rural poverty.

Food security expects to satisfy at least one of two conditions: supply side and demand side capacities. The supply side condition includes i) state policies and positions to deal with food security; ii) state mechanisms and instruments for effective implementation of policies, programmes and strategies, iii) enough measures and capacity to provision and implement safety net provisions during emergency and disaster, support to the elderly and other disadvantaged peoples and iv) private sector capacity to deal with local and external markets. The demand side includes i) secure and equitable access to production resources, ii) a sustainable increase in production capacity for sufficiency, import substitution and export promotion of relevant commodities, iii) options to deal with the state in securing access to basic services especially during emergencies and disasters including economic shocks. In order for the demand and supply sides to converge, there is a need to adopt a holistic approach of looking at food and livelihood issues as a package and considering a targeted approach to ensure that gender and inclusion issues are mainstreamed. These include access to basic education, health, clean water supplies and sanitation (Khan et al. 2002).

Based on the FAO concept, forty to fifty years ago food availability issues tended to dominate the discussions and debates, following neo- Malthusian perspectives. The original theorem of Malthus stated that while food production levels grow at a linear rate, human population grows at geometric rate if unchecked. The perspective predicted a decrease of available food per capita with ensuing famines and the eventual extinction of the human race.

In recent decades, the discourse of food security has been dominated by a market-based approach following neoliberal growth policies. Many multilateral organisations such as the International Monetary Fund (IMF), the World Bank (WB), the World Trade Organisation (WTO), the United Nations (UN), the Food and Agriculture Organisation (FAO), the International Fund for Agricultural Development (IFAD) and the World Food Program (WFP) are dealing with food security within different mandates and frameworks. More importantly, the FAO and the IFAD deal with overall agrarian reform and pay special attention to small scale, peasant and landless farm production. The WFP in comparison is mandated to respond to emergency and relief packages and related interventions for the short term. However, the worldwide hunger situation is worrisome as there are increasing numbers of vulnerable populations due to natural disasters and political instability, disparities among the north and south, regional imbalances of food situations, geographical and other variations within the country and gender-based discriminations within households. Looking holistically at the food security situation worldwide, reducing poverty and increasing food production and distribution are of major importance, both of which are directly linked to food security and human security (Spring 2009). It is argued that food security frameworks often overlook the structural issues built into the social and cultural factors of food, nutrition and the provision of land rights, seeds, credit, family ties and social relations of production and consumption patterns (ibid). It therefore provides minimal information on whether there is enough food to eat and where the food comes from, who produces it and how and under which conditions it has grown (FAO 2007). As a result, small farmers, fisher folks and women-headed households are more vulnerable from hunger and malnutrition. In recent decades, food governance led by international trade

Diagram 5.1 State obligations

Source: Designed by the authors

arrangements has often created additional obstacles to achieving food security in an equitable and unconditional manner. In this regard, overall growth and beneficial sharing in order to be equitable and inclusive towards poor and discriminated categories of the communities remain a serious concern.

Realising the limitations of food security, the concept of food sovereignty emerged. 'Food sovereignty' is a term coined in 1996 by members of Via Campesina to refer to a policy framework advocated by a number of farmers, peasants, pastoralists, fisher folk, indigenous people and environmental organisations.

They claimed the 'rights' of peoples to define their own food, agriculture, livestock and fisheries systems, in contrast to having food largely subject to international market forces. It was a movement to put peasants' food and food producing resources, both natural and man-made, under their own control in order to wipe out the problem of hunger (Khadka 2005), putting those who produce, distribute and consume food at the heart of food systems and policies rather than the demands of markets and corporations. The concept prioritises local and national economies and markets and empowers peasant and family farmer-driven agriculture, artisanal fishing, pastoralist-led grazing and food production, distribution and consumption based on environmental, social and economic sustainability (Boonchai and Sedsirot 2007). Food sovereignty includes support for smallholders and for collectively owned farms, fisheries etc. rather than industrialising these sectors in a minimally regulated global economy (Rosset 2003). The concept focuses on human relationships in terms of mutual dependence, cultural diversity and respect for the environment (Schanbacher 2010).

The right to food was recognised in the UN Declaration of Human Rights in 1948. The Declaration states that "everyone has the rights to a standard of living adequate for the health and wellbeing of himself and of his family, including food" (Art. 25.1). Subsequently, Article 11 of the legally binding International Covenant on Economic, Social and Cultural Rights (ICESCR), adopted in 1966, entered into force in 1976 and as of 2008 ratified by 158 states, mentions that "the State Parties to the present Covenant recognise the rights of everyone to an adequate standard of living including adequate food and that it is the fundamental right of everyone to be free from hunger". Similarly, General Comment 12 of the Covenant 1999, further interprets the rights to adequate food as follows: "The right to adequate food is realised when every man, woman and child, alone or in community with others, has physical and economic access at all times to adequate food or to means of its procurement." In this discourse, the concept of the right to food (RtF) is further elaborated by the FAO with implementation guidelines as shown in the schematic diagram 5.1.

However, largely following the work of Amartya Sen (1981) on famines, the debate around food security, sovereignty and the rights to food has become dominated by issues of entitlement and access to food (Gill et al. 2003). Rejecting the framework of Malthusian theory about population growth, food insecurity and human insecurity in the early 1970s, Sen developed a more comprehensive famine framework in his famous book on 'Poverty and Famines: An Essay on Entitlements and Deprivation'. In his seminal study he highlighted that access to food, rather than a lack of food production, caused famine (Schumbert 2005). Sen in his theory introduced the concept of endowments, entitlement and capabilities. He focused on the access and entitlement of individuals and households to food (Tiwari 2007). His work argues that the problem of food insecurity is actually the problem of access and entitlement to food and the means of gaining it by all people at all times. Entitlement failure occurs when it is not possible for a person to acquire commodity bundles with enough food to survive (Sen 1981; Rubin 2009). In the same vein, Alkire (2003) defines the capability dimension of human security. The definition focused on the ability of people to be free from hunger and thus food secure. The capability approach evaluates policies according to their impact on people's capabilities. It asks whether people are healthy and whether the means or resources necessary for this capability are present, such as clean water, access to doctors, protection from infections and diseases and basic knowledge of health issues. It also asks whether people are well- nourished and whether the conditions for this capability, such as having sufficient food supplies and food entitlements, are being met (Robeyns 2005). The ultimate concern of food security is not the size of nutritional intake, but the extent of nutritional wellbeing, being free from hunger and the capability to achieve that wellbeing.

5.3 Instruments ratified by the Government of Nepal

Being part of the global community, the Government of Nepal (GoN) has felt the need to associate and align itself with many different global and regional instruments to work towards the commitment to combat hunger. Being associated with these different instruments requires strong state commitment to remain a responsible duty-bearer towards its citizens, especially those who are economically poor and discriminated based on gender, age, religion, physical ability and geographic variation. To fulfill the conditions to deliver these services requires creating an enabling environment for better and equitable production relation, facilitating distribution mechanisms and ensuring proper safety net provisions during emergencies and disasters, including political instability-fuelled displacement and social unrest. Some of the major instruments that have been ratified are presented below in Table 5.2.

Table 5.2 Some major instruments related to poverty and hunger ratified by the Government of Nepal

S. N.	Instruments	Date of Signing/ Ratification	Major provisions
1	Universal Declaration on Human Rights (UDHR)		Article 25: Right to food, clothing and shelter for all
2	International Covenant on Civil and Political Rights, 16 December 1966	14 May 1991 a	Art. 1: ...pursue their economic, social and cultural development, Art. 6; Right to life

S. N.	Instruments	Date of Signing/ Ratification	Major provisions
3	International Covenant on Economic, Social and Cultural Rights, 16 December 1966	14 May 1991 a	Art. 1: ...pursue their economic, social and cultural development; Art. 2.1 and 3: .... full realisation of the rights and guarantee economic rights, Art. 7: employment and fair wages, Art. 9: social security, Art. 11: adequate food, clothing and housing
4	Convention on Elimination of all forms of Discrimination against Women (CEDAW)	22 April, 1991	Art. 14g: Equal treatment in land and agrarian reform as well as in land resettlement schemes; Art. 15: ...Contracts and to administer property
5	Convention of Biological Diversity (CBD)	15 September 1993	Local community rights over biodiversity, its use and benefit sharing
6	World Trade Organisation (WTO)	23 April 2004	Article 27.3b of TRIPs: Patent rights
7	Convention on Child rights (CRC)	14 September 1990	Art. 24c: Provision of adequate nutritious foods and clean drinking water,
8	International Treaty on Plant Genetic Resources for Food and Agriculture (ITPGRFA)	2 January 2007	Art.1: Fair and equitable sharing of the benefits arising out of their use; Art. 5: Exploration, conservation and sustainable use of plant genetic resources for food and agriculture; Art. 6: Sustainable use of plant genetic resources; Art. 9: Farmer's rights: protection of traditional knowledge, right to equitably participate in sharing benefits and right to participate in making decisions
9	International Labour Organisation (ILO) 169	22 August 2007	Rights of local and indigenous communities over natural resources e.g. Art. 14.1: The rights of ownership and possession over territorial land; Art. 15.1: The rights of the peoples concerned to the natural resources, rights to participate in the use, management and conservation; Art. 17.1: transmission of land etc.

Source: Compiled by the authors from various sources

The instruments shown above are crucial as all of them directly and indirectly relate to the food security situation as they deal with farmer's rights to genetic resources, trade facilitation of goods and services including agricultural products, access and control over natural resources with special rights of the indigenous communities, local communities, farming communities, women and children. Despite state commitments towards these instruments, their implementation are constrained due to political instability, economic fragility and social discrimination rooted in the values, norms and practices of Nepali society. Further expanding the focus of the National Human Rights Commission on food security issues and the food-related provisions of the Comprehensive Peace Agreement (CPA) are other instruments.

5.4 Major policies and plans of the Government of Nepal

The Government of Nepal has introduced different development policies and planned interventions to improve the livelihoods and food security of all development regions of the country (Table 5.3). In the late 1970s, it adopted a policy of providing basic needs to people focusing on marginal groups and areas (Adhikari and Bohle 1999). Over the period of time, the government has introduced targeted programmes to address the issues of excluded regions. As an example, since the Second Five-Year Plan (1963-1966), the government has been implementing the 'Remote Area Development Programme' focusing on the marginal Mid- and Far-Western development regions. The Ninth Five-Year Plan (1997-2002) introduced a crucial plan known as the Agricultural Perspective Plan (APP), a 20-year master plan formulated by the government in 1995 with the support of the Asian Development Bank (ADB) to increase food production and reduce the poverty of marginal farmers (NPC 1995). More specifically, the government has been providing transport subsidies through the Nepal Food Corporation (NFC) to provide food in remote food-deficit area since the 1980s (Adhikari 2010). At the same time, the World Food Programme (WFP) has been implementing its Food for Work (FfW) programme and providing food assistance for vulnerable populations affected by conflict, high food prices and natural disasters (WFP 2010).

Table 5.3 Major food security policies and programmes in Nepal

Production	Distribution/Access	Consumption/ Nutrition
• Land Act 1964 • Forestry Act 1993 • APP 1995 • Seed Act and guidelines 2054 BS Livestock Act 2055/56 BS • National Agriculture Policy 2061 BS • Agricultural Input Policy (irrigation, seed, insects/ pests, fertilizer) 2004 • Agreement with haliya, kamaiya 2010	• Food aid through WFP and other international organisations 1971 • Public food distribution through NFC (Nepal Food Corporation) 2034 BS • Food Act 2052 BS • Provision of cheap market food depots, food credit cards in 2007 • Programme for Ghodeto, rope way, road to reduce price of food in 2007 • Provision of food stock (10%, 7%, 5% in Tarai, Hills and Mountains) in 2007 • Road, electricity, communication, depots provisions in remote area in 2007	• Health policy 2046 BS • Drinking water policies 1992 • Consumer protection act and regulation 2054/56 BS • Nutrient policy-2061 BS • Vitamin (tablets, hen) for pregnant women in 2007 • Nutrition allowances for child below 5 years of Dalit and Karnali people 2010

Source: Compiled by the authors from different sources

Among these food security policies and programmes, land reform and providing agricultural inputs are of major importance in Nepal. However, land reform has not been achieved as expected (Nepali 2010); for example, agricultural inputs have not reached landless and mountain people. Improvements in people's livelihoods and food security objectives have not been achieved as expected (NPC 2007). Some of the reasons often cited for the poor performance of the interventions are bad governance and discontinuation of the targeted programmes (UNDP 2009). Also, evidence shows that the food distribution systems through the NFC and the WFP have increased the dependency of rural people on external food. Adhikari (2010) claims that such interventions have caused significant changes in the food habits of these groups, such as increased dependency on rice and the discontinuation of traditional food production and preparation practices.

5.5 Food security and implementation

Nepal is highly diversified in terms of social heterogeneity and physiographic location. Despite its efforts to implement bottom-up planning processes and remote area development programmes starting from the Seventh Five-Year Plan (1986-1990), poverty reduction and food security from the Eighth Five-Year Plan (1993-1997), broad-based economic development and targeted programmes including social inclusion from the Tenth Five- Year Plan (2002-2007).

For the past several years, Nepal has not been self-sufficient in food, as its production growth rate is slower than its population growth rate (Adhikari 2010). In the early 1960s, Nepal had the highest level of agricultural productivity in South Asia, but by the early 1990s its agricultural production was the lowest in the subcontinent (Tiwari 2007). Forty-three of Nepal's 75 districts are unable to produce sufficient food to meet the minimum requirements of the people in these districts (Adhikari 2010) and 60.2 per cent of households experience food insufficiencies (Upreti 2010). Poverty and food security issues in Nepal have important spatial, social and now political dimensions. Food insecurity has close correlations with physiographic variations (altitude) and development regions: the people of the Mountain region are poorer than the Hills and the Hills people are poorer than people in the Tarai (Gill et al. 2003). The Mountain physiographic region and the Mid- and Far-Western development regions are the traditionally food deficit regions (Adhikari 2010). In terms of food production in Nepal, the Tarai produces a surplus of about 7 per cent, the Hills have a deficit of 36 per cent and the Mountains have a deficit of almost 80 per cent (Gill et al. 2003).

Simultaneously, continuing gender, caste, ethnicity, age and disability- based discriminations in access to means of living and food and opportunities in Nepal's social, political and economic spheres considerably marginalise the poor and excluded (DFID and WB 2006; Adhikari 2010). The incidence of poverty is higher amongst Nepal's Dalits and Janajati. There is also evidence of intra-household nutritional discrimination against girls and women, especially pregnant and lactating women (Gill et al. 2003). These groups have limited control over and access to strategic resources (NPC 2007). In this regard, the unequal distribution of household assets such as land, labour and input (Upreti 2010) and differential access and control over common property resources such as forest, water and infrastructure (Pokharel and Nurse 2004; Dev and Adhikari. 2007) are the major hindrances to achieving the groups' food needs. The rigid social system dominated by unequal power positions traps the available resources in the outside world. Because of the low productivity of agricultural crops, the income and purchasing power of the rural poor - 75 per cent of whom work as wage workers - remains stagnant (Adhikari 2010).

Labour migration is the main livelihood strategy to secure food in Nepal (Müller-Böker and Thieme 2007). Rural youths out-migration is continually increasing. The majority of the poor and rural youths are forced to migrate as a livelihood strategy (see chapter 7 for detail). The findings of NLSS-III show that at least 80 per cent of rural youths have migrated for better employment and income opportunities within and outside the country (CBS 2011). At a particular point in time, at least 20 per cent of this population was away from home (57 per cent within and 43 per cent abroad). As a result, Nepal's agricultural sector has become feminised and with a minority youth work force. Moreover, as migration is a class- based phenomenon it has also brought different dynamisms and means to agrarian development, creating both opportunities and challenges to rural livelihoods. However, remittances are used to purchase imported food and thus have negative implications on rural production patterns. Additionally, remittances are not used in the productive sector, which makes the agrarian system further vulnerable. Conversely, migration has also brought opportunities to promote women as farm managers, re- orienting farming towards cash crops. As road connections in many rural areas are improving, returnee migrants are starting to opt for commercial farming with the knowledge and skills gained abroad.

There are always risks that certain communities will fall into the trap of hunger and food insecurity. The major potential risks associated with migration are health risks such as HIV/ AIDS, natural calamities, development-led displacement, market deregulation and political conflict. In many cases, such violations are considered localised phenomena and a single relief package constitutes the response mechanism. In such situations, the rights of the individuals/communities are compromised and left for charity services to deal with. These kinds of situations directly affect the food security and livelihoods of the population, which in the long run has complex implications on people's psychological wellbeing. Negligence on food security assistance causes a sense of helplessness and mistrust (particularly towards the state) among recipients and may lead them to fall into the trap of other forms of violation due to displacement. One of the reasons why such issues are brought forward as rights and deal with systematic response mechanisms is due to the lack of documented evidence. Therefore, documenting food rights violations gives a very strong basis for litigation and to inform and organize the rights holders and their supporting alliances to formulate an agenda to make the state aware of and seriously respond to the issue of human security. Some cases documented by the Food First Information Action Network (FIAN) Nepal are presented below (Source: Provided by FIAN Nepal):

Case 1: HIV/AIDS-affected women denied their rights to food in Achham District

HIV/AIDS became a widespread disease in the Payal Village Development Committee (VDC) of Achham, where the majority of men migrate to India for seasonal work. As a consequence, many women are getting infected through their husbands. The bitter truth is that once the husband dies, women are denied access to nutritious food and treatment and in the majority cases they are also denied access to the entitled property. This is a violation of the human right to food according to the UNDHR Article 25 (1) of the right to food, shelter and medical treatment.

Case 2: People at risk of displacement around Lakshmanpur Dam

More than 3000 families living in five VDCs (Holiza, Betahani, Fattepur, Gangapur and Matahaiya) are badly affected by the inundation and land erosion caused by the Lakshmanpur Dam built on the Rapti River. The yearly flooding caused by the closure of the floodgates remains a reality to these local inhabitants. According to the international provision, no construction that obstructs natural water flow can be built within an eight kilometre radius. However, the Kalkalwa Afflux is located about 500 meters from the border and is a major reason for the inundation. Its construction is a clear violation of the rules and consequently affects local communities through insecurity, displacement, lack of proper safety measures and compensation.

Case 3: Vulnerability caused due to natural disaster in Bajura District

In August 2011, eight families of Juwa Pani Village of Barha Bis were affected by landslides. The families received temporary relief packages through the Nepal Food Corporation for immediate relief. However, the government did not made any further intervention towards their safe settlement, reviving their production potential and supporting them to find alternative livelihood options.

Case 4: Denial of equitable water-sharing mechanisms

Eighty-five Kumal families in Pipaltar VDC of Dhading District were denied access to irrigation water, which ledthem towards starvation due to insufficient food production. With the support of human rights organisations and civil society initiatives, the case was filed at the district administration office.

Case 5: Expansion of wildlife reserves and the eviction of people, Western Region

The expansion of the Sukla Phanta Wildlife Reserve in the Western region of Nepal forcibly evicted 207 families who lived in the Reserve's proximity. The evicted families were provided with food and clothes as compensation. However, they are still struggling to find a permanent solution in terms of settlement and livelihood options.

There are many progressive examples put forward by other developing countries to deal with hunger and food security issues. These cases show that hunger is a political issue and requires a high level of political commitment to deal with it, knowing that hunger can lead to social unrest, communal conflict and national and broader-level instability. In long run, hunger impacts economic growth and the overall development of the country. In the worst case scenario, food can become a political weapon and national sovereignty can be compromised for the sake of food. Some of the examples of other developing countries are presented below:

India: India is the second-largest wheat producer in the world after the green revolution of the late 1960s. The green revolution focused on the cultivation of High Yielding Varieties (HYVs) and Genetically Modified Breeds (GMBs) of food crops which needed greater agricultural input and consolidation of land. It also focused on trade liberalisation and globalisation which meant that natural resources, production systems, markets and trade were handed over to global Agro-business. As a result, small farmers and landless labourers were disempowered and dispossessed and new forms of slavery and bondage were created (Siva 2002). Now, India has the largest number of undernourished people in the world. According to the FAO, fifty per cent of the world's hungry people live in India, with 200 million food-insecure people. According to Global Hunger Index 2008, India ranked 66th out of 88 nations. There is evidence that many riots and suicides occurred because farmers could not pay the cost of agricultural input and landlessness (Welthungerhilfe et al. 2008). More than 17,500 farmers killed themselves every year between 2002 and 2006 due to debt and crop failure (Patel 2007). Some also became involved in armed conflicts in response to their difficulties (Shaban 2007). However, the Supreme Court of India took the commendable initiative to provision food security as the fundamental rights of its people.

Brazil: Brazil is the world's fourth-largest food exporting country and one-third of Brazil's export earnings come from agriculture. In 1964, the government adopted policies that reinforced the agricultural export model. This caused millions of people to be expelled from their land and increased rural and urban poverty (Amaral and Peduto 2010). As a critical mass movement against hunger in 2004, President Luiz Inácio Lula da Silva adopted the 'Zero Hunger' programmes for which the government prepared a plan against Hunger. The Zero Hunger programmes fall into four spheres: i) increased physical and economic access to food; ii) promoting family agriculture; iii) income generation activities; and iv) social mobilization and education. In these programmes, the government implemented subsidied fertilizer, a food bank to redistribute surplus food from market to insecure families, a school fund programme to provide scholarships to food insecure groups, a food fund for providing nutritious food to pregnant women, etc. By adding social mobilisation to the Twin-Track formula, Brazil enhanced the returns of Zero Hunger, increasing participation of not only the poor but also of any member of the community who wanted to be part of the solution (ibid). The Brazilian Government also uses a guaranteed minimum price policy to stimulate agriculture (ibid). Now, hunger is legally considered a national shame and the poor are claiming their lawful rights from their nation (FAO 2007). As a result, poverty was reduced by 31.4 per cent between 2003 and 2006, meaning that fourteen million people overcame extreme poverty during this period (Patrus 2009). Brazil is making progress towards achieving the targets of the World Food Summit and the Millennium Development Goals.

Cuba: During the 1990s Cuba lost Soviet and Eastern Bloc trade preferences and per capita caloric consumption fell 18 per cent from 3,050 in 1985-1989 to 2,513 in 1990-1994 (Ross 2000). Rationed foods were not adequate to meet the population's nutritional needs and many Cubans were surviving through the informal market and/or were suffering malnutrition. Cuba then signed the Trade Sanctions Reform and Export Enhancement Act (TSRA) with the United States (US) which allowed American firms to sell food and agricultural products to Cuba. Cuban purchases from these firms amounted to $4.319 million in 2001, $138.635 million in 2002 and $256.9 million in 2003 (Koont 2004). Cuba became the thirty-fifth most important food and agricultural export market for the United States in 2003, up from last (226th) position in 2000 (Ross 2000). Furthermore, because current US legislation requires that all Cuban purchases from the United States be conducted on a cash basis, the lack of credit risk associated with these sales makes Cuba one of the most attractive export markets for American firms. As Cuba focuses on food purchases, with several options available outside of the Libreta, under the present Cuban system of distribution access to basic goods is strongly delineated along income lines and/or access to dollars (ibid). Then monoculture cultivation of sugarcane to increase the non-farm income has focused (Golzalez 2003).

5.6 The importance of inclusion and multiplicity in food security approaches

Ensuring people's rights to food is the duty of the state, which has to adopt multiplicity in its approach to ensure that people from different age, gender, geographical region, religions and health situations have access to this right. The state also has to deal with emergencies and disasters. Given this mandate, the state has to remain consciously present in three different situations. The first situation is emergency and disasters: in the situations of natural disasters as well as human-induced, conflict- led displacement or epidemics, the state is responsible for ensuring that affected people have access to adequate food according to their needs. The second situation is enabling the environment: for this most crucial aspect, the state needs to remain consistently committed to adopting multi-pronged programmes to ensure equitable access to means of production, fair distribution and protection from post-harvest losses, links with better markets, fair prices and food quality assurance through standard practices. The third situation is insulating the poor, especially against market-led shocks through price hikes, artificial food shortages and deregulated markets, as well as crop failure due to poor input supply or weather. The state, with these commitments, is the best possible means of protecting people from falling into the hunger trap. In all these situations, the inclusion of the rights holders in decision-making processes and the recognition of their needs and rights is crucial, particularly the needs, rights and voices of those who are the most vulnerable to food insecurity especially women, land-poor producers, people with disabilities and the elderly who desperately need special care in setting the standards and/

or implementing the programmes (Gill et al. 2003).

Though food security within the right to food framework is enshrined in many international instruments as briefed above, its implementation obligations are still ambiguous. In many cases, the intention of the state to be party to such instruments is left up to the jurisdiction of the members to oblige it on moral grounds. Moreover, there is little guidance on the implementation of provisions as parties are in different states of development, with different understandings and political commitments.

Members who are more politically stable and economically robust opt for multiple measures to deal with food insecurity in different situations; they are in a much more advanced position compared to many developing and or under-developed countries. Nevertheless, having a common understanding and guiding principles and tools are always helpful to set milestones. In this context, the FAO Council created the Intergovernmental Working Group (IGWG) and after two years of discussions and negotiations adopted the Voluntary Guidelines by consensus at its fourth session on 23 September 2004. The guidelines have set common implementation standards in support of the 'Progressive Realization of the Rights to Adequate Food in the Context of National Food Security' in 2004. Among many other tools, case documentations against the violations of the rights to food are one of the fundamental and grass roots-based initiatives which can be promoted with the support of the rights holders (Ghale and Upreti 2008).

5.7 Barriers to food security

5.7.1 External barriers

Globalisation, liberalisation and privatisation have brought both opportunities and challenges (Ghale 2010). Countries such as Nepal with weaker economies and other socio-political constraints are likely to have a less capacity to harness the benefits of globalisation processes. The main threat to subsistence farming-based economies is a company's concentration of power in over-production and creation of food chain. This process directly impacts farmers with small holdings as they are more likely to be displaced from their profession as they become less competitive with the world market, which will affect their food security and livelihood. The process further promotes out-migration, displacement and conflict.

People finally become mere consumers of imported inputs, technologies and products. Nepal being a bio-diverse and small farmer-led country, there is a chance that resources, including technologies, could be concentrated in the hands of private companies which will not consider right to food as their core business until there is a strong state presence to regulate the market. The scenario of resource concentration and its effects on the food chain is presented in Diagram 5.2

Diagram 5.2 Power concentration

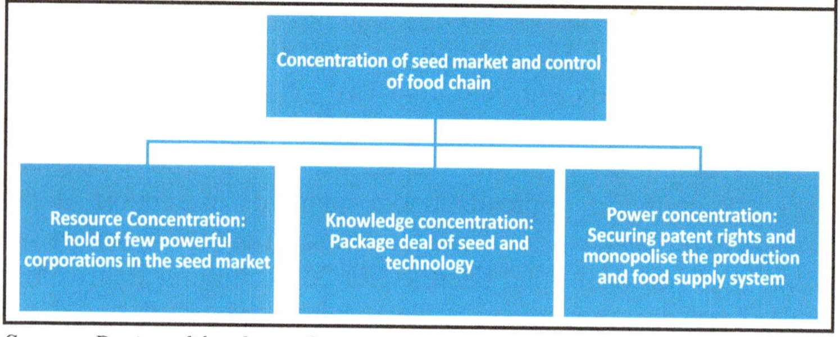

Source: Designed by the authors

When a country's food security situation becomes more and more vulnerable and largely depends on imports, it will lead to a weaker balance of payment situation and help for a negative trade balance; food can ultimately become a political weapon. The privatisation of water and land, combined with the incompetence of public institutions to regulate the market, ultimately lead to uncertainty and pose a great threat to national sovereignty.

5.7.3 Internal barriers

Situations of hunger and food insecurity are affected by many reasons. Some of these technical, social and political reasons as described below:

Social: Socially excluded groups (Dalits, women including single women, indigenous people, landless households and elderly people) are the most vulnerable groups in Nepal. Evidence shows that both formal institutions (such as land tenure, markets and state policies) and informal institutions (such as the caste system, rules which establish gender-based occupations, patron-client relations, untouchability and caste-based discrimination, social networking, institutions of bargaining power and political engagement) are primary sources of exclusion and inclusion in Nepal. These systems mean that certain people have greater access to the limited production resources, available food reserves and the means to access food. Simultaneously, access to food is determined by the purchasing power of the people (FAO 2008). It was found that low caste groups in the study area could not rear buffalo and sell milk - the main source of dairy products and cash income - because of prevailing practice of untouchability. More importantly, Nepal's policies to increase food access capabilities, particularly in the sectors of health, education and employment, are unable to reach marginal groups. To compound the problem, many people from marginal groups lose their labour power due to regular ill health. The only employment opportunities in the area are available to teachers; there is no vocational or skills-based education which is essential for socially excluded groups. As a result, landless socially excluded people are in fear of how they can manage their daily food needs.

In caste-based patron client institutions like bista[1] and haliya[2] of Bajura and Achham districts and kamaiya[3] of Kailali district, lower caste and indigenous people work for higher caste people, and are paid in grain at harvest time. Sometimes, they are also paid in nominal cash. There is a local culture that the Brahmin

---

1 In this institution, low caste people make tools, sew clothes and make shoes as required by the socially advantaged people; in return, they are paid in grain at harvest time (Coplan 1972).

2 It is ploughman and master relationships between low and socially advantaged households. It is one kind of slavery (Coplan 1972).

3 System of bonded labour where one group of indigenous people called Tharu work for their masters to pay debt.

caste (priest) may not plough the land. Low caste groups must plough the land of these caste groups. These sorts of practices oblige the client to face any kind of exploitation from their patron. Practices that promote untouchability still exist in rural areas of Nepal. Evidence shows that there are separate water sources for Dalit communities, often located in dirty areas where the livestock of higher caste groups use the water. This situation limits the water security and food consumption of such people. In some cases, they are forced to collect water from rivers contaminated with water-borne diseases.

Social networks and relatives are Safety Nets during times of food insecurity (Deressa et al. 2009). Groups other than those most discriminated against often have the widest networks and the wealthiest relatives to gain support from during emergencies and disasters. There are also limited informal relationships among the resource holding and discriminated groups including friendships, colleagues and school mates, relationships which are less bonded than family relationships. The sharing of capital and food during periods of crisis and starvation favors socially advantaged people rather than others. In this regard, bargaining power is determined by social and legal recognition of the legitimacy of the claim. Dalits are largely denied space to articulate their needs and demands before other caste groups and women hesitate to speak in front of men due to social relationship patterns. Thus, these people are unable to frame issues such as wellbeing and deprivation, which are crucial to understanding and mitigating vulnerability. To reduce the hunger situation in the study areas, the Nepal Food Corporation (NFC) and the World Food Programme (WFP) has initiated the provision of food distribution through their plan (NPC 2007). Evidence shows that affected households which are more politically engaged get more support from the provision. It is also reported that a lot of food is wasted in the preparation of alcohol, mostly by people who are politically influential.

Political: Among many factors, land is one political determinant towards food security. The land tenure system in Nepal is skewed and holding size is too small. More importantly, the recently formulated land management policy is still not in effective implementation. It has resulted in landlessness among tillers, limited fertile land being used for non-agricultural purposes and land parcels being occupied by corporate houses. Historically, tenure is determined by the institution and set of rules which allow socially advantaged young males to own land in the form of Birta[4], Jagir[5] and Rakam[6] (Nepali 2010). These sorts of systems not only make the groups food self-insufficient but, most importantly, limit their means of income of command over food. The preliminary finding of this co-author's PhD study from the Far-Western Development Region of Nepal shows that socially advantaged male groups who own the land have more livestock, which is the major source of income. Power relations in the area are based on the size of land and Brahmin has benefitted more from the public food distribution system.

Technical: Nepal was a food exporter country in the 1980s but did not become a net food importing country. The production capacity of the country has diminished due to the lack of proper assessment of the potential niche-based commodities for internal consumption and for the export market, the poor service delivery capacity of the state institutions, the low investment environment for the private sector, food quality regulations and poor stock and/or reserve management for emergencies and disasters. The problem also remains devising and implementing the targeted programmes for needy communities suffering from multiple socio-political and economic barriers. Likewise, the state lacks mechanisms to recognise the diversity of food according to cultural richness, ecological variation and age-related requirements. Therefore, the state in most cases fails to organise its

---

4 Birta means an assignment of income from the land which provides individuals with a livelihood. It was granted in favour of priests, teachers, religious heads, soldiers, members of the nobility and the royal family (Regmi 1999).

5 Before 1952, it was a common practice in Nepal to assign the income of Raikar lands as emoluments to government employees and functionaries. Such assignment was known as Jagir (Regmi 1999).

6 Rakam refers to a particular category of land grants and assignments similar to Raikar, Jagir Guthi lands on which cultivators are required to provide unpaid labour to meet government requirements.

plan, programme and resource allocation according to four major pillars of food security: availability, accessibility, affordability and utilisation. The state in many cases fails to recognise its own role of duty bearer and the need to deliver services to the best of its ability.

5.8 Conclusion

The discussion shows that hunger and food security are critical dimensions of human security. Food is one of the most important basic needs and achieving food security is a fundamental right of every individual and community.

There are major three concepts regarding the contribution to human security through food security. The concept of food security emerged after the Second World War as a market-based approach following neoliberal economic growth policies based on a free market. Many international organisations such as the IMF, the WB and the WTO, as well as UN organisations including the FAO, the IFAD and the WFP use the term 'food security' to describe global efforts to eliminate hunger and malnutrition. They focus on agricultural reform and small-scale, peasant and landless farm production and aim to curb poverty, with food production and distribution playing integral roles in this process. In this regard, the FAO and the IFAD focus on reducing gaps through cheap prices and increasing small farmer food production. These recommendations directly link food security with human security (Spring 2009) but these goals are not achieved. Inequalities within countries and between countries of the global North and South are core elements for the world's failure to eradicate hunger and poverty. Some groups are more vulnerable from hunger and malnutrition. It is argued that financial governance and international trade arrangements often create additional obstacles to achieving food security. In this regard, how growth will be beneficial to the world's poor is a critical issue of food security. Also, food security follows the model of globalisation that reduces human relationships to economic values.

Realising the limitations of the concept of food security, the idea of the right to food emerged. This right is realised when every man, woman and child, alone or in a community, has physical and economic access at all times to adequate food or to means of its procurement. Like components of food security, the right to food also articulates the dimensions of availability, physical and economic accessibility, adequacy and sustainability. Right to food being a human rights concept and an agenda for policy action, it obliges governments to acknowledge people's rights to food by fulfilling the obligation to respect, protect and fulfill. Simultaneously, the concept of food sovereignty emerged, which focuses on human relationships in terms of mutual dependence, cultural diversity and respect for the environment. Peasants are exploited, discriminated and even tortured by feudal landlords in rural areas. Therefore, food is a major factor of human security with technical, political and social dimensions governed by external and internal factors. The promising concept of food sovereignty, which keeps the producer, consumer and national competence at its core, is one of the most viable options to consider. There is an urgency to deal with these issues before food becomes a political weapon and the state and its people lose their sovereign rights.

5.9 Recommendations

Based on the discussion in previous section, we would like to make the following recommendations:

5.9.1 Revisit the human security framework

So far, most of the debate around food and human security is focused on the material dimension of food. Though there are conceptual debates and discourses around the issue of rights, there is one important missing link in the concept itself, which can cause long term damage if not managed properly. Worry, fear and helplessness through the potential and actual loss of livelihoods are strong risk factors of human insecurity. Evidence from the field shows that there is psychological fear among vulnerable groups relating to how to feed their family, how to secure quality food and how to manage limited available food

- some of the major threats against the right to be free from want. Therefore, hunger and food security are major aspects of human security. The situation gets worse in emergencies and disasters or by the displacement of women from their families, eviction of landless people and abandonment of children. Linking short-term measures with long-term support mechanisms can promote equitable production relations, enhance productivity and manage resources to secure adequate food for all. Once people are free of fear, they can deliver at their best. The following framework is proposed in order to consider food as part of one's psychological wellbeing and therefore one of the major factors in non-traditional human security:

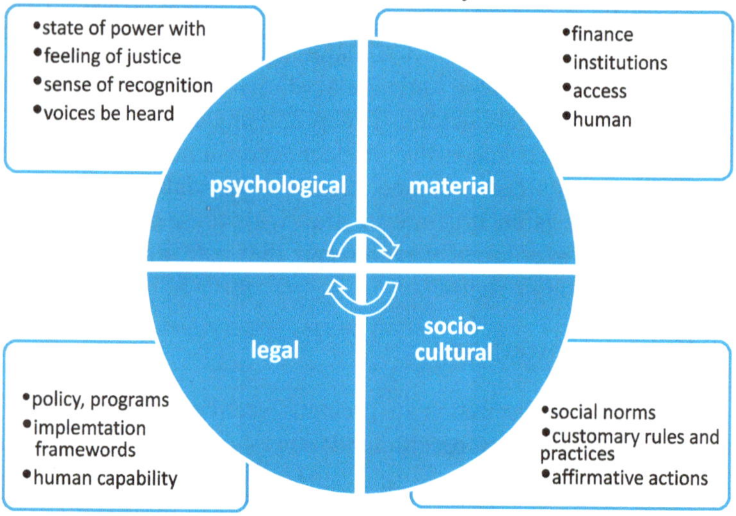

Source: Proposed model by the authors with specific emphasis on psychological wellbeing as an important aspect of human security.

5.9.2 Food security for peace

Sustainable access to adequate food has a strong connection to human rights principles. Most importantly, the Interim Constitution of Nepal has adopted a food sovereignty principle, which gives a legal basis to devise policy procedures and effectively implement them (GoN 2007). The National Human Rights Commission (NHRC) has also gradually considered and worked on economic deprivation-led poverty, food insecurity and human death. Nepal being a signatory of different international instruments, it is obliged to protect the rights of its citizens including that farmers have rights over seeds, indigenous communities have rights over genetic resources and production bases within their historically significant territories and that women have rights over production resources like land. Likewise, the trade agreements such as the World Trade Organisation (WTO) and the South Asian Free Trade Area (SAFTA), to which the Government of Nepal is a signatory, oblige it to utilise market opportunities and also protect citizens and the nation from the potential negative impacts of global initiatives (Bhandari et al. 2005). On the political front, the CPA of 2006 set forth the importance of the nexus between socio-political affairs and economic frontiers and equitable production relations. From the experiences of other countries in the world, political instability-led conflict and social unrest have brought major challenges to food insecurity, which further lead to violence. As Nepal is in a phase of political transformation, it has the potential to abolish all existing social, political, cultural, geographical and economic inequalities through short-, medium- and long-term milestones, including the participation of all actors especially the rights holders, civil society members, academia, media and legal communities, drawing on global best practices.

5.9.3 Remove institutional barriers

Evidence shows that both formal and informal social, economic and political institutions increase the food insecurity of marginal groups. For successful intervention in securing the food security of such groups, this institutional aspect should be restructured and the barriers of caste and gender-based wage labour and patron-client relationships removed and converted to market-level exchange. In this regard, the institutions of microfinance, community funds, insurance and safety nets focusing on the marginal community may support sustainable food security (MoAC 2010). Also, access to health institutions, information sharing and employment opportunities are vital for building the resilience of the poor.

References

Adhikari A, Bohle HG. 1999. *Food Crisis in Nepal.* New Delhi: Adroit Publishers.

Adhikari J. 2010. Food Security, Conflict and Livelihoods Threats in Nepal. *In:* Upreti BR, Booker UM, editors. *Livelihoods, Insecurity and Social Conflicts in Nepal.* Kathmandu: South Asia Regional Coordination Office of the Swiss National Centre of Competence in Research (NCCR North- South), pp 73-130.

Alkire S. 2003. *A Conceptual Framework for Human Security.* Crise Working Paper 2. Oxford: University of Oxford.

Amaral WAN, Peduto A. 2010. *Food Security: The Brazilian Case. Trade knowledge network: Series on Trade and Food Security.* Policy Report. Manitoba: International Institute for Sustainable Development (IISD).

Barrett CB, Maxwell DG. 2005. *Food Aid After Fifty Years: Recasting Its Role.* London: Routledge.

Bhandari S, Shrestha SM, Ghale Y. 2005. *Nepal's Accession to the WTO: Challenges and Opportunities for Nepal.* Kathmandu: Action Aid Nepal, Law Associates Nepal.

Bhattarai R. 2010. Broadening Nepal's Security Agenda: Armed Conflict, Migration and Environmental Perspective. *In:* Bhattarai R, Wagle GS, editors. *Emerging Security Challenges of Nepal.* Kathmandu: Nepal Institute for Policy Studies (NIPS).

Bishokarma NK. 2010. Maoist People's War and community adaptation: A case of Community Forestry User Groups Nepal. *Journal of Forest and Livelihood* 10(1):57-61.

Boonchai K, Sedsirot B. 2007. *The concept and the policy of Food Resource Base.* Paper presented on the International Development Studies Conference on "Mainstreaming Human Security: The Asian Contribution" held in Bangkok, October 4-5, 2007.

CBS [Central Bureau of Statistics]. 2011. *Nepal Living Standard Survey, Volume I and II.* Kathmandu: Central Bureau of Statistics, National Planning Commission, Government of Nepal.

Defra [Department for environment, food, and rural affairs]. 2006. *Food Security and the UK: An Evidence and Analysis Paper.* London: Food Chain Analysis Group, Department for environment, food, and rural affairs.

Deressa T, Hassan RM, Ringler C, Alemu T, Yesuf M. 2009. Determinants of farmers' choice of adaptation methods to climate change in the

Nile Basin of Ethiopia. *Global Environmental Change* Vol. 19 (2): 248–255.

Dev OP, Adhikari J. 2007. Community Forestry in the Nepal Hills: Practice and Livelihoods Impact. *In Forest, People and Power: the political ecology of reform in South Asia*. London: Earthscan.

DFID [Department for International Development] and WB [World Bank]. 2006. Unequal Citizens: Gender, Caste and Ethnicity Exclusion in Nepal: Summary. Kathmandu: Department for International Development, World Bank.

FAO [Food and Agriculture Organization]. 1995. *50th Anniversary Symposium*. Quebec: Food and Agriculture Organization.

FAO [Food and Agriculture Organization]. 2007. *Right to food lesson learned from Brazil*. Rome: Food and Agriculture Organization.

FAO [Food and Agriculture Organization]. 2008. The State of Food Insecurity in the World, Rome: Food and Agriculture Organization. Available at: http://www.fao.org/publications/sofi/en/; accessed on 27 April 2010.

Gasper D. 2005. Securing Humanity: Situating 'Human Security' as Concept and Discourse. *Journal of Human Development* 6(2): 221-245.

Ghale Y, Upreti BR. 2008. Concentration and monopolization of seed market: Impact on food security and farmer's rights in mountains. Mountain Forum. archive.mtnforum.org/rs/ol/browse.cfm?tp=aui&st=list2&authorID=2902&authorName=Yamuna%20Ghale.

Ghale Y. 2010. Corporate Globalization: Hunger and livelihood insecurity in Nepal. *In:* Upreti BR, Müller-Böker U, editors. *Livelihood Insecurity and Social Conflict in Nepal*. Kathmandu: South Asia Regional Coordination Office of the Swiss National Centre of Competence in Research (NCCR North- South), pp 131-177.

Gill GJ, Farrington J, Anderson E, Luttrell C, Conway T, Saxena NC, Slater R. 2003. *Food Security and the Millennium Development Goal on Hunger in Asia*. Working Paper 231. London: Overseas Development Institute.

GoN [Government of Nepal]. 2007. *Interim Constitution of Nepal*. Kathmandu: Government of Nepal.

Gonzalez CG. 2003. Seasons of Resistance: sustainable agriculture and food security in Cuba. Tulane Environmental Law Journal16: 685-732.

Hastings DA. 2010. The Human security index: An update and a new release. *Human Security Index*. www.humansecurityindex.org/wordpress/wp-content/uploads/2012/02/hsiv2-documentation-report1_1.pdf; accessed on 23 August 2012.

Heukelom TSV. 2010. *A Human Approach to Food Security*. Paper presented at the 15th International Humanitarian Conference, Access to Resources and the International Community, Webster University Geneva, 18–19 February 2010. Geneva: International Conference Centre. Also available at: http://content.undp.org/go/newsroom/publications/poverty- reduction/poverty-website/mdgs/beyond-the-midpoint.en; accessed on 27 April, 2010.

Homer-Dixon T. 1994. Environmental Scarcities and Violent Conflict: Evidence from Cases. *International Security* 19(1): 5-40.

Khadka K. 2005. *Food Sovereignty as Peoples' Fundamental Right: Nepalese Perspective*. Kathmandu: All Nepal Peasants' Association, South Asian Alliance for Poverty Eradication.

Khan SR, Kazmi S, Ahmad Z. 2002. Structural Adjustment and Food Security in Pakistan: An aggregate Analysis. *In* Siva, B. and Bedi, G. *Sustainable Agriculture and Food Security: the impact of globalization*. New Delhi: Sage Publication.

Koont. 2004. Food Security in Cuba. *Monthly Review* 55(8).

Kumar D. 2012. *Militarization and threat to democracy*. Discussion paper prepared for Martin Chautari, Kathmandu.

Lang T. 2002. Food Security: Does it Conflict with Globalization. In Siva, B. and Bedi, G: *Sustainable Agriculture and Food Security: the impact of globalization*. New Delhi: Sage Publication.

McDonald B. 2010. *Food security*. Cambridge: Polity Press.

MoAC [Ministry of Agriculture and Cooperatives]. 2010. *Crop and Food Security Update: Summer Crop Nepal 2009/2010*. Kathmandu: Ministry of Agriculture and Cooperatives.

Müller-Böker U,Thieme S. 2007. *Livelihood Strategies in a Marginal Area of Nepal (Far West Nepal), with an emphasis on labor migration to India*. Issues in Geographical Marginality: Paper presented during the Meetings of the Commission on Evolving Issues of Geographical Marginality in the Early 21st Century World, 2001-2004. Grahamstown: Rhodes University. Also available at: http://www.nccr-nepal.org/publications.html; accessed on 27 April 2010.

Nepali PB. 2010. *Access to land resources: Dalits and their social exclusion and inclusion*. Lalitpur: Samata Foundation.

NPC [National Planning Commission]. 1995. Agricultural perspective plan. Kathamndu: National Planning Commission.

NPC [National Planning Commission]. 2007. *Three-year Interim Plan (BS.2064/65-2066/67)* [in Nepali]. Kathmandu: National Planning Commission.

OECD [Organization for Economic Cooperation and Development]. 1981. *Food Policy.* Paris: Organization for Economic Cooperation and Development.

Patel R. 2007. *Stuffed and Starved.* London: Portobello Books.

Patrus A. 2009. Implementing the human right to food in Brazil. *World Hunger Note*.www.worldhunger.org/articles/08/hrf/ananias.htm; accessed on 13 August 2012.

Pokharel BK, Nurse M. 2004. Forests and People's Livelihoods: Benefiting the poor from community forestry. *Journal of Forests and Livelihoods* 4(1): 19-29.

Quilop RG. 2007. National Security and Human Security: Searching for their Nexus in the Philippine Setting. Paper presented on the International Development Studies Conference on "Mainstreaming Human Security: The Asian Contribution" held in Bangkok, October 4-5, 2007.

Robeyns I. 2005. The Capability Approach: a theoretical survey. *Journal of Human Development* 6(1): 93-117.

Ross JE. 2000. *Food Security in Cuba, economictransition.* pp 115-125. Also available at: http://web.gc.cuny.edu/dept/bildn/publications/documents/Ross9. pdf; accessed on 14 August 2012.

Rosset P. 2003. Global Small-Scale Farmers' Movement Developing New Trade Regimes. *Food First* News & Views 28 (97):2.

Rubin O. 2009. The Niger famine: a collapse of entitlements and democratic responsiveness. *Journal of Asian and African Studies* 44 (3): 279-298.

Schanbacher WD. 2010.*The politics of food: The global conflict between food security and food sovereignty.* Santa Barbara: ABC-CLIO.

Schubert J. 2005. *Political Ecology in Development Research: An Introductory Overview and Annotated Bibliography*. Bern: NCCR North-South.

Sen A. 1981. *Poverty and Famines*. Oxford: Oxford University Press.

Shaban A. 2007. Food Security Issues in India with Special Reference to Western Region Paper presented on the International Development Studies Conference on "Mainstreaming Human Security: The Asian Contribution" held in Bangkok, October 4-5, 2007.

Siva B. 2002. Globalization of agriculture, food security and sustainability. *In* Siva, B. and Bedi, G. *Sustainable Agriculture and Food Security: the impact of globalization*. New Delhi: Sage Publication.

Spring UO. 2009. Food as new human and livelihoods security challenges. *In:* Brauch HG, Grin J, Mesjasz C, Kameri-Mbote P, Spring

UO, editors. *Facing global environmental change: Environmental, human, energy, food,* health and Water Security Concepts. Berlin: Springer, pp 476-501.

Tiwari M. 2007. Chronic Poverty and Entitlement Theory. *Third World Quarterly* 28(1): 171-191.

UNDP [United Nation Development Programme]. 1994. *Human Development Report*. New York: Oxford university press.

UNDP [United Nation Development Programme]. 2009. Nepal Human Development Report 2009. Kathmandu: United Nation Development Programme.

Upreti BR. 2010. A Decade of Armed Conflict and Livelihoods Insecurity in Nepal. *In*: Upreti BR, Müller-Booker U, editors. *Livelihoods, Insecurity and Social Conflicts in Nepal.* Kathmandu: South Asia Regional Coordination Office of the Swiss National Centre of Competence in Research (NCCR North- South),pp 73-130.

Upreti BR. 2012. Water and Food Insecurity: Nontraditional Security Challenges for Nepal. In Sridhar K. Khatri and Bishnu Raj Upreti. *Nontraditional Security Challenges in Nepal.* Washington, D.C.: The National Bureau of Asian Research.

Wall de A. 2005. *Famine that kills*. Darfur: Oxford University Press..

Welthungerhilfe, International Food Policy Research Institute, Concern Worldwide. 2008. *Global Hunger Index : The Challenge of Hunger 2008*. Bonn/ Washington, D.C./Dublin: Welthungerhilfe, International Food policy research Institute, Concern Worldwide.

WFP [World Food Programme]. 2010. *The Cost of Coping: A collision of crisis and the impact of sustained food security deterioration in Nepal.* Kathmandu: World Food Programme.

World Food Summit. 1996. Rome Declarationon World Food Security. FAO Corporate Document Repository. *FAO.* www.fao.org/docrep/003/w3613e/w3613e00.htm; accessed on 28 April 2010.

****

Chapter 6

Health and human security

Damodar Adhikari, PhD

6.1 Health as a security concern

We live in an age of globalisation when the separation between national and international boundaries on the issue of health no longer exists. Today's global flow of goods, services, finance, people and images spotlight the many inter-linkages in the security of all people. The security of one person, one community and one nation rests on the decisions of many others - sometimes fortuitously, sometimes precariously (UNDP 2003). Thus, the territorial concept of state governance has been gradually diminishing and replaced by global governance, which has created different dimensions in health and security issues in recent years. There is no dividing line between 'foreign' and 'domestic' infections.

As highlighted in Chapter 3, it is a fact that poverty lies at the root of many ills and that ill health, in its turn, has a devastating effect upon the survival, livelihood and dignity of individuals and the economies of both developed and developing countries (Figure 6.1). If we are going to break this vicious circle and ensure human security for the world's people, we will have to make a major investment in public health in the developing world (Gutlove 2002).

6.1.1 Health and human security: A global scenario

From a health security perspective, child and maternal deaths are of global importance, particularly in developing countries. According to the estimate of the World Health Organisation (WHO) et al. (2012), an estimated 287,000 maternal deaths occurred globally in 2010, a decline of 47 per cent from levels in 1990. With 245,000 maternal deaths, Sub- Saharan Africa (56%) and South Asia (29%) accounted for 85 per cent of this figure. Two countries account for a third of global maternal deaths: India at 19 per cent (56,000) and Nigeria at 14 per cent (40,000). The global Maternal Mortality Rate (MMR) in 2010 was 210 maternal deaths per 100,000 live births, down from 400 maternal deaths per 100,000 live births in 1990. The MMR in developing regions (240) was 15 times higher than in developed regions (16). Sub-Saharan Africa had the highest MMR at 500 maternal deaths per 100,000 live births, while Eastern Asia had the lowest among Millennium Development Goals (MDGs) developing regions, at 37 maternal deaths per 100,000 live births. The MMR of the remaining MDGs in developing regions, in descending order of maternal deaths per 100,000 live births are South Asia (220), Oceania (200), South- eastern Asia (150), Latin America and the Caribbean (80), Northern Africa (78), West Asia (71) and the Caucasus and Central Asia (46).

As per the WHO 1995, the fifth MDG aim to improve maternal health, with a target of reducing the MMR by 75 per cent between 1990 and 2015. The percentage reductions for the 10 countries that had achieved MDG 5 by 2010 are: Estonia (95%), the Maldives (93%), Belarus (88%), Romania (84%), Bhutan (82%), Equatorial Guinea (81%), the Islamic Republic of Iran (81%), Lithuania (78%), Nepal (78%) and Vietnam (76%). The WHO scenario shows positive trends in general, but there is a very discouraging picture of many developing countries (WHO 1995). Millions of mothers, children and elderly people living in developing countries are dying from preventable diseases.

The WHO projected the following global scenario (1955-2025) showing challenging health security issues (Table 6.1)

Table 6.1 Health and human security: A global scenario

Key Indicators	1955 (actual)	1995 (actual)	2025 (projected)
Demographic indicators			
Global population	2.8 billion	5.8 billion	8 billion
Rural population (%)	68	55	41
Urban population (%)	32	45	59
Proportion of older people requiring support from adults of working age	10.5	12.3	17.2
Old/young ratio (under 20)	12/100	16/100	31/100
People aged over 65 years	n/a	390million	800million
Average no. of babies per women of child-bearing age	5.0	2.9	2.3
Life expectancy			
Average life expectancy at birth (years)	48	65	73
Age structure of deaths			
Deaths among children under 5 years (%)	40	21	8
Deaths among 5-19 years olds	10	7	3
Deaths among adults aged 20-64	28	29	27
Deaths among people over 65 years of age	21	43	63
Health of infants and small children			
Infant mortality rate (per 1000 live births)	148	59	29
Leading causes of global deaths (deaths in millions)		1997	2025 (projected)
Infectious and parasitic diseases	n/a	17.3	n/a
Circulatory diseases	n/a	15.3	n/a
Cancer	n/a	6.2	n/a
Respiratory disease (mainly chronic obstructive pulmonary disease)	n/a	2.9	n/a
Perinatal conditions	n/a	3.6	n/a

Source: WHO (1995) n/a : not available

As shown in Table 6.1, the number of people aged over 65 will rise from the present figure of 390 million to 800 million by 2025, eventually accounting for 10 per cent of the total population

(WHO 1995). The size and proportion of people requiring support from adults of working age will increase from

10.5 per cent in 1955 and 12.3 per cent in 1995 to 17.2 per cent in 2025. By 2025, the older population of many developing countries, especially in Latin America and Asia, is set to increase by up to 300 per cent (ibid). As a result, there will be an increased level of population dependency, as well as social issues creating potential risks for human security (ibid).

The average life expectancy in 1955 was just 48 years; in 1995 it was 65 years; in 2025 it will reach 73 years. More than 50 million people live today in countries with a life expectancy of less than 45 years (WHO 1995). By the year 2025, it is expected that no country will have a life expectancy of less than 50 years (ibid). By 2025 there will still be 5 million deaths among children under five per year; 97 per cent of them in the developing world and most of them due to infectious diseases such as pneumonia and diarrhea, combined with malnutrition (ibid). Children who survive may suffer illness, stunted growth or other problems into adult life. Thus, the WHO projection, based on the trend, shows that there are existing and potential human security issues in developing countries in the years to come, which need to be addressed seriously to minimise human security threats.

6.2 Health and human security: A conceptual framework

This section examines the conceptual links between health and human security and examines the health-poverty-human security nexus by exploring the evidence and causality between health and poverty. It does not use any disease-specific illustration, but presents a generic conceptual framework to highlight how human security may be advanced by addressing critical health issues to address the difficult dimension of poverty. As human security is people-centred (UNDP 1994), there is a close link between health and human security. On the one hand, poverty and inequality, humanitarian emergencies, communicable and non-communicable diseases, conflict and natural disaster lead to illness, injury, disability and finally to death. On the other hand, all these issues pose threats to different dimensions of human security including survival, livelihood and dignity. If health systems - particularly service delivery - are not responsive enough, effective and efficient responses to addressing critical threats to human security will be much more severe. Figure 6.1 above illustrates the conceptual link and interrelationship between health and human security.

Figure 6.1 The health and human security link

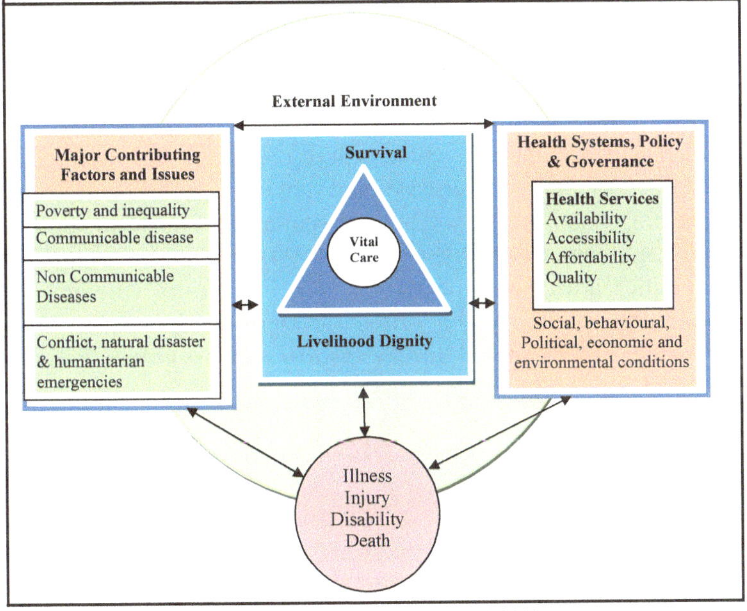

Source: Developed by the author based on CHS (2003)

When people's livelihoods are deeply compromised, when people are uncertain where the next meal will come from, when their life savings suddenly plummet in value, when their crops fail and they have no savings - human security contracts. People eat less and some starve. They pull their children out of school. They cannot afford clothing, heating or health care. Repeated crises further increase the vulnerability of people in absolute or extreme poverty. As a result, poor people may suffer worse health and may die younger than others. Poverty and inequality create insecurity not only to those who live in extreme poverty but also to the community, society, country and ultimately, the rest of the world. Health is one critical component of development that helps people exit the cycle of poverty, or makes them fall into the cycle to start with (UNDP 2003).

Health systems and policy shape health service delivery. Similarly, social, behavioural, political, economic and environmental conditions shape health outcomes to a large extent. While many avoidable deaths can be prevented by better health behaviour such as stopping smoking, eating more healthy foods, getting more exercise and practicing safe sex, many other avoidable deaths, especially those due to infectious diseases, nutritional deprivation and unsafe childbearing and childrearing, can be prevented only by reaching people trapped in poverty or conflict. Disease and poverty go hand in hand. Therefore, good health is both essential and instrumental to achieving human security (UNDP 1994). Similarly, disturbing inequalities are compounded 'hot spots' of health emergencies around the world. Health crises threaten the interdependence and solidarity of global health efforts and consequently pose human security challenges (ibid).

6.3 The evolving concept of health and human security

A true understanding of the broad concept of security firmly recognises that human security - protecting and empowering people, at the individual and community levels - is essential to national and international security (OSAA 2005). Human security represents an effort to re-conceptualise security in a fundamental manner. It is a people-centric concept, originally evolved from traditional territorial security concepts, primarily focused on ensuring security for the individual, not the state. It is essential because at the very heart of security is protecting human lives (CHS 2003).

Health security is at the vital core of human security (CHS 2003). Health and security have long been distinct fields, to the detriment of both. Health has been seen as a 'medical problem' and security, as a matter of military defense (ibid). However, such concepts have drastically changed since the 1990s. Good health is not only the absence of disease but it is a positive state of physical, mental and social well-being (WHO 1946). Consequently, good health is directly related to human dignity, the ability to exercise choice and not fear the future. Poor people are particularly vulnerable to malnutrition, poor reproductive health, immune deficiency and communicable diseases; conversely, ill health is a sure route to poverty. Families may lose their homes and lifetime savings because of ill health. Therefore, health is one of the key building blocks of society and essential component for economic growth, poverty reduction and social justice (Gutlove 2002).

Health security incorporates relative freedom from disease and infection and the ability to access better survival, livelihood and dignity (CHS 2003). A people-centric approach to health, which is the essence of human security, is also a fundamental component of public health policies. Public health provides a unique opportunity for deeper understanding and implementation of human security. Conversely, human security offers a new opportunity to re-define public health within a context of rights-based development (Gutlove 2002).

There is a growing trend of defining health from human rights perspectives. The WHO Constitution of 1946 defines the rights to health as a fundamental right, stating that the health of all people is fundamental to the attainment of peace and security. According to the constitution the enjoyment of the highest attainable standard of health is one of the fundamental rights of every human being without the distinction of race, religion, political belief, economic or social condition (WHO 1946).

The belief in a right to health care has its basis in two moral principles: the 'social justice' argument that health care maintains an individual's normal functioning and therefore preserves the ability to participate in the social and economic life of society; and 2) the 'utilitarian' view that guaranteeing health services increases the welfare of the greatest number of people (Engelhard and Garson 1992). Health is both a direct component of human well-being and a form of human capital that increases an individual's capabilities (Appleton and Teal 1998). Better health significantly contributes to economic development and to the reduction of poverty and income inequality (RTI 2010).

6.4 The health security situation in Nepal

This section provides a general overview on health-related policies, plans and programmes in Nepal. Further discussion on key issues based on the conceptual framework continues in the next section.

6.4.1 Health sector performance and human security

Despite the fact that health is a fairly new concept in the Nepali context, the country has started making significant progress in terms of health outcomes and impact since the 1980s and this progress has continued progressing despite more than a decade of armed conflict. Key health indicators such as life expectancy, infant and child mortality and maternal mortality show gradual but steady improvements. The maternal mortality rate is declining and the number of child deaths has halved during the past 10 years (MoHP et. al 2012). Fertility has declined from an average of 5.1 children per women in 1980s to the current level of 2.6 and nearly one in every two women use a modern method of family planning (ibid).

Table 6.2 shows the progress made in Nepal since 1991, as well as the outcomes and impact indicators. Nepal's targets to 2015 were chosen to reflect the MDGs health targets.

Table 6.2 Trends in key health indicators and MDGs targets

MDGs/Key Impact Indicator	Status				Targets	
	1991	1996	2001	2006	2011	2015
MDG 4: Reduce Child Mortality						
Under-five mortality rate (between birth and fifth birthday)	158	118.3	91	61	54	38

MDGs/Key Impact Indicator	Status				Targets	
	1991	**1996**	**2001**	**2006**	**2011**	**2015**
Infant mortality rate (between birth and first birthday)	106	78.5	64	48	46	32
Neonatal mortality rate		49.9	43	33	30	16
Prevalence of underweight children under 5 years of age (%)		49.2	48.3	38.6	34	29
MDG 5: Improve Maternal Health						
Maternal mortality ratio	539	539	415	281	170 (WHO estimate)	134
Total fertility rate (15-49)	4.8	4.6	4.1	3.1	2.6	2.5
Adolescent fertility rate (15-19 years)	n/a	127	110	98	85	70
CPR (modern methods)	24	26.0	35.4	44.2	43	67
MDG-6: HIV/AIDS						
HIV prevalence among people aged 15-49 years	n/a	n/a	n/a	n/a	n/a	0.30
Population aged 15-24 years with comprehensive knowledge of HIV/ AIDS (%)	n/a	n/a	n/a	M-43.6 F-27.6	M-33.9 F-25.8	M-50 F-40
TB treatment success rates (%)	n/a	79	89	89	90	90
Malaria annual parasite incidence per 1,000	n/a	0.54	0.40	0.28	0.2	Halt and reverse

Source: Compiled by the author from different sources:, MoHP, (2010a), MoH (1993), MoH (1986), MoHP et.al. (2007) and MoHP (2012), WHO et al. (2012).

n/a: not available

The data outlined in Table 6.2 demonstrate positive trends in health outcomes and impact level indicators in the country. The Table provides an overall view of the substantial progress that Nepal has made on health during the past two decades. Tuberculosis case detection and treatment success rates are improving and malaria annual parasite incidence is declining.

6.4.2 Key security issues in Nepal's health sector

In the health sector of Nepal, key human security issues are related to maternal health (MDG 5) and child health (MDG 4), nutrition (MDG 1) and HIV/AIDS (MDG 6). Therefore, this section focuses on these key areas.

a. Maternal and child health

Table 6.3 shows key maternal care indicators in a comparative perspective:

Table 6.3 Key maternal care indicators

Key Indicators	1996	2001	2006	2011
Anti Natal Care from a skilled provider (%)	23.6	27.9	43.7	58
Births assisted by skilled provider (%)	9	10.9	18.7	36
Births delivered in the health facility (%)	7.6	9.1	17.7	35

Source: MoH et al. (1997), MoHP et al.(2002), MoHP et al.(2007) and MoHP et al.(2012).

Table 6.3 shows that there are steady improvements in Anti-Natal Care (ANC) visits, births assisted by skilled providers and deliveries at health facilities. Nepal has been quite successful in designing and implementing innovative programmes to address child and maternal health-focused issues. The country has received international attention and acclaim for its progress on reducing maternal and child mortality. Nepal is one among very few developing countries in the world on track to achieve the MDGs related to maternal and child health for 2015. This fact shows that Nepal has been improving the health security situation in the country, although its policies were not necessarily designed and implemented from a human security perspective but from peoples' welfare perspectives.

Table 6.4 Immunisation indicators

Key Indicators	1996	2001	2006	2011
BCG	76	85	93	96
DPT3	54	72	89	91
Polio3	51	92	91	92
Measles	57	71	85	88
All vaccines	43	66	83	87
Children 12-23 months receiving no vaccinations	20	0.9	2.7	3

Source: MoH et al. (1997), MoHP et al.(2002), MoHP et al. (2007) and MoHP et al.(2012)

Table 6.4 shows that 87 per cent of children in Nepal have all the WHO- recommended immunisations. Nepal Demographic and Health Survey (NDHS) 2011 found that immunisation coverage is highest among children living in the Far West region (94%) and those living in the wealthiest households (96%). Three per cent of children (12-23 months) have not yet received any type of vaccinations. Both indicators show that poverty and inequality are still issues in child immunisation, which has raised health security concerns.

b. Childhood illness

Universal and free primary care was introduced in January 2009 by the government to improve the availability, accessibility and affordability of primary care. It was the first step towards implementing the Interim Constitution's provision for health service delivery. However, in reality, access and coverage to primary care have remained critical issues, as only 42 per cent of children with fever and only 39 per cent of diarrhea cases are taken to a health facility (Table 6.5). The dataset shows that only 50 per cent of children with diarrhea were given Oral Rehydration Treatment (ORT) or increased fluids, which are quite limited; such cases illustrate that there is a high level of health insecurity caused by preventable diseases.

Table 6.5 Treatment status (Maternal and child health)

Description	1996 (1991-1995)	2001 (1996-2000)	2006 (2001-2005)	2011 (2006-2010)
Percentage of children for whom advice or treatment was sought from health facility/ provider				
ARI Symptoms	18.2	23.7	43	50
Fever	N/A	23.7	34	42
Diarrhea	13.8	21.2	26.9	39
Percentage given fluid from ORS packet during diarrhea	25.9	32.2	29	39
Percentage given ORT	28.6	46.5	40.7	45
Percentage given Zinc	N/A	N/A	Less than 1	6
Anaemia in children				

Description	1996 (1991-1995)	2001 (1996-2000)	2006 (2001-2005)	2011 (2006-2010)
Any anaemia	n/a	n/a	48	46
Mild	n/a	n/a	26	27
Moderate	n/a	n/a	22	18
Severe	n/a	n/a	Less than 1	Less than 1
Anaemia in women				
Any anaemia	n/a	n/a	36	35
Mild	n/a	n/a	29	29
Moderate	n/a	n/a	6	6
Severe	n/a	n/a	Less than 1	0.3
Households using adequately iodised salt	n/a	n/a	n/a	80

Source: MoH et al. (1997), MoH et al. (2002), MoHP et al. (2007) and MoHP et al.(2012). n/a: not available

Among other childhood illnesses, diarrhea and Acute Respiratory Infections (ARI) are the primary killers of children in Nepal. Nearly 12 per cent of children in Nepal were found to suffer from diarrhea and almost 5 per cent from Acute Respiratory Infections. Hand washing with soap alone has been estimated to contribute to cutting deaths from diarrhea by half and ARIs by one quarter (MoHP 2012).

c. Nutrition

A number of surveys and studies conducted since 1975 look at the nutritional status of children and women in Nepal. They found a very high prevalence of under-nutrition and nutritional disorders (Adhikari 2010). National Nutrition Strategies developed in 1978 and 1986 focused on improved agricultural productivity to improve the availability of food (ibid); however, subsequent government plans in nutrition identified the need for improved food utilisation within households to improve nutritional status. An attempt to develop a National Plan of Action in 2007 identified household food security, child care practices, women's status and responsive health services as the key determinants of childhood nutrition (ibid). The most recent effort in this regard had been to conduct a Nutrition Assessment and Gap Analysis (NAGA) (ibid). One important finding of this assessment is the gap in knowledge on various food behaviours including intra-household food use, diversity of diet, food quality and quantity, breast feeding and complementary feeding practices, food handling and hygiene practices and emergency preparedness and its impact on nutritional status (ibid). The consequences of under-nutrition are the most serious for fatal development and for children under 24 months of age (ibid). Nepal is not making effective enough progress toward the underweight target of the first MDG of 'Eradicating Extreme Poverty and Hunger'.

Chronic energy deficiency and anemia in mothers is a substantial problem, with 24.4 per cent of women of reproductive age with a Body Mass Index (BMI) of less than 18.5 kg/m^2 and a third of Nepali women anemic (MoHP 2007). Anemia can lead to increased risk of maternal mortality due to postpartum hemorrhage and Low Birth Weight (LBW) infants. The prevalence of LBW is also high; although accurate, population-based data are not available. Between 14 to 34 per cent of newborns are estimated to be less than two kilograms at birth (Pokharel 2009). One hospital-based study of 3,500 mother-infant pairs from four major hospitals in various regions showed that 27 per cent were LBW and of those, 70 per cent were small-for-date indicating intrauterine growth retardation (ibid).

Nevertheless, Nepal has made significant progress on nutrition interventions as described in the 2008 Lancet Nutrition Series on Maternal and Child Under-nutrition (Adhikari 2010). This is particularly the case for Vitamin A supplementation, which is among the evidence- based interventions listed in the Lancet. Nepal won international acclaim for scaling up its Vitamin 'A' programmes (ibid). In 2006, the Vitamin 'A' coverage rate for children 6 to 59 months of age was 87.5 per cent nationally (ibid). This has likely had a large effect on decreasing under- five mortality rates. Iron folate supplementation for pregnant women is increasing; rates of anaemia have decreased by 44 per cent since 1998 (ibid). Fortification programmes (salt iodisation and iron fortification of wheat flour) are largely on track to expand over the next few years. The more difficult challenge now is decreasing the levels of under-nutrition, which are driven by cultural and social factors that determine food-related practices, as well as food scarcity in some regions.

The government, in recent years, has been giving increased attention to improving the health and nutritional status of the Nepali population, especially for poor and marginalised groups. Table 6.6 shows the trend in the nutritional status of children under five years of age.

Table 6.6 Trends in the nutritional status of children under five years of age

Description	2001	2006	2011
Stunting (height-for-age)	57	49	41
Wasting (weight-for-height)	11	13	11
Under-weight (weight-for-age)	43	39	29

Source: MoH et. al (2002) , MoHP et. al (2007) and MoHP et. al (2012).
Note: The data are based on the WHO Child Growth Standards.

Table 6.6 shows that the prevalence of stunting has continuously declined between the 2001, 2006 and 2011, although the rate is still very high at 41 per cent. Wasting actually saw a small increase in 2011, returning to the 2001 level of 11 per cent. This is an alarming result indicating more immediate dietary deficits and/or potential serious health complications. Underweight showed significant improvements (29%), but is still high. There is also a progressing trend in exclusive breast feeding and complementary feeding among children aged more than six months (Table 6.7).

Table 6.7 Breast and complementary feeding

Description	2001	2006	2011
Children 0.5 months exclusively breastfed	n/a	53	70
Children given complementary feeding	53	63 (6-7 months)	66 (6-8 months)

Source: MoH et. al (2002) , MoHP et. al (2007) and MoHP et. al (2012).

In Nepal, health and nutrition behaviour remain a key obstacle to improved health and nutrition of women and children (Adhikari 2010). Poor Infant and Young Child Feeding (IYCF) practices are a particularly serious obstacle to improved nutrition. Poor hygiene and sanitation and recurrent infections such as diarrhea in young children can further exacerbate the inadequate feeding practices by reducing absorption of nutrients.

Given the rich diversity of culture, geography, ethnicity and beliefs in Nepal, programmes that attempt to change nutrition-related practices must begin by understanding both the negative and positive behaviours in a particular location as well as the community level barriers to optimal nutrition behaviours.

In recent years, it has been widely recognised that the MDG 1 for reducing hunger will not be achieved without dramatic improvements in the overall health and growth of young children.

d. HIV/AIDS

The first case of AIDS in Nepal was reported in 1988. By August 2010, more than 16,000 cases of HIV infection were officially reported to the National Centre for AIDS and STD Control (NCASC), with three times as many men reported to be infected as women (MoHP and NCASC 2010).

HIV/AIDS remains a concentrated epidemic in Nepal with continuing risks associated with a large migrant worker population. According to MoHP and NCASC (2010) as of 2009, national estimates indicate that approximately 64,000 adults and children are infected with HIV, although most of them were not aware of their infection, with an estimated overall prevalence of about 0.4 per cent in the adult population (15-49 years old). About 4,500 people received Antiretroviral (ARV) therapy, of which 270 are children. Referring to UNICEF, MoHP and NCASC (2010) it states that the number of women over age 15 who are living with HIV in Nepal is estimated at 20,000. In 2009, 2,600 children aged 0 -14 were estimated to be living with HIV.

Further, MoHP and NCASC (2010) reveals that as in other countries in the region, people who inject drugs (PWID), men who have sex with men (MSM) and female sex workers (FSW) are the groups most at risk of HIV, but there are also other groups who have an elevated risk of HIV such as seasonal labour migrants. Nepal's 1.5 million to 2 million labour migrants, who are potential clients of sex workers abroad, account for the majority of the HIV-positive population. Nepal's labor migrants make up almost 40 per cent of the total estimated HIV infections in the country, followed by the wives and partners of migrant men infected with HIV. One of the newest challenges for Nepal's HIV prevention programme is to reduce transmission among migrants and their spouses and partners.

This is especially important for migrants to Mumbai where the risk of HIV infection is high. Table 6.8 shows progress made over last 15-20 years and overall trends in HIV/AIDS reduction:

Table 6.8 Key indicators related to HIV/AIDS and current status (%)

Description		1996	2001	2006	2011
Heard of AIDS	Women	26.8	49.6	72.6	86
	Men	n/a	71.7	91.7	97
Knowledge on preventive methods	Among women				
	Using condoms	n/a	32.6	58.3	74
	Limiting sex to one uninfected partner	n/a	36.9	64.6	79
	Among men				
	Using condoms	n/a	62.5	83.5	89
	Limiting sex to one uninfected partner	n/a	54.3	82.6	89
Multiple sexual partners: Men	Percentage who had 2+partners in the past 12 months	n/a	n/a	2.8	4
	Mean number of sexual partners in lifetime (%)	n/a	n/a	2	ever married -7 never married - 3

Source: MoH et. al (2002), MoHP et. al (2007) and MoHP et al. (2012).
n/a: not available

Nepal appears to have a high level of NGO, government and donor capacity in terms of the overall response to HIV; however, there are weaknesses. The response focuses on Most at Risk Populations (MARPs) and in doing has remained vertical and unconnected to the broader health system. The lack of integration of HIV programmes and services into the health system is a concern for both the government and the NGOs working in the field. The epidemic outside the urban centres is heavily influenced by poverty and HIV and other health and development programmes have been slowed and sometimes halted by political violence, instability and insurgency. Advocacy on HIV-related law and policy is weak; HIV legislation was drafted but has been stalled for over seven years.

6.4.3 Initiatives to improve the health security situation in Nepal

The Interim Constitution of Nepal, 2007 (Article 16), for the first time in the country's history, stipulated basic health as a citizen's fundamental right. Defining basic health as a fundamental right shows the state's firm commitment to human security. However, there is long way to go to translate the constitutional provisions into practice.

Nepal, with significant support from external development partners (EDPs), is working towards achieving the MDGs by 2015. The goals 4, 5 and 6 are directly related to health; namely, reducing child mortality, improving maternal health and combating HIV/AIDS, malaria and other major diseases.

The Government of Nepal introduced a Sector-Wide Approach (SWAp) in the health sector in 2004. During the first phase of the Nepal Health Sector Programme (NHSP 2004-10), progress has accelerated and has been accompanied by significant improvements in equal access to health services. The Government and the EDPs jointly prepared a Health Sector Strategy in 2003, followed by the first Nepal Health Sector Programme-Implementation Plan (2005-2010) (MoHP 2010a). The NHSP was a milestone in the health sector of Nepal for programme harmonisation and gradually building country ownership.

It is estimated that Nepal Health Sector Programme-1 (NHSP-1) prevented 96,000 deaths and nearly 3.2 million disability-adjusted life years (DALYs)[1] at a cost of $144 per DALY saved (MoHP 2010a). The current plan Nepal Health Sector Programme - 2

1 DALYs = Disability Adjusted Life Years. It means the sum of years of potential life lost due to premature mortality and the years of productive life lost due to disability (WHO).

(NHSP-2) represents a continuation and further refinement of earlier policies and plans based on the implementation of cost-effective, evidence-based health interventions. If the targets of NHSP-2 are broadly achieved in line with a 'middle case' scenario, this achievement would be broadly maintained, saving a further 45,000 deaths and nearly 1.5 million DALYs at a cost of $147 (ibid).

6.5 Major contributing factors and issues

Several features hinder health security in Nepal. These factors are discussed in this section with reference to the conceptual framework presented and discussed in section 6.2.

6.5.1 Poverty and inequality issues in health service delivery and outcomes

a. Equity in Anti-Natal Care (ANC) utilisation

Table 6.9 shows the trends in ANC visits provided by doctors and nurses by wealth quintile:

Table 6.9 Trends in four or more ANC visits by wealth quintile in percentage

Wealth quintile	1996	2001	2006	Change in percentage points
First (poorest)	2.7	5.1	10.5	7.8
Second	3.4	6.0	20.2	16.8
Third	5.8	9.5	27.7	21.9
Fourth	9.6	18.0	38.0	28.4
Fifth (richest)	31.5	46.8	60.0	28.5
Total	8.8	14.3	29.4	20.6
Difference between poorest and richest quintiles	28.8	41.7	49.5	20.7

Source: RTI (2008)

Table 6.9 shows that inequality has gradually increased from 29 to 50 per cent between the poorest and richest quintiles in four or more ANC visits between 1996 and 2006. ANC utilisation increased by almost fourfold in the poorest quintile, although the rate is still very low; compared to utilisation almost doubling among the richest. The trend shows that wealthier people have been far more likely to benefit from four or more ANC visits than the poor and that this gap has widened over the 10 years. This statistic provides evidence that health insecurity (in terms of ANC- related service delivery) among the poor has not improved significantly; rather, inequality has increased over the years.

b. Equity in the use of Doctors, Nurses and Auxiliary Nurse Midwives during delivery

The Safe Delivery Incentive Programme (SDIP) was introduced in 2006 to promote the use of Skilled Birth Attendants (SBAs), particularly by the poor and excluded. Since the introduction of the Safe Delivery Incentive Programme (SDIP), the utilisation of skilled birth attendants during delivery has increased sharply and is expected to enroll more poor mothers in the future.

Inequity, however, has been widening markedly in the utilisation of SBAs - Doctors, Nurses and Auxiliary Nurse Midwives (ANMs) - during delivery. The difference between the poorest and richest quintiles grew from 32 per cent in 1996 to 53 per cent in 2006 (Table 6.10). The greatest rate of change was observed in the fourth quintile, which changed by more than 200 per cent, from 7 to 23 per cent in the last decade (Table 6.10).

Table 6.10 Trends in deliveries attended by Doctor, Nurses and Auxiliary Nurse Midwives (ANMs) by wealth quintile in percentage

Wealth quintile	1996	2001	2006	Change in percentage points
First (poorest)	2.6	2.5	4.8	2.2
Second	4.9	4.7	10.1	5.2
Third	6.1	6.7	12.4	6.3
Fourth	7.0	12.6	22.9	15.9
Fifth (wealthiest)	35.0	43.9	57.8	22.8
Total	9.0	10.8	18.7	9.7
Difference between poorest and richest quintiles	32.4	41.4	53.0	20.6

Source: RTI (2008)

Although the rates of change among the poorest and second quintiles are large, the percentages of deliveries attended by SBAs remain very low.

c. Equity immunisation services

Table 6.11 shows the disparity between the poorest and richest quintiles for fully immunised children:

Table 6.11 Proportion of fully immunised children aged 12-23 months by wealth quintile in percentage

Wealth quintile	1996	2001	2006	Change in percentage points
First (poorest)	30	55	67	37
Second	34	55	82	48
Third	42	63	87	45
Fourth	49	79	89	40
Fifth (wealthiest)	73	86	95	22
Total	43	65	82	39
Difference between poorest and richest quintiles	43	31	28	-15

Source: RTI (2008)

As Table 6.11 shows, inequality has gradually decreased between the richest and poorest quintiles. The disparity between the poorest and richest quintiles for fully immunised children decreased from 43 percentage points in 1996 to 28 percentage points in 2006. Considerable progress has been achieved, particularly among children in the second and third quintiles, in which the proportion of fully immunised children increased from 34 per cent in 1996 to 82 per cent in 2006 and from 42 per cent to 87 per cent, respectively (Table 6.11). The change in percentage of these two quintiles is more than twice the change of the richest quintile.

6.5.2 Conflict, natural disaster and humanitarian emergencies

Conflict may increase the prevalence and incidence of infectious diseases and may also lead to humanitarian emergencies, thus leading to human insecurity (Figure 6.1). It poses threats to both national and international security in the current context of globalisation. The concentration of mobile populations fleeing the destruction of armed violence increases the spread of viruses and bacteria from carriers and vectors. Thus, the global burden of infectious diseases is highly concentrated in conflict zones. For example malaria, a preventable and curable infectious disease, kills on average 20 per cent of children under five in conflict zones (O'Donovan 2008). Most of these deaths are concentrated in Africa, where both poverty and conflict are endemic. Mapping the incidence of malaria against the location of conflict zones reveals a pattern of disease and poverty exacerbated by conflict (WHO 2008a).

Nepal faced 10 years of armed conflict and human security threats continued even after the Comprehensive Peace Agreement was signed. During the armed conflict period in Nepal (1996-2006), public health services were seriously interrupted and conflict destroyed the means for a basic livelihood among populations, resulting in conditions of exacerbated poverty, poor hygiene and forced displacement. Nepal continues to struggle to restore peace and progress towards democracy and prosperity.

6.5.3 Communicable diseases and human security issues

Nepal has been facing a range of communicable and non-communicable diseases and is now being expanded with a third category of diseases (NHRC 2006). Among the communicable diseases malaria, HIV/AIDS, Tuberculosis (TB), Acute Respiratory Infections (ARI), diarrhea and H1N1[2]are the major killers and threats to human security. While communicable diseases are still an important cause of preventable deaths, in current years, chronic non-communicable diseases have emerged as major killers. Injuries and disasters, along with emerging and re-emerging diseases associated with changes in environment, constitute the third category of diseases.

The presence of infectious diseases in Nepal is widespread and their epidemiology is mostly unknown. There are mainly two categories of infectious diseases in Nepal: a) food and

---

[2] It is a scientific name of influenza A virus

waterborne diseases (bacterial diarrhea, Hepatitis A and typhoid fever) and b) vector borne diseases (Japanese encephalitis, malaria and dengue fever) (WHO 2008b).

Both categories of infectious diseases are preventable; however, serious efforts to focus on intervention are vital to this success. If prevented, morbidity and mortality would be significantly reduced, thus increasing survival rate, improving livelihood and human dignity.

6.5.4 Non-communicable diseases and human security issues

Bovet and Paccaud (2012, p 4) provided a good framework showing the relationship between Non-Communicable Diseases (NCDs) and poverty (Figure 6.4): it explains how the populations in low and middle income countries are exposed to modifiable risk factors in the globalised context and lose their household incomes due to the high cost of health care.

Figure 6.2 Relationship between NCDs and poverty

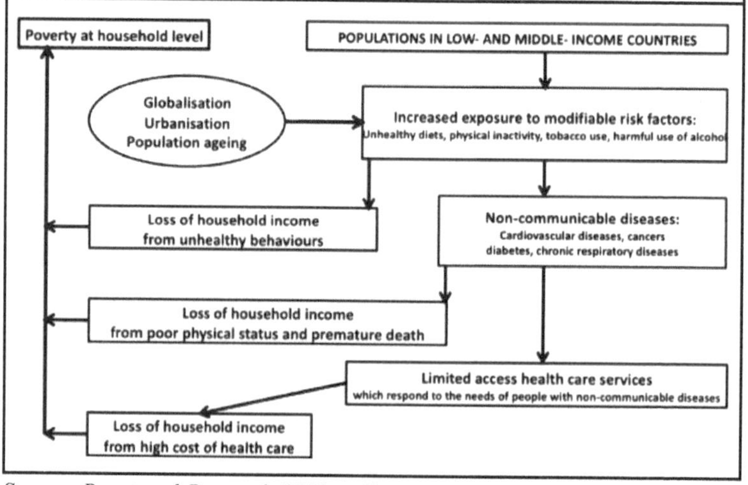

Source: Bovet and Paccaud (2012, p 7)

Nearly 52 per cent of deaths and 44 per cent of the Burden of Diseases (BOD) in the South Asia Region (SEAR) are related to Non-Communicable Diseases (NCDs) (WHO 2008c). The major NCDs in the region are cardiovascular disorders, cancer, diabetes mellitus, chronic lung diseases and conditions arising from accidents and injuries. A recent survey shows that Nepal has a remarkably high prevalence of risk factors for NCDs (ibid).

With regard to this challenge, it is estimated that the annual cost per capita for implementing a set of highly cost-effective interventions could amount to only USD 1 for population-based measures aimed at reducing tobacco and harmful use of alcohol and to another approximately USD 2 for scaling up multi-drug therapy for all persons at high risk of cardio vascular disease (CVD) (Bovet and Paccaud 2012). If it is not addressed with preventive measures, treatment of NCD will be very costly, probably beyond the capacity of the health system.

Table 6.12 Prevalence of diabetes in South Asia (Projected in 1998)

Country	2000	2025
Bangladesh	2.2 (1 564)	3.1 (4,032)
Bhutan	2.1 (19)	2.3 (39)
India	4.0 (22 878)	6.0 (57,243)
Maldives	2.5 (3.2)	3.0 (9.2)
Nepal	2.2 (263)	2.6 (638)
Pakistan	7.1 (5 310)	8.7 (14,523)
Sri Lanka	2.6 (318)	3.5 (617)

Source: White and Rafique (2002)

Table 6.12 shows the prevalence of diabetes in South Asia in 2000 and 2025 (projected in 1998).[3] Values are given in percentages (number of people with diabetes, in thousands). It clearly indicates that the prevalence of diabetes in South Asia (SA) is rapidly increasing, largely due to changing lifestyle and behavioural factors.

The Annual Health Report 2002 explained that degenerative Non- Communicable Diseases (NCDs) in Nepal accounted for 42 per cent of the cause of all deaths and contributed 23 per cent of loss of all Disability Adjusted Life Years (DALY) (WHO 2008c). It was also estimated that within 15 years, degenerative

3 For detail see: http://www.ncbi.nlm.nih.gov/pmc/articles/PMC383378/table/tbl2/.

diseases and all other NCDs would account for almost 30 per cent of the DALY lost (ibid). Nepal World Health Survey of 2002 revealed that NCD deaths were 41.96 per cent of all deaths. Similarly, the World Health Report 2003 estimated NCD-related deaths constitute 48 per cent of the total deaths in Nepal, which is quite high in comparison to related deaths in the region (MoHP 2002 as cited in WHO 2008c). If NCDs are not prevented, they may substantially hold back human development and impede progress towards the Millennium Development Goals (MDGs).

According to the WHO Report (Gobocan 2000 as cited in WHO 2008a), tobacco-related disease mortality in Nepal due to lung cancer was 39.9/1000,000 for men and 7.5/1000,000 for women. Similarly, oral and pharynx cancer was 51.8/100,000 for men and 23.2/100,000 for women (WHO 2008a). All these estimates show that human security threats caused by NCDs are significantly high in Nepal. Tobacco use, excessive alcohol consumption, low intake of fruits and vegetables, physical inactivity, weight, height and blood pressure were identified as major key risk factors for major NCDs (Table 6.13).

Table 6.13 Risk factors for non-communicable diseases (2007-2008, population aged 15-64 years)

Risk factors		Both Sexes (%)	Males (%)	Females (%)
Tobacco use	Who currently smoke tobacco daily	23.8	31.2	15.5
Alcohol consumption	Current drinkers (who drank alcohol in the past 30 days)	28.5	39.3	16.5
Fruit and vegetable consumption	Who ate late less than five of combined servings of fruit and vegetables per day	61.9	60.5	63.5
Physical activity	Low levels of activity (defined as <600 MET-minutes/week)	5.5	5.2	5.9
Physical measurements	Who are overweight or obese (BMI $\geq$ 25 kg/m2	7.2	7.3	7.1
	Who are obese (BMI $\geq$ 30 kg/m2)	1.7	1.1	2.4

Risk factors		Both Sexes (%)	Males (%)	Females (%)
Blood pressure (BP)	Raised BP (SBP $\geq$ 140 and/ or DBP $\geq$ 90 mmHg or currently on medication for raised BP	21.5	24.5	18.1
Combined Risk Factors				
Low Risk	None of the risk factors included above	22.0	20.9	23.3
Raised Risk	At least three of risk factors included above), aged 15-44 years old	5.7	8.4	2.7
Raised Risk	At least three of risk factors included above), aged 45-64 years old	20.1	24.2	15.2

Source: WHO (2008)

Table 6.13 shows that among adults aged 15-64 years, 23.8 per cent consume tobacco products; 28.5 per cent drink alcohol; and 60.5 per cent men and 63.5 per cent women do not take recommended amount of fruits and vegetables on daily basis. The prevalence of common behavioural risk factors varies among age groups and sex. Seven per cent of people are overweight and 24.5 per cent of men and 18.1 per cent of women are hypertensive. The number of people facing high risk factors is increasing and currently 8.4 per cent men and 2.7 per cent women are at heightened risk with a combination of at least three risk factors. The percentage of the population facing high risk factors has been rapidly increasing as the urban population increases, thus threatening the country's human security situation. Lifestyle adjustment is critical to this population.

6.6 Health system, policy and governance

Health systems, policy and governance provide the framework to systematically address poverty and inequality in health, communicable and non-communicable disease and health-related issues associated with conflict, natural disaster and humanitarian emergencies and consequently to promote human security.

Therefore, this section discusses these systemic dimensions of health security.

Service delivery issues

Although Nepal's health sector has seen significant progress in the past decade, many people suffer from diseases that are long forgotten in the developed world. As discussed earlier, Nepal has seen significantly reduced maternal and child mortality rates nationally; disparities, however, persist in access to and use of Essential Health Care Services (EHCS) the health status between the poor and the wealthy and between deprived and privileged castes or ethnicities.

In a country with difficult geographical terrain and roughly 80 per cent of the population living in rural areas, delivery of EHCS is focused on both community- and facility-based health services. Due to the absence of critical human resources for health and other reasons, basic services have been interrupted at the grassroots level. Poor and marginalised groups have suffered more than other groups during this transition. Due to weak delivery systems and weak responsive nature of public institutions, the legitimacy of the public sector is in question (Adhikari 2010).

Based on the analysis presented above, the key service delivery issues in Nepal include a) weak access to and utilisation of EHCS, particularly by the poor and marginalised, b) the centralised health service delivery mechanism and practices, c) weak public-public and public-private partnerships, d) weak sector management including planning, programming and budgeting practices, e) uncertain health financing and sustainability issues, f) weak retention of human resources in rural and remote health facilities, g) weak supervision, monitoring and reporting, h) poor quality of health services, i) weak ownership of local level institutions, j) unmet family planning needs, k) higher levels of stocks of essential drugs, particularly at district and lower levels and l) inadequate diagnostic tools and equipment in the facilities. All these issues have resulted in a high level of morbidity and mortality threatening human survival, livelihood and dignity.

a. Availability of health services

Nepal has a vast network of health facilities down to the community level. Each Village Development Committee (VDC) has at least one health facility (HP-675, or SHP-3,127, or Primary Health Care Centres (PHCCs). -208). Outreach clinics (ORC), Female Community Health Volunteers (FCHVs) (48,489) and PHCC/ORC Clinics (13,180) link static health facilities to communities at the grassroots level (DoHS 2012a). There are 75 District/ Public Health Offices (D/PHOs) in each district, 65 district hospitals, 10 Zonal hospitals, three regional and two sub-regional hospitals in addition to a few specialty and super-specialty hospitals in urban areas (ibid).

This network is particularly striking in service delivery at the community level where Female Community Health Volunteers (FCHVs) have been mobilised to provide key life-saving interventions such as preventing postpartum hemorrhage during home deliveries, treating childhood pneumonia and diarrhea, making non-clinical family planning methods available at the household-level and teaching simple techniques for newborn care. They are the pillar of community-level health activities and the backbone of health services and health education that provides results in rural areas. As outlined above, there are a number of supply- and demand-side challenges in health service delivery. Major challenges include making quality and equitable Essential Health Care Services (EHCS) services more accessible to remote communities; ensuring that necessary drugs and supplies and sufficiently trained and motivated staff are available; and making services more results-focused and accountable to the population. Demand-side constraints include the utilisation of services that are available through different levels of health facilities. Demand-side challenges involve different barriers (cultural, financial, geographical, social, institutional) in accessing services. A number of initiatives have been introduced in the health sector to improve access to and coverage of these services; for example, through the extension of free EHCS and through support to help meet transport and other costs for accessing services. Improvements also include action to tackle other factors that prevent people from using services, including improving knowledge and helping to empower women and socially excluded groups to demand the services which, under the Interim Constitution, they have a rights to receive (MoHP 2010b).

b. No provision for Nepal's aging population

The size of the aging population in Nepal is increasing due to changing population structures and extended life expectancy. This issue is further complicated by new social problems such as the increased prevalence of nuclear families and the out-migration of the young generations. There is no provision for preventative and curative health care for the aging population (geriatric care). Geriatric care is different from other healthcare, as it is a unique approach to primary healthcare focused on the needs of older adults.

c. Universal free primary health care: Some issues and challenges

Since mid-December 2006, the Ministry of Health and Population (MoHP) has introduced primary health care services (emergency and inpatient services) free of charge to poor, disabled, senior citizen and Female Community Health Volunteers (FCHVs) at up to 25 bedded district hospitals and Primary Health Care Centres (PHCCs). From mid-January 2008, the MoHP has instituted a policy of free care at Health Posts (HPs) and Sub- Health Posts (SHPs) and expanded free drug schemes at primary health care centres (PHCCs) and district hospitals. The government has assigned 40 types of medicines to be provided free of cost through health institutions across the country. However, many people in remote districts have no access to this service. Due to difficult terrain, most of the health institutions could not get medicine in time. Delay in the supply of the medicines, non-delivery of medicines as per the demand and lack of health workers in health institutions are the main reasons for this situation.

The purpose of abolishing user fees is to increase access to and utilisation of health services and to improve the health status of poor and marginalised citizens, particularly women, who have little control over economic resources but who require frequent health care for themselves and their children. But the implementation of the policy seems to be in weak in most part of the Hill and Mountain districts, especially in the Mid- and Far-West regions. People in these parts of the country do not have access to health facilities within a one hour walk. The health facilities do not even have medicine for most illnesses.

Delivery services for all pregnant women have been free of charge at all government institutions since 2010/11 and a Safe-Delivery Incentive Programme (SDIP) has been implemented to address other financial barriers. The trend of institutional delivery has been significantly increased and thus deaths from complicated delivery have decreased in recent years.

These reform initiatives are further improving access to and use of Essential Health Care Services (EHCS), including deliveries at facilities, among the poor and excluded, but health facility and household surveys continue to identify barriers and inequalities. For example, although 60 per cent of households had heard of free health care services in 2009 (RTI 2010), including 65 per cent of women, less than half of the poorest interviewees had heard of them compared to 85 per cent of the wealthiest interviewees. Among the poorest pregnant women, 56 per cent expected to deliver at home and fewer than 2 per cent expected to deliver in a district hospital. The reason most frequently mentioned for not delivering at a health facility was distance, followed by high fees, transportation costs, no help at home and poor quality of services (ibid).

d. Health seeking attitudes, behaviour and utilisation

A household survey of 13 districts (RTI 2010) shows that about 88 per cent of all respondents would take a pregnant household member for antenatal care (ANC), but only 76 per cent from the poorest households compared to 97 per cent from the wealthiest. The most common reasons for not seeking antenatal care were 'Belief in traditional treatment,' 'Do not feel it is necessary to take a pregnant woman to a health facility,' and 'The hospital is too far.' Among recently delivered or pregnant women, more than half sought ANC but almost all the wealthiest women did.

The RTI study (2010) shows that 61 per cent of household respondents had used a government health facility in the last six months and over half of them had also utilised a NGO or private facility. Dalits were the least likely to use an NGO or private facility. The poor were most likely to use Health Posts (HPs) and Sub-Health Posts (SHPs) whereas the wealthy were more likely to use hospitals. Twenty-nine per cent of households received health care free of charge. Households from the poorest quintile were most likely to have received services free of charge (43 %), whereas the wealthiest were most likely to have paid (86 %). The cost of health services decreased moving across Nepal from the East to the Far-West region. As expected, drugs were the greatest expense. On average, the poorest people were still paying about NPR 1,400 (USD 15) per visit and wealthiest were paying almost NPR 3,000 (USD 35).

The same patterns emerged for non-medical expenses. The poorest households paid NPR 520 (USD 6) for food, lodging and transportation and the wealthiest paid almost NPR 900 (USD 10) per visit. Non-medical expenses per visit also decreased from east to west. Dalits, Janjatis and Muslims paid the least. The total out-of-pocket expenditures for the poorest households averaged about NPR 1,900 (USD 21) per visit, whereas the wealthiest spent NPR 3,800 (USD 42) (RTI 2010). Delivery services became free of charge for all women at institutions in January 2009; however, 52 per cent of women who recently delivered paid for services (ibid). The poorest were the most likely to have paid and the wealthiest the least likely; presumably because the wealthier women were better informed about the new policy. About 75 per cent of women who recently delivered received a cash incentive, but fewer of the poorest quintile than the wealthier quintiles received the incentive.

e. Access to health care and human insecurity

The study (RTI 2010) also shows that among the poorest quintile, 90 per cent cited Health Posts (HPs) and Sub-Health Posts (SHPs) as the nearest facilities, compared to only 45 per cent of the wealthiest. Fifteen per cent of respondents cited hospitals as the nearest facility, but the wealthiest did so at three times that rate. Among the women, hospitals were cited as the nearest facility significantly more often than among the household respondents, especially among the poorest quintile. However, the number of women responding that they did not know what the nearest facility was four times the household rate in the case of the respondents from the poorest two quintiles. Travel time ranged from five minutes to four hours to reach the nearest maternal care facility (ibid).

Another recent survey (MoHP 2012) shows that the percentage of women with antenatal care from a skilled provider[4] has improved significantly over the last five years and is currently at 58 per cent (urban 86, rural 55).

f. Barriers to health care

One in three respondents reported problems in accessing health care services during the previous six months. Respondents from the poorest quintile were only slightly more likely than their peers in other quintiles to report problems, but overall the rate of complaint was remarkably similar across all wealth quintiles. 'High fees at facility' was the most common complaint, followed by 'Facility too far' and 'Drugs/supplies unavailable.' For the poorest respondents, distance to the nearest facility was a more pressing concern. 'No one to look after household activities' was cited by the poorest at a rate nearly ten times that of the wealthiest.

The proportion of women who received health care in the previous six months was highest (90 per cent) among the wealthiest quintile (RTI 2010), while the greatest proportion of women who had not received health care services was among the poorest quintile. The incidence of complaints was highest among the poorest women and lowest among the wealthiest. Among the poorest women, getting enough money, the distance to the nearest facility and transportation affected at least half the respondents.

---

4 Skilled providers include doctors, nurses and midwives.

g. Quality of services

Persistent lack and ineffective deployment and management of human resources continue to plague health service delivery and the sector at large. Due to poor retention of human resources in rural and remote parts of the country, logistics systems are adversely affected. Weak supervision, monitoring and reporting practices also further complicate the situation. All these factors result in a poor quality of health service delivery in remote and rural parts of the country.

There is a shortage of adequately trained staff to handle the logistics functions. Frequent transfer of trained personnel - often outside of the health sector - makes developing and retaining capacity a daunting task.

h. Shortage of critical human resources for health

There is also a chronic shortage of obstetricians, gynaecologists, paediatricians, general practitioners, medical officers and nurses in the district and zonal hospitals. To reduce the shortage of these care providers, the Government made an effort to purchase these categories of services by contracting with the private sector; however, the attempt did not succeed because long-term contracts could not be made.

Nepal also faces serious challenges providing safe-delivery services nationwide. Only 36 per cent of deliveries took place in health facilities in 2006-2010 (against a target 60 per cent by 2015) (MoHP 2010b). The managers of the Aama programme (a recent version of safer motherhood) recognise that the current government health workforce is inadequate to achieve desired levels of utilisation. The root cause of safe-delivery staffing shortages in the government facilities was not a lack of trained staff but the inability of the Government to attract and retain them in the remote areas where they are most needed. About 75 per cent of medical doctors reside in the capital city, where only 20 per cent of the population lives (ibid).

6.6.2 Health governance: Decentralisation, transparency and accountability

Nepal's health sector still carries a tradition of a top-down approach to resource allocation, planning and implementation. Almost all health programmes are vertically controlled; planning and resource allocation and major decisions are taken at the central level, underestimating local capacity and multi-sectoral perspectives. As a result, there is currently a very limited scope to be responsive to local health needs. Current planning and implementation practices do not encourage local innovation or local ownership, which threatens sustainability.

In Nepal, communities are willing to participate in the development process and they are proactive in local development activities. In this positive setting, trusting the community is vital and should be the foundation of any model of participatory development (Adhikari 2010). As evident in the health sector, the role of Mother's Groups and Female Community Health Volunteers (FCHVs) in reducing child and maternal mortality is vital. However, transparency and accountability mechanisms in other vertical programmes are not very effective in the health sector.

Recently, the MoHP with the support of External Development Partners (EDPs) designed a local health governance strengthening programme, which is being implemented in four districts of the country. Exciting and potentially far-reaching progress is evident with improving local governance of health services, but future progress will depend to some extent on decisions made by the central government regarding decentralisation and federal forms of governance.

6.6.3 Policy and institutional issues

a. Lack of comprehensive health service act

Nepal has a series of policies, strategies and disease specific legal frameworks (a total of 19 acts and 13 Regulations) (MoHP 2011). The Health Service Act of 1996 created separate health services and different groups and sub-groups of services outside of the Civil Service Act. It includes major but complicated provisions to manage human resources in the health sector of Nepal. Unfortunately, Nepal does not yet have a comprehensive Health Service Act that provisions and ensures that quality health services be provided from different levels of health facilities. Therefore, there is a policy and institutional gap between constitutional provisions and health service provisions. To ensure health security such legal frameworks are vital.

b. Health financing and human security issues

The Government has been continuously increasing finance to health services, but sustaining and building on these achievements still require sustainable health financing strategies and dependable support from the External Development Partners (EDPs) under the Sector-Wide Approach (SWAp). However, the increased level of expenditure is not effective enough to reduce the out-of-pocket expenditure in health, which is still among the highest in the region in Nepal (56% in 2006) (MoHP 2009a). Evidence shows that increasing the ratio of the health budget by 10 per cent with the assurance of good governance, the Child Mortality Rate (CMR) may decrease by 4.5 per cent and life expectancy rate may increase by 0.6 per cent (MoHP and RTI 2010). Increasing the real per capita income by 10 per cent will cause the Infant Mortality Rate (IMR) to fall by 7 per cent, child mortality by 11 per cent and increase life expectancy rate by almost 2 per cent (ibid). There is a direct correlation between health financing (with good governance) and human security.

Total Health Expenditure is funded from several sources. The largest single source of health care financing is the private sector, which accounts for 56 per cent of the total health expenditure in 2005-06. General government financing is the second largest source of funds, contributing 23.7 per cent, while External Development Partners (EDPs) contributed 20.8 per cent of the total in 2005-06 (MoHP 2009b). These statistics show that there is a significant potential human security threat in Nepal compared to the other countries in the region such as Sri Lanka, the Maldives and Bhutan (ibid).

c. Absorbing capacity and irregularities

The MoHP has been receiving increased budget support from both government and External Development Partners (EDPs) every year. However, its absorbing capacity has not been improved as expected. In terms of irregularity clearance, it has improved quite significantly in last three years (Table 6.14).

Table 6.14 Budget vs expenses status-DOHS and irregularities clearance status

FY	Expenditure (%)	Irregularity Clearance (%)
2010/11	79.70	45.90
2009/10	80.65	33.00
2008/09	81.60	28.00
2007/07	80.6	n/a
2003/04	69.7	n/a

Source: DoHS (2012b) n/a: Not available

Natural disasters, pandemics, new and re-emerging diseases

Due to unregulated urban expansion, population increase, climate change and other challenges, every year natural disasters have been damaging Nepal's human, financial and physical capital. In recent years, disease patterns have been rapidly changing which means that communicable disease surveillance is facing new challenges such as drug-resistant strains and the potential deliberate release of infectious agents. The centrality of health issues to the realisation of human security is illustrated by the tremendous human costs of new diseases such as HIV/AIDS, re- emerging old diseases such as tuberculosis, widespread environmental degradation, gender-based and other forms of violence, famine, all forms of discrimination and recurrent social strife and territorial occupations (Gutlove 2002).

Two serious pandemics [Severe Acute Respiratory Syndrome (SARS)] and virulent swine flu, H1N1 have raised public health security alarms around the world in the last 10 years. Nepal is prone to the avian flu virus, which has emerged quite frequently in the country. Awareness of this potential human security threat is very low and epidemic alert and rapid response systems are not effective enough. Improved preparedness is critical to respond to future unexpected risks and enhance the human security.

The Nepali health sector is not well prepared to respond to epidemic challenges and health hazards resulting from natural disasters. There is an urgent need to envision such challenges and prepare coping strategies to face potentially adverse situations before they occur. Unfortunately, there are no preparedness plans or effective institutional mechanisms in place for this purpose. There is also the increased possibility of new and re-emerging diseases in recent years, which need to be addressed by the health system well in advance.

6.6.5 The threat of biological and chemical weapons

Communicable disease surveillance and the threat of biological and chemical weapons are areas in which national security overlaps directly with the public health system. The threat of biological or chemical weapons is a growing human security concern globally. While biological and chemical weaponry is a low probability risk, it may carry important consequences, leading to security concerns both in developed and developing countries. Nepal, however, does not have surveillance and preventive systems in place.

States that have not joined the relevant international conventions and non-state actors, pose a threat. International public health policy provides a framework within which to build a global health partnership. The WHO and other international agencies are working on a response to these threats that aims to improve technical support to member states. The challenge is to increase public health infrastructure to enhance the potential for greater global cooperation (Gutlove 2002).

6.7 Ensuring health security in Nepal: Some recommendations

The analysis presented above shows that there is a high level of human insecurity in Nepal that is related to health. Most of the issues are systemic in nature rather than programmatic. Therefore, a systemic approach is needed to sustain health outcomes and address these issues. This section provides perspectives to strengthen the existing initiatives and suggests some initiatives needed to ensure the health security of all Nepal's citizens.

6.7.1 Adopting a human security approach in health sector reform

As discussed above, Nepal has achieved significant improvements in terms of health outcome and impacts, particularly in relation to MDGs 4 and 5. There are still wide gaps and significant inequalities in accessing quality health services that need to be improved through systemic approaches. These gaps and inequalities are evident in the health outcome and impact levels once the information is segregated and analysed.

A human security approach is needed to streamline the inequality in the health sector. Promoting this human security approach requires a policy framework of protection, empowerment and social inclusion which provides an enhanced role for civil society organisations and local communities supported by national institutions.

There are potentially significant levels of trauma and many adverse psychosocial impacts resulting from the decade long-conflict and gender- based and domestic violence. There has been a dramatic increase in suicides among women of reproductive age, such that it is now the leading single cause of death (MoHP 2010a).

The conflict also harmed interpersonal relations and trust and community networks, which are fundamental to social capital. In addition, the broader issues of the breakdown of law and order in the extended transition imposed pressure on the vibrancy of social capital at the local level, which has to be properly addressed as soon as possible (Adhikari 2009). Without solid coping strategies, people who have undergone traumatic experiences can come to feel a profound sense of shame, hopelessness and mistrust, which can often lead to increased criminal activity and domestic and gender-based violence. In addition to psychological care and counselling, family members and communities need to be reunited and the missing identified, located and accounted for.

Human security is about building effective political, economic and social institutions that value human beings as their core element. It is also about promoting local governance by putting the 'human factor' at the centre and improving public policy and budgeting practices for the benefit of all. Adopting a human security approach in the health sector requires constitutional, regulatory and policy provisions, which are discussed in the sections below.

6.7.2 Constitutional, regulatory and policy provisions

For the first time in Nepal, basic health services were included as a people's fundamental rights in the Interim Constitution. These constitutional provisions, however, pose a challenge to the health sector and raise a series of questions in their implementation. Essential Health Care Services (EHCS) have been defined by Nepal Health Sector Programme - 2 (NHSP- 2), but basic health care has not yet been defined in the health sector of Nepal. Furthermore, there is no legal framework that enforces and regulates the constitutional provisions. The constitutional provisions also provide an opportunity for the state to design, plan and implement the basic health care package, which does not yet exist in Nepal. The Government and its partners need to see these provisions as valuable opportunities to strengthen the health system from a human security perspective.

6.7.3 Adapting local governance approach and improving human security

Through tradition and socio-politico structure, the Nepali Health System is largely dominated by a centralised mentality. Health planning, management and service delivery are seen as 'top-down' processes, sometimes led and imposed by outside actors detached from the ground reality, rather than as processes to be owned by national and local institutions and people. Therefore, to date, little attention has been given to building local civil society and communities or to involving and strengthening their capacity at the local level. Such arrangements and traditional practices have raised serious governance and accountability concerns over the years. To address this issue and create local ownership in managing health services, about 40 per cent of local health facilities (a total of 1,433 Sub-Health Posts (SHPs), Health Posts (HPs) and primary health care centres (PHCCs)) have been handed over to local government units to be managed by Health Facility Operation and Management Committee (HFOMC) but without prior consultation, readiness assessment or serious preparation. Therefore, this process has created serious confusion in leading and managing these health facilities. There is as yet no clear policy and programme targeted to address related issues. The Local Self Governance Act of 1999 gives full authority to local government units to establish and manage local health facilities, but related legal provisions have not yet been realised or practiced, largely because of the absence of elected officials in local government units since mid-July 2002 and partly due to the unwillingness of central-level institutions to decentralise resources and authority.

Health outcomes and impacts are largely determined by multi-sectoral efforts, usually beyond the health sector (for example in water and sanitation, education and infrastructure), but health institutions are not effective enough to adopt a multi-sectoral approach from the centre to the local levels. Sometimes coordination with other sectors is emphasised, but not integrated well at the programme and institutional levels.

Both local level health systems and service delivery therefore have to be reconceptualised as part of the broader democratic local governance, where multiple local level actors act and interact regularly and manage governance activities so that health-related security issues and equality issues are identified and addressed locally. This process is multi-sectoral by nature and the effectiveness of the system and service delivery in particular relies upon this level of interaction between policy makers, service providers and citizens.

Nepal has a vibrant social capital that provides an enabling environment and an effective platform for people to participate, express their views and hold decision-makers accountable (Adhikari 2006). From the demand-side perspective, a key element for effective service delivery is the empowerment of people as citizens, which can improve or limit access to and quality of services. These can include a variety of forms of citizen participation in public service delivery and policy making through a set of instruments like:

- Public Expenditure Tracking Surveys (PETS) y Citizen monitoring of public service delivery y Citizen advisory boards
- Citizens charters
- Social/public auditing and public hearings
- Integrity pacts, citizen score cards, etc.

6.7.4 Social security schemes, insurance and human security

There is no comprehensive social security system in Nepal. A few partial and targeted social security schemes have been implemented through the Ministry of Local Development and other public agencies, but these do not necessarily address critical contemporary health issues. These schemes are not well coordinated, are mostly fragmented and not focused on long-term vision and policies. Some schemes are introduced on an *ad hoc* manner and sometimes discontinued without achieving any significant impact.

Global experience shows that human security is easier to ensure through early prevention than later intervention. It is also less costly to meet these threats upstream than downstream. For instance, the direct and indirect cost of HIV/AIDS was roughly $240 billion during the 1980s (UNDP 1994). Even a few billion dollars invested in primary health care and family planning education could have helped contain the spread of this deadly disease. Social security and protection mechanisms are vital to ensure human security. The timely design and implementation of preventive approaches is critical for developing countries like Nepal.

The root causes of Non-Communicable Diseases (NCDs) in Nepal are mostly related to life-style and behaviour, which require consistent efforts through information communication and behaviour change. At the same time, public health systems also need to be strengthened and scaled up to improve health care to detect, treat or refer hypertensive, diabetics and overweight individuals (WHO 2008a).

The prevention and control of NCDs is multifaceted and complex, but a critically important task for Nepal to ensure human security. The treatment, care and support for NCDs patients is very expensive, which makes them not easily accessible or affordable to most people. Therefore, an alternative approach (such as early detection and lifestyle adjustment) and support systems like insurance and catastrophic protection systems are required. To address the issue, the MoHP designed and implemented community health insurance schemes in a few VDCs in the past; however, these schemes needs to be reviewed and adjusted based on experiences and learning. A few public hospitals [e.g. B.P. Koirala Institute of Health Sciences (BPKIHS)] also introduced hospital-based insurance schemes, but these are not effective enough in practice.

Broad-based health insurance can be an alternative to improve access to quality health care services, but government subsidies will be needed for those who cannot afford regular premium payments. There is a need to carry out research to introduce health insurance schemes in Nepal as an initial step in moving towards fully effective health insurance services.

6.7.5 Addressing disparities to achieve human security

There are striking health gaps in Nepal: between urban and rural areas, between different ecological zones, between men and women, between more and less educated sections of the population. Generally, different types of disparities overlap and interact with each other. For example, poorer and less educated families are also likely to be those without adequate access to water and sanitation and their children are at greater risk of malnutrition. As a result, improvements in just one aspect of their lives might not make much difference to their health.

Breaking this vicious cycle requires robust strategies and targeted programmes, such as:

- Social protection and health insurance policies and programmes.
- Effective implementation of Gender and Social Inclusion Strategy.
- Pro-poor focused health financing and targeted programmes for poor and marginalised groups of people.
- Effective implementation of behaviour change and communication (BCC) campaigns.
- Collaboration with multiple sectors at different levels.
- Addressing social determinants of health like gender, class, ethnicity, caste, language and religion, stigma and discrimination (in the case of HIV/AIDS, leprosy, etc.).
- Promotion of good governance in general and particularly in the health sector, including participatory planning and management, transparency and strengthened accountability.

Social issues of inclusion are critical to ensure health security in Nepal. For example the Dalit population (the most disadvantaged group) account for about 13 per cent of the country's population, yet their participation in the health care workforce is negligible. Therefore, the process of including Dalits in the health care workforce remains a challenge to the health system. They have not been able to compete with advantaged groups in the selection process due to several social and economic barriers. Learning from the education sector, Nepal Health Sector Programme- 2 (NHSP-2) can create temporary positions (Rahat) reserved for Dalit auxiliary nurse-midwives (ANMs) in underserved communities. This will increase the availability of care providers in underserved areas as well as promoting the participation of Dalits in the health care workforce and improving their access to primary health care services.

6.8 Conclusion

Health security is a fundamental component of human security and therefore, health related policies, regulations, programmes and implementation practices should be guided by human security frameworks. The data presented and analysed in this article clearly shows that there are significant levels of health insecurity in the health sector of Nepal. These issues are associated with child and maternal health, HIV/ AIDS, communicable and non-communicable diseases, poverty, potential disaster-led health crises and inequality. The state's role in ensuring health security is fundamental, so that it is necessary for the state to provide appropriate enabling policies and institutional frameworks, service delivery, regulations and social protection provisions. In the context of changed morbidity and mortality patterns, the participation of local government, civil society, development partners and individual is vital. The state's role is particularly vital in developing countries like Nepal, where health systems have not been developed to provide minimum protection to its citizens, particularly in saving the lives of women, children and the poor and marginalised.

There is no question that the state should provide minimum protection from disease, but unhealthy behaviour and lifestyle are going to be growing health security concerns in the coming years. Therefore, an individual's roles and responsibilities are important in the context of unhealthy behaviour and lifestyle-related health security threats.

References

Adhikari D. 2006. *Towards Local Democracy in Nepal, Power and Participation in District Development Planning*. Dortmund: Faculty of Spatial Planning, University of Dortmund.

Adhikari D. 2009. Restructuring of Local Democracy in Nepal under a Federal System. *In:* Hill A, Weiss K, editors. *Spatial Planning with Obstacles - 40 Years of Spatial Planning in Crisis Regions and Developing Countries*. Dortmund: Institute for Spatial Planning (IRPUD), Technical University of Dortmund, pp 203-227.

Adhikari D. 2010. *A Study on the Service Delivery of the Local Bodies* (Draft). Economic Policy Network II. Kathmandu: Ministry of Finance, Government of Nepal and Asian Development Bank.

Adhikari RK. 2010. *Food Utilization Practices, Beliefs and Taboos in Nepal: An Overview*. Kathmandu: USAID. Also available at: www. ghtechproject. com/resources; accessed 30 June 2012.

Appleton S, Teal F. 1999. *Human capital and economic development*. Background paper prepared for the African Development Report 1998. Oxford: Oxford University Press.

Bovet P, Paccaud F. 2012. Cardiovascular disease and the changing face of global public health: A focus on low and middle income countries. *Public Health Reviews* 33(2):1-19. Also available at: http://www. publi- chealthreviews.eu; accessed on 30 June 2012.

CHS [Commission on Human Security]. 2003. *Human Security Now*. New York: Commission on Human Security (CHS).

DoHS [Department of Health Services]. 2012a. *Report to the Joint Annual Review (JAR)*. Kathmandu: Department of Health Services (DoHS), Ministry of Health and Population (MoHP).

DoHS [Department of Health Services]. 2012b. *Annual Report 2067-68*. Kathmandu: Department of Health Services (DoHS), Ministry of Health and Population (MoHP).

Engelhard C, Garson A. 1992. *The Right to Health Care and The Role of Govern- ment in Health Policy*. Washington, DC: Miller Center of Public Affairs, University of Virginia. Also available at: www. medicine.virginia.edu; accessed on 1 July 2012.

Gutlove P. 2002. *Cairo Consultation on Health and Human Security* Massachusetts: Institute for Resource and Security Studies. Also available at: www.irss-usa.org; accessed on 8 December 2011.

MoH [Ministry of Health], New ERA and Macro International Inc. 1997. *Nepal Demographic and Health Survey 1996*. Kathmandu: Ministry of Health, New ERA and Macro Internationl Inc.

MoH [Ministry of Health]. 1986. *Nepal Fertility and Family Planning Survey Report*. Kathmandu: Nepal Family Planning and MCH Project.

MoH [Ministry of Health]. 1993. *Nepal Fertility and Family Planning Survey Report. 1991*. Kathmandu: Family Planning and Maternal and Child Health Division, Ministry of Health.

MoHP [Ministry of Health and Population] and NCASC [National Center for AIDS and STD control]. 2010. *Let's Know Our Epidemic, Fact Sheet No.1 and No. 4*, Kathmandu: Ministry of Health and Population, National Center for AIDS and STD control..

MoHP [Ministry of Health and Population] and RTI [Research Triangle Institute]. 2010. *Assessment of Health System Performance in Nepal*. Kathmandu/Triangle Park, N.C.: National Center for AIDS and STD control, Research Triangle Institute..

MoHP [Ministry of Health and Population], New ERA and ICF International Inc. 2012. *Nepal Demographic and Health Survey (NDHS) 2011*. Kathmandu: Ministry of Health and Population, New ERA and ICF International Inc.

MoHP [Ministry of Health and Population], New ERA and Macro International Inc. 2007. *Nepal Demographic and Health Survey (NDHS) 2006*. Kathmandu: Ministry of Health and Population, New ERA and ORC Macro.

MoHP [Ministry of Health and Population], New ERA and ORC Macro. 2002. *Nepal Demographic and Health Survey 2001*. Kathmandu: Ministry of Health and Population, New ERA and ORC Macro.

MoHP [Ministry of Health and Population]. 2009a. *Nepal Nutrition Assessment and Gap Analysis (NAGA)*. Kathmandu: Ministry of Health and Population. Also available at: http://nepal.usaid.gov; accessed 23 November 2011.

MoHP [Ministry of Health and Population]. 2009b. *Nepal National Health Accounts II (2004-2006)*. Kathmandu: Ministry of Health and Population.

MoHP [Ministry of Health and Population]. 2010a. *Nepal Health Sector Pro- gramme - II (2010-2015)*. Kathmandu: Ministry of Health and Popula- tion.

MoHP [Ministry of Health and Population]. 2010b. *Human Resource Strategies: Options for Safe Delivery*. Kathmandu: Ministry of Health and Population.

MoHP [Ministry of Health and Population]. 2011. *Compilation of Health Acts and Regulations*. Kathmandu: Ministry of Health and Population.

MoHP [Ministry of Health and Population]. 2012. *M&E Framework, Nepal Health Sector Programme II (2010-2015)*. Kathmandu: Ministry of Health and Population.

NHRC [Nepal Health Research Council]. 2006. *Assessment of Burden of Disease in Nepal*. Kathmandu: Nepal Health Research Council.

O'Donovan. 2008. The Nexus Between Health and Security: A Case-based Ap- proach to Evaluating Health Conditions and Delivery in Conflict Zones. *In:* Kim G J, Fernandez M D, editors. *The Atlas of Health*. London: Earth- scan, pp 68-69.

OSAA [Office of the Special Adviser on Africa]. 2005. *Human Security in Africa*. New York: Office of the Special Adviser on Africa.

Pokharel RK, Houston R, Harvey P, Bishwakarma R, Adhikari J, Pant KD, Gartoulla R. 2009. *Nepal Nutrition Assessment and Gap Analysis (NAGA). Final report of Nutritional Assessment Team.* Kathmandu: Child Health Division, Ministry of Health and Population (CHD/ MOHP). Also available at: http://nepal.usaid.gov/; accessed on 30 June 2012.

RTI [Research Triangle Institute]. 2008. *Equity Analysis of Health Care Utilization and Outcomes*. Triangle Park, N.C.: Research Triangle Institute.

RTI [Research Triangle Institute]. 2010. *Pro-Poor Health Care Policy Monitoring, Household Survey Report from 13 Districts*. Triangle Park, N.C.: Research Triangle Institute.

UNDP [United Nations Development in Programme]. 1994. *Human Development Report*. New York: Oxford University Press.

UNDP [United Nations Development in Programme]. 2003. *Human Security Now*. New York: Oxford University Press. Also available at: http:// www. policyinnovations.org; accessed on 2 January 2012.

White F, Rafique G. 2002. Diabetes prevalence and projections in South Asia. *The Lancet* 360(9335):804-805. Available at http://www.thelancet. com/ journals/lancet/article.

WHO [World Health Organisation], UNICEF [United Nations International Chil- dren's Emergency Fund], UNFPA [United Nations Fund for Population Activities] , WB [World Bank]. 2012. *Trends in Maternal Mortality: 1990 to 2010*. Geneva: World Health Organisation, United Nations International Children's Emergency Fund, United Nations Fund for Population Activities, World Bank.

WHO [World Health Organisation]. 1946. *Preamble to the Constitution of the World Health Organization as adopted by the International Health Conference.* New York: World Health Organisation.

WHO [World Health Organisation]. 1995. *Fifty Facts: Global Health Situation and Trends 1995-2025*. New York: World Health Organisation. Also available at: http://www.who.int/whr.

WHO [World Health Organisation]. 2008a. *World Malaria Report*. Geneva: World Health Organization. Also available at http://www.searo.who. int; accessed on 30 June 2012.

WHO [World Health Organisation]. 2008b. Communicable Disease Research. *WHO*. www.nep.searo.who.int; accessed on 1 July 2012.

WHO [World Health Organisation]. 2008c. *STEPS Surveillance: Non Communicable Disease Risk Factors Survey*. Kathmandu: World Health Organisation.

****

Chapter 7

Changing migration patterns and their impacts on human security in Nepal

Anita Ghimire, PhD

7.1 Introduction

The diversification of migration in magnitude, geography and the consequent changes in meaning and outcomes of migration, has shifted the focus back to migration-security relations (Truong and Gasper 2011). In the twenty-first century, the trend of migration has diversified in every imaginable dimension. It has increased exponentially in numbers, in geography (origin, destination and transit), in patterns (such as temporary, circular) and in the numbers of institutions that shape this movement of people (see for example, IOM 2010). Virtually every nation of the world has been involved in this migration cycle, either as a host country, a place of origin or a transit country, or in more than one position (see for example, IOM 2011). This exponential increase in different dimensions of migration and its outcomes has in recent years framed migration from security perspectives. In the wider discourse this has led to the scrutiny of migration from a security perspective and this has brought migration into the security agendas of different states (Poku and Graham 2010).

Nepal also is caught in this migration cycle. It has been a country of origin for different types of migrants, a host for refugees from Bhutan and Tibet for many decades, a host for Indian flood-induced refugees and seasonal and permanent migrants and most recently to Somali refugees. Because of these movements, it is important to critically examine the nexus of migration and security in Nepal. The objective of this chapter is to analyse how these different forms of international migration pose threats to the security environment in Nepal from a human security perspective. It does so by problematising the present tendency to overtly link migration and security and instead critically examining the various kinds of security concerns for the people. Though individual human security and state security are intricately linked, this paper delves into the former only. The aim is to move beyond the frontiers of foreign employment and the labour-centric understanding of international migration and call for fresher debate around issues of international migration-related human security.

7.2 Background

Industrialisation and urbanisation had a great influence on the movement of people after the nineteenth century, accelerating the pace of migration (Martin and Widegreen 1996). With the growth of cities and the corresponding decline in village labour markets, more people from villages started coming into cities to look for jobs or establish factories (Hall 1998). The development of road networks, along with means of transportation such as bicycles, steamships and trains at first and motor cars later on, further accelerated the process and led to massive international migration (see for example, Foner 2000). Cities across the world became centres of growing cultural, economic, political activity and ever more people started to migrate (Hall 1998).

Migration today has become a global phenomenon. With more and more people on the move, migration has become multidirectional. The number of migrants today has reached 215.8 million, 3.2 per cent of the world's total population (IOM 2011). While this number considers only international migrants for labour purposes, if we take into account people migrating for other reasons the number becomes much higher. At the same time, different wars around the world have increasingly led to forced migration. The collapse and partition of large empires and conflicts have forced people to leave their place of habitual residence (Korn 1999). These movements have important connections with the human security of the migrants and non-migrants of the states involved.

In Asia, there will be interesting changes in demography that will make the issue of migration and human security more relevant in the coming years. Data reveals that India will overtake China as the world's most populous state and Pakistan's population will triple that of Russia by 2030 (NTS Asia 2007). Additionally, to face challenges like climate change, armed violence and mass unemployment, people from Asia will continue to seek opportunities abroad (ibid). In contrast, demography in Europe will be an outlet to the population boom in Asia. Due to low fertility rates, there will be a rise in the ageing population. It is predicted that the working age population in the European Union (EU) will decrease by 52 million by 2050 (ibid). The percentage of the population aged between 0 and 14 will also be reduced, from 16.4 per cent in 2004 to 13.4 per cent by 2050, while the proportion of elderly people (aged 65 and more) is expected to almost double over this period, from 16.4 per cent in 2004 to 29.9 per cent in 2050 (ibid). The proportion of very old people (aged 80 and more) is expected to almost triple in the EU, from four per cent in 2004 to 11.4 per cent in 2050 (Islam 2007). The growing demand for both skilled and unskilled services in Europe versus a pool of young population in Asia will make the migration of foreign youths to European countries inevitable. This will have several implications on the migration-human security nexus of Europe and Asia.

Furthermore, Islam (2007) is of the opinion that immigrants' income and tax revenues are needed to cushion Europe's dwindling pension funds and health care system. On one hand, there is an increase in migration of people into Europe to fulfil its need for young and working population and bolster its economy to sustain older people; on the other hand, due to increasingly visible migrants, hostility towards migrants demonstrated by political parties and the general public is on the rise. Though these hostilities may have arisen for strategic causes like election campaigns, they will have manifold impacts on the human security of both the migrants and the native population. The following observation by Islam (2007, p 4) best describes the situation of migration and human security conditions in Europe:

> "French politicians used strong words to condemn renewed violence in France's largely immigrant suburbs in October last year, twelve months after riots in poor neighbourhoods spread across the country. French conservative Presidential frontrunner Nicolas Sarkozy calledthe disaffected youth 'scum' in autumn 2005 and the Socialist politician Laurent Fabius has described violent young men as 'bastards.' Immigrants, meanwhile, complain of discrimination by public authorities in employment, housing and education, while Europe's minorities increasingly complain of racism and discrimination generally. With far-right and xenophobic political parties attracting more and more support, Muslims in Europe warn of a rise in Islamophobia across the continent".

Similarly, due to the expansion of EU member states and provisions to allow Eastern European population to obtain jobs in Western European countries, there is a growing sentiment against immigration (Horowitz 2010). A report by Horowitz (2010) says that more than nine in ten Italians (94%) considered immigration to be a big problem, including 64 per cent who said it was a very big problem in Italy. The report says that due a sharp rise in immigrants, outbreaks of hostility has been seen towards foreigners, mostly from the Muslim and non-white community, because they are seen as a threat to jobs, livelihoods, culture and identity. The right wings party in Europe have been able to capture this sentiment and have turned opposition to immigrants into a new political agenda. Horowitz (2010) notes that individuals who are unprepared or unable and unwilling to adjust to this novel situation of having significant number of immigrants support right wings agendas as a good alternative. This has helped right wing parties to gain strength and hence put restrictions on migration to western countries. Similarly, growing illegal migration from African and Asian countries is becoming a matter of concern to the governments of the receiving societies which take a liberal view of legal migration. This will have an impact on the framing of migration and security policies in the coming years.

Even within Asia, inter-regional migration and the securitisation of migration will have an impact. For example, NTS Asia (2011) identifies that Pakistani identity and internal security is threatened by the influx of Burmese and Bengali migrants. The rules for immigration of Indian, Pakistani and Sri-Lankan nationals to other South Asian countries shows that the image of migrants from those countries has been what calls "enemy" and "other" (Ghimire and Gurung 2011). However there are important overlaps between state-centred security issues like the activities of transnational armed groups, drug traffickers and fake currency dealers, extremism and terrorism and issues of human security like poverty and unemployment which create a permissive environment for such activities in Asia. For Nepal, too, the issue of migration and human security will have important implications given its location neighbouring the 'Drug Triangle' (Burma, Vietnam, Laos and Thailand) and the 'Golden Crescent' (Afghanistan, Iran and Pakistan).

7.3Conceptual framework: Linking migration and human security

The concept of human security is derived from the concept of 'security' used in the field of international relations and foreign policy (Alkire 2003). It got wide attention after the Human Development Report in 1994 (UNDP 1994) systematically explained the idea. The core concept, however, already existed in the background and was prescribed in many religious norms. For example, the Hindu philosophy 'Loka Samasta Sukhino Bhavantu' in which there is an emphasis of the 'Sukha' (the wellbeing of the 'Loka' - all people or the Buddhist philosophy of freeing oneself from desire and fears), is related to the notion of wishing for the well being of other human beings and the wellbeing of the state. However the term came into practical and widespread use in the humanitarian and development arena after 1994.

Regarding migration and security, the idea of surveillance of human movement is said to have begun in Europe in the sixteenth and seventeenth centuries. Foucault (1975) traces the history of surveillance of human movement to government efforts to check mobility of people to control plague at this time. People who were mobile needed to be registered in a given territory and documentation was later extended to the mobile population. Thus the notion was to control movement. Gradually this in/ security related with migration led to the confinement of the mobile populace in places like workhouse, schools and the like.

Though in modern times, human mobility has come to be accepted as a natural human phenomenon, in its earlier history it was strictly regarded as negative, at least from the perspective of state. Thus the issue of security in migration originated. It was the impact of migration on the security of the immobile population that was of concern. This concern led to the origin of different methods of securitising migration.

The history of the migration-security nexus cannot be conceptualised without the notion of state and the citizenship and identity that the state provides. Gradually the notion of security in migration and the state's need for controlling migrant populations led to the emergence of policy agendas, institutions and processes of migration (Torpey 2011). In geography, this security concern reinforced notions of physical borders and boundaries. In social aspects it gave birth to the notion of the 'alien' and the 'native' and the rationale that forms the basis of social interaction between them and the state. On the political front, it reasserted the legitimacy of the state to control 'alien' populations and the state's capacity to provide identity and define who would be 'native' and 'alien'. These interdependent systems then led to the birth of processes of immigration and documents related to identity and movement, such as passports. As Torpey (2011, p 4) notes, "modern states and the international systems of states of which they are a part, have expropriated from individuals and private entities the legitimate means of movement particularly, though by no means exclusively, across international boundaries. The result of this process has been to deprive people of the freedom to move across certain spaces and to render them dependent on the state and the state's authority.

A critical aspect of this process has been that people have also become dependent on the state for possession of an 'identity' from which they can escape only with difficulty and which may significantly shape their access to various spaces. However along with this securitisation of migration through methods like visas and policies, the phenomenon of migration itself has come to be institutionalised.

There are two different views on the nexus of migration and security. According to Huysmans and Squire (2009), the migration-security nexus in recent times has been approached from two perspectives: from a security perspective and from a migration studies perspective. From a security perspective, migration is taken as a central dimension of the security agenda. This perspective highlights the importance of inculcating migration in the natural security strategy and national security in the migration policy. This realm of thought analyses to what extent the movement of people in different forms like refugees, IDPs and labour forces affects issues of national security (eg. Loescher 1992; Rudolph 2003; Heisbourg 1991). In the other realm of thought on the migration- security nexus, scholars analyse how migration policies affect security policies (eg. Rudolph 2006; Weiner 1993). In this perspective, security is taken as a condition and its link to migration consists of questioning how the movement of people would affect that condition. While all the above discourses focus on the state as the subject of study, the human security approach in migration takes the individual migrant as a subject of security discourse.

The issue of migration as a human security threat is said to have re- emerged in the present decade primarily due to the overwhelming increase in different forms of migration. Refugees, IDPs induced by conflict, development interventions, climate change, internal and international labour migrants, student and highly skilled migrants and the general increase in mobility of people have made certain issues relevant for the security of the state as well as that of the people.

A survey of literature on the migration-human security nexus finds that the nexus is discussed on two fronts. One realm of discourse (for example, UN 2008; Huda 2006) highlights the human insecurity of the migrant population, mostly from a humanitarian perspective. These studies depict the plight of different forms of migrants like refugees, IDPs and labour migrants from humanitarian concerns. The other realm (for example, Kicinger 2004) is concerned with the possible participation of migrants in illegal and violent activities. It is however important to note that these two issues are not separable as each of these issues can fuel the other.

For example, Islam (2007) highlights that problems over identity and integration which result from the immigration of desperate people of different ethnic, religious and cultural backgrounds is leading to the breakdown of Europe. She is of the opinion that these insecurities perceived at the individual level contribute to violent activities in the form of terror attacks, bomb alerts, race riots and public confrontation between the mainstream population and the minority migrants. She reveals that the participation of 'home grown' Muslim youths in incidences like the riot over caricatures of Prophet Mohammed show that the alienated population can easily be radicalised and become a threat to both human security and the state itself.

Thus migrants affect states and regions in different ways: as countries of origin, as transit countries and as (long/short term) host or destination countries. The home countries may be concerned by the change in social and family relations which affect individual migrants and non-migrants, as well as workforce availability and the macro scale impact on the labour market. Taking examples from Europe, Kicinger (2004, p 2) aptly listed the consequences to the destination country of incoming masses: insecurity in the areas of social stability, demographic security, cultural identity, social security systems and state welfare philosophy, as well as internal security threats due to growing crime rates and other illegal activities like the trade of drugs and arms and human trafficking. For transit countries, as shown by research on drug routes and human trafficking in several countries of South and Central Asia (UN 2008; Huda 2006), internal security dangers emerge when territory is used for illegal activities. The native population may take risks and get involved in such activities, for example acting as mediators for drug trafficking.

For Asia, as shown by NTS Asia (2007), concerns over human security are greater than state-centred security. So there is a need to look closely at human security issues as most individuals, groups and societies in Asia face non-traditional security threats. The clustered nature of distribution of ethnic and religious group across different countries of Asia, as well as porous border systems, could induce cross-border migration and thus affect the population of the whole region, irrespective of national borders. This movement of people could later create tension among host societies and migrants, alienation of the newly urbanised population, economic and social inequality and threats to the wellbeing of individuals who often compromise their physical and psychological safety. So these issues are best considered through the lens of 'security framing'.

This chapter takes the concept of human security (Leaning and Arie 2000) as a conceptual framework for analysing the migration human security nexus. This perspective of human security emphasises the fulfilment of four basic psychosocial needs to foster security in individual or groups: the need for identity[1], recognition[2], participation[3] and autonomy[4]. This approach argues

---

1 Identity at a level of the individual means that a person knows who he is, where he came from socially and geographically, can lay adequate claim to a history and a set of possessions can prove or establish these facts without much fear of challenge from external groups or authorities (Leaning and Arie 2001 p 16).

2 Recognition is the certainty that the above mentioned facts of existence and history are acknowledged and accepted by others within a network of family and social relationships. Recognition confers dignity (Leaning and Arie 2001 p 16).

3 Participation for an individual is the opportunity and capacity to engage with others in economic, political, or social relationships, networks enterprises (Leaning and Arie 2001 p 16).

4 Autonomy is an attribute of being empowered and standing in the world, speaks to a person's ability to determine his own path, independently think about and shape his own future resist confinement in subject, victim, or passive modes (Leaning and Arie 2001 p 16).

that individuals and communities have greater resilience if their core attachment to home and community remains intact and the future holds promise. These links underpin a sense of identity and facilitate participation in the constructive collective project. When these attachments are undone, as they are when populations are uprooted and dislocated, when families and communities are broken up and when arbitrary violence and discrimination render the future distant and unpredictable, individuals turn to other sources for participation, recognition and empowerment. These sources take the shape of identity groups formed around race, religion, geography or age, and are characterised by an aggressive stance towards established institutional processes. This approach has used the economic term "discount rate" (ibid, p 33) to analyse human behaviour and perceive an individual's or group's sense of future. Within the concept of human security, the discount rate is the rate at which the people trade off their future priorities (continuing education, investing in their future, preserving natural resources, etc.) against more current urgent needs and perceived and real threats. People with short planning horizons and high discount rates will be more likely to consume resources than to invest in them for the future.

7.4 Migration and human security in Nepal

For Nepal, the issue of migration and human security will become important as the country is recovering from the decade-long conflict. People have been caught between a decade of conflict and a very rapid incidence of globalisation and booming technology. So the changes currently taking place in Nepal are due on the one hand to the experience of conflict; and on the other, the phenomenon of globalisation and technological outreach has induced significant changes in the physical day-to-day activity as well as the psyche of the people of Nepal. As Giddens (1984) says in his structuration theory about the impact of structure on agency, these changes in the macrostructure and institutions have affected people's daily livelihoods and led to change in people's agency which is in a dialectical relationship with the structure. It has influenced the range of decisions that people tend to take to make in their daily lives. The experience of different phases of conflict guides people's vision towards future livelihoods, their perception of threats and security and their ways to deal with these issues. Their ways of coping with daily livelihood dilemmas has changed with this experience. The rise in different forms of migration is one of the visible outcomes of this interplay of experience, perception and decision-making of structure and agency, or of changes in the 'social fields' and its affect on the 'habitus' of people (Bordieu 1977).

As elsewhere around the world, the phenomenon of migration has increased in volume and diversified geographically (NIDS and NCCR North-South 2011). On the one hand, conflict induced a new form of forced displacement with the majority of Internally Displaced Persons moving from rural to urban areas. On the other hand, conflict increased international migration of various forms like labour migration and migration for education. Similarly, the gender dimension to migration has changed. There is an increasing feminisation of migration, with women now estimated to make up around 10 per cent of the total Nepali migrant population (ibid).

The trend in migration has seen a steep rise. Analysing the available data from the Ministry of Labour and Transportation (MoLT), it can be seen that migration for foreign employment has increased dramatically, from 3,259 people in 1996/97 (the start of conflict) to 27,796 in 1998/99 when the conflict escalated. In terms of spatial dimensions, the choice of destination has increased to 109 countries for foreign employment and to 70 countries for educational migration (NIDS and NCCR North-South 2011).

Besides these forms of internal and international migration, Nepal has also become a hub for migrants from various countries in its position as a country of asylum, a transit country or a country for touristic activities and holidays and business of all kinds (see for example, Mikilan 2009).

Its location neighbouring the 'Drug Triangle' (Burma, Vietnam, Laos and Thailand) and the 'Golden Crescent' (Afghanistan, Iran and Pakistan), combined with the relative ease of entry in comparison to other regional countries (Ghimire and Gurung 2011), could make it a transit point for people involved in illegal activities. Though less studied (notable exceptions includes for example, Mikilan 2009), we can assume that this location easily affects the social aspect of the daily lives and human security of people in Nepal.

It is worthwhile to note that while literature discusses the human security concerns posed by migration, the two phenomena may be self- perpetuating. For example the sense of economic insecurity has driven a large number of people to seek foreign employment or to conduct illegal business, taking high risks in doing so. As long as the poor environment for economic security, livelihood participation in collective and constructive projects and identity and recognition persists, Nepali people will have a high incidence of human insecurity. This fact has promoted migration as one of the coping strategies. However due to the above-mentioned circumstances in Nepal, people have high "discount rates" (Leaning and Arie 2001) and continue to oversee long-term future implications and migrate under risky conditions. Before going into the analysis, I present here the conceptual part of the chapter: the discourse regarding the nexus between human security and migration.

7.5 Nepal as a host, destination and transit and its impact on the people living in Nepal

The following section is the main argument of the article and it analyses the different positions which Nepal occupies in the migration trajectory. It also considers the insecurities which these positions pose to migrants, as well as to the wider society, from a human security perspective.

7.5.1 Nepal as country of origin

Nepal is a country of origin for two types of migrants: labour migrants going overseas for foreign employment and student migrants leaving the country to pursue higher education.

a. Migration for foreign employment and human security

Given the existing conditions of the working age population and the lack of employment opportunity in Nepal, it is no surprise that the number of migrants going abroad for foreign employment has increased dramatically. It is estimated that the number of working age Nepalis currently unemployed is 2.5 million.[5] The labour participation rate stands at 83.4 per cent of Nepal's total population, with at least 30 per cent either unemployed or underemployed and with 400,000 people entering the labour market every year (NIDS and NCCR North-South 2011). So it is inevitable that young Nepalis are looking for income and job opportunities outside Nepal. According to the Department of Foreign Employment, 240,269 Nepalis left for overseas employment in the first nine months of the fiscal year 2010-11. On average, 1,099 Nepali migrant workers fly out of the country every day. Though there is evidence that migrants mostly re-migrate after their first migration, it is not recorded if all the above migrants are first-time migrants. The statistic does not, however, include migration to India and undocumented migration, which are at large. Migration to India remains unaccounted for due to the open border and the lack of systems in both countries to keep track of population movement. Undocumented migration occurs largely when people migrate illegally with fake documents and travel through India. In terms of destination, the Government of Nepal permits migration for employment in 109 countries, though Nepalis are found to have migrated mainly to 24 countries (ibid). However, there is evidence that despite the government banning migration to certain countries like Iraq for security reasons, Nepalis continue to take the risk and travel there for work. The killing of 12 Nepali youths in Iraq in 2004, at a time when the government had banned migration to Iraq, is a concrete example of this.

b. Human insecurity of labour migrants

The primary human insecurity concern of these labour migrants is their labour employment prospects. Most labour migration

---

5 This estimate of unemployment is disputed by a number of economists as a gross understatement. Deependra Bahadur Chettri, former governor of Nepal Rastra Bank, also disputes this figure, saying the ostrich-like attitude that ignores ground realities is unlikely to solve the problem of unemployment.

from Nepal depends on the demand from Gulf countries, so when there is a financial crisis in those countries, Nepalis have to bear the brunt in two ways. Prospective migrants will find it harder to migrate and those migrants already there will face uncertainties and may have to take greater risks to get jobs, thus compromising their human security. For the families left behind, it may result in less remittance, which would affect their life here. The financial meltdown of 2008-9, when there was a great decline in job demand, has indicated this fact. In addition, growing technology capabilities means that manual labour is in less demand. As a large proportion of Nepali labour migrants are unskilled or semi-skilled, they will fare very poorly in comparison to migrants from other regions like Sri Lanka and the Philippines where governments have taken great initiatives to send highly skilled labour migrants.

The second concern lies in the cost of migration and the risks which migrants take in order to pay these costs. It is estimated that a migrant pays around NPR 200,000 (USD 2,255) to manpower agencies to cover different kinds of formal fees (NIDS and NCCR North-South 2011). Additionally, they pay a large sum of extra money to the agents to get the work done, as well as additional charges for passports and other needs. Several reports[6] emphasise that migrants have paid large sums of money in the hope of getting a job overseas and have been duped. For labour migrants, much of this money comes from the sale of land or other assets, or from taking loans at high interest rates. Labour migrants often have family members in Nepal who are dependent on them which results in psychological and economic pressure to take on risky jobs or to accept abuse faced in the workplace. Also, once they return, the lack of environment for secure livelihoods makes them rethink their decision.

Another cause of insecurity is the migration process. Though there are no quantitative data, a large number of migrants take illegal migration routes and travel there undocumented. This later undermines their security; for example, they cannot charge the

---

6 See for example UNIFEM and People's Forum (2006) and NIDS and NCCR North-South (2011) for documentation of such cases.

agents for any problems as their status is undocumented. They have to stay as illegal migrants and thus are denied protection and services. Ghimire and Gurung (2011) found that there is a high prevalence of this process among female migrants. Most female migrants are lured into going overseas by local agents who work in villages. These agents are reluctant to take legal procedures. If the women later have complaints, the agents cannot be charged. A report by UNIFEM[7] and People's Forum (2009) shows that 96 per cent of fraudulent cases are carried out by individual agents rather than by registered employment agencies.

Insecurity of Nepali migrants in Malaysia

According to a newspaper report, Malaysia is the preferred destination for Nepali migrant workers, but the country is turning out to be a graveyard for many of them. It is reported that 81 Nepali migrant workers have died between January and June 2010. Some 113,982 migrant workers from Nepal left for Malaysia in the 2009-10 fiscal year and the total number of Nepali migrant workers in Malaysia is over 400,000. The newspaper, quoting an official at the Nepali embassy in Kuala Lumpur, said the cause of death of 45 Nepalis was "not known" but five died in the workplace, nine in road accidents, one from chronic disease and seven committed suicide. It is reported that the number of suicide cases has gone up among Nepali migrant workers while road accident deaths have gone down. At least five to six Nepalis commit suicide every month.

Source: The Himalayan Times, 8 September 2010.

Besides the risks migrants take to travel illegally, there are cases of suicides, abduction, murder and physical and psychological exploitation and abuse of migrant workers in the destination country, causing grave insecurity for the migrants. When the host country is unwilling or unable to share the problems related to migration, it becomes a grievance to the home country because according to the notion of sovereignty, these migrants become the liability of the place of origin. For example, in 2009 Israel banned incoming Nepali migrant workers, citing that there were many illegal Nepali migrants in Israel. For Israel, there are growing concerns over the children of migrants of Nepali origin whose father or mother is unknown. In Israel alone there are

[7] It is changed to UN Women in 2010.

around 800-1200 such children whom Israel is going to deport back to Nepal (NIDS and NCCR North-South 2011).

Such incidences have important implications for the human security of these migrants. The reaction of the Israeli government to the case of illegal children from people of Nepali origin is telling: The children of migrant workers "are liable to damage the state's Jewish identity, constitute a demographic threat and increase the danger of assimilation," Israeli Interior Minister Eli Yishai was quoted as saying (NIDS and NCCR North-South 2011, p 16). Migrants are stereotyped as unwanted and as people whose assimilation into Jewish society should be restricted, as they constitute a demographic threat and could harm the Jewish identity. This mentality already highlights a great threat to migrants' psychosocial need for wellbeing in the destination country. As they are often in a poor state to negotiate their rights in the face of such assumptions, they are often deprived of their rights as migrants, which increases their insecurity.

There have already been severe concerns about returned Nepali female migrant workers not being accepted back to the society due to the stigma attached to the migration of women to certain countries. There is increasing pressure to build shelter homes in Nepal and in destination countries for women who are ostracised by society. Due to this lack of acceptance by their home and society, they have lost both their physical security as well as fulfilment of need for identity, participation and recognition which gives them psychosocial security. In this condition, it is hard to imagine that children who are deported will easily integrate into society and that their human security concerns will be met.

c. Migration for education

The technological advancement in communication and modes of knowledge and information exchange, as well as the expansion of "social imaginaries" and "consumer desire" fuelled by this advancement, have become intertwined and reinforce each other to form complex pull factors to entice students to study abroad. As Brooks and Waters (2011, p 28) put it, the "full submission of education to pursuits of global economy" has led to the commoditisation and marketing of education.

On the macro global level, there has been a huge change in the education policies of receiving countries. Until recently, many countries were geared towards attracting foreign students. There are two important factors for this: firstly, the interests of organisations like the World Bank and UNESCO; and secondly, the interests of the nation states and the educational institutions themselves. There was a significant reduction in state funding to education in many developed countries in the last two decades of the twentieth century. In this situation, the individual institutions turned to student migrants to fill the gap. As such, international students provided significant income to these institutions. For example in Australia, which is one main education destination for Nepali students, when state funding decreased by 30 per cent between 1995 and 2003, revenue from international students helped recover 14 per cent of the loss. Today Australia reaps USD 12 billion a year from foreign students. Similarly, the UK gets economic benefits of USD 3.48 billion to USD 40 billion annually (NIDS and NCCR North-South 2011).

In the specific case of Nepal, a generalisation can be proposed for the push factor for education. On the macro level, Nepal's economic and political system vis-a-vis the global system is perhaps one of the main factors: students have migrated because of the unstable political situation, weak prospects for quality education in Nepal and the need of a quality education to get better rewards in the competitive labour market. Discourses around the relationship between employability and oversees study show that overseas qualifications are highly valued in the labour market. Employers are of the opinion that overseas qualifications help broaden horizons towards 'otherness' and a broader global outlook (Brooks and Waters 2011), besides the obvious networking opportunities it brings. This outlook, they feel, benefits both the individuals and the organisations that employ them. Thus the emphasis on education in employability is not only academic excellence and formal degrees but also other implicit skills, attributes and abilities which come from exposure and experience. The possibility of gaining all these skills in Nepal is very low. In addition, an overseas degree provides better opportunities for employment overseas.

There are also social factors. The decision to study abroad is a family decision and involves the participation of the family, although it may be initiated by an individual student. Abjuring the previously held belief that student migration is an 'elite migration,' more students now come from middle class families. As Vincent and Ball (2006) observe, in today's parenting style of the middle class, the child is a 'project' and the parents' vision is to provide social and educational resources for the child. Sending a child abroad for study is thus a strategic move towards accumulating what the family sees as the most important capital for rewarding employment and is also increasingly related to accumulating cultural capital and ensuring the social mobility of the whole family. For individual migrants, overseas education is again related to higher and rewarding employment status and a global experience. It is also an opportunity to study subjects of interest not available in Nepal.

According to the data taken from the Ministry of Education (MoE 2011), a total of 62,391 students requested the 'No Objection Letter' to migrate to 70 destination countries as students between December/January 2010 and December/January 2011. However, the number of students is probably much higher as not all universities require those letters and students also go by various scholarship schemes.

Human security issues of Nepali migrant students

The main security concern of the Nepali students is in the changing policies towards semi-skilled and low-skilled migrants which are growing more restrictive in nature. The recent change in policy towards migrants among the top destination countries mostly geared towards curtailing unskilled migration will have an impact on Nepali student migration. The United Kingdom, the most popular destination among Nepali students, has already started initiatives to cut net in-migration. The coalition government has announced plans to reduce the number of student visas to be issued by 70,000-80,000 and its impact is already huge in Nepal.[8] After the introduction of the Point Based System in 2008,

---

[8] See The Kathmandu Post, 4 June 2010.

Nepali student applications increased from 581 in 2008 to 10,104 in 2009. But after the system was closed, the number declined to 2,333 in 2010.[9] Australia is also tightening its immigration policy. The Australian Government aims to reduce net overseas migration by 20 per cent, cutting down 20,000 visa applications.[10] Among South Asian countries, Nepal has the second largest community in Australia after India. The prospects of permanent residency and job placement were the major attractions for Nepali students. However, with the recent tightening of the policy, the 23,000 Nepali students already there and those aspiring to go will be affected. There is a drastic cut from 400 to only 181 categories in the listed occupations in demand by the Australian Government. As per the new change, applications for permanent residency by students who intend to take up occupations not cited on the new list and who do not meet the requirements for skilled migration visas will not be eligible. Due to this, many Nepali students are forced to return home.[11] However, the expansion in the choice of destination countries will provide an alternative to the student flow. Thus the number of student migrants in total is unlikely to decrease significantly while challenges to their human security will prevail.

There are other personal and societal factors which affect the risks that student migrants take. On the one hand, students have invested a huge amount of money to meet different needs associated with their migration process; while on the other hand, some of them have obligations and expectations to help their siblings to enter foreign education or maintain the status quo of their families back in Nepal by regular remittance and/ or retaining their title as 'foreign educated'. Such financial and social obligations force the students to take risks and continue their stay in the host countries under adverse conditions. Firstly they have to lose their legal status and resort to the category of illegal migrants which hampers the kind of services and opportunities they can enjoy in the host country. Secondly, this

---

[9] UNESCO. Global Education Digest 2009. Canada: UNESCO.

[10] See The Kathmandu Post, 4 June 2010.

[11] See The Kathmandu Post, 8 February 2011.

illegal status severely cuts down their legal earnings and they have to compromise on the wages they receive and the kinds of job they do. This hampers other dimensions of their personal wellbeing.

7.5.2 Nepal as a host country

Nepal has been a host country to refugees from three countries: Bhutan, Tibet and Somalia. The following section discusses the status of human security and its relationship with the below mentioned phenomenon in Nepal.

a. Tibetan refugees in Nepal

According to Joshi (2011), following the exile of the His Holiness the Dalai Lama, many Tibetans settled in Nepal, India and Bhutan, most of them migrating without any property. Those who managed to bring animals, gold, coral and other precious metals sold them at throw-away prices to Nepalis to buy food. At present, Tibetan refugees have been settled in the districts of Solukhumbu, Mustang, Lalitpur, Pokhara, Rasuwa, Walung, Manang, Baglung, Tanahun and Kathmandu by the Government of Nepal. Joshi (2011) stated that there are 20,000 Tibetans living in these different settlements.

Nepal is not a signatory to the Refugee Convention and the recognised refugee categories have been based and distinguished on ethnicity and groups (Joshi 2011). The Government of Nepal has provided refugee cards which allow refugees residence permits but does not give them permission to work. Previously, services in the form of food and relief aid were given and handicraft centres were created to make them self-reliant. However, there are no provisions to meet the demands of the growing population who are now more educated. Younger and better educated refugees want to enter new labour markets rather than the handicraft business, but the unavailability of citizenship restricts them. So they resort to working in small offices doing work which does not correlate to their academic qualifications and they remain highly dissatisfied (ibid).

The situation for Tibetans who have refugee cards is very difficult in terms of livelihoods but more so for Tibetan youths born in Nepal after the 1990s. They have neither refugee cards nor citizenship documents from the Government of Nepal. They are listed in the name of their parents. The lack of documents has highly impeded their academic pursuits and mobility; for example, they cannot undertake medical study or careers due to their lack of citizenship. Many Tibetan youth say that, knowing the restrictions, they do not think of studying beyond a Bachelors' degree and applying for jobs in offices or doing business (Joshi 2011). Most aspire to go abroad and many also have relatives outside the country which makes it easier for them to migrate. But the Government of Nepal cannot give them migration-related documents like visas and so they take risks and use illegal means for migration. Some of the Tibetan refugees have dreams and aspirations but hardly any options to fulfill them legally, which means that they either go back to the same livelihood choices that are available and open for them or take risky measures to pursue their dreams.

There are also incidences of confrontation and tension between the refugees and the Government of Nepal. It is widely held that these tensions are due to the refugees' lack of assimilation into the local population in terms of their culture, language and so on. It is also perceived that the aspirations for political participation among the refugees living in the northern part of Nepal remain unfulfilled. This leads to sense of alienation and often creates tension in the host-refugee relationship incurring insecurity among both populations. These difficulties have caused severe frustration among the youth groups, often manifested through protests which can deteriorate into riots. The refugees' lack of hope in the future and their inability to participate in constructive and collective jobs in society constitutes a chief element of psychological insecurity and augments their feelings of exile, retaliation and helplessness, which contributes to human insecurity.

For the Government of Nepal, this psychological insecurity augments several concerns. There is firstly a concern that the land of Nepal is being used to meet the political interests of several groups and countries. Incidences like the Khampa Rebellion (Norbu 1996) and the protest in Nepal in march 2008 before and during the Beijing Olympics have implications for Nepal as a state and for its internal governance. For example, these activities were viewed by China as examples of how Nepal's land can be used for anti-China activities. This recognition hampers the Nepal-China relationship and may lead China to suggest it be allowed to have a say in Nepal's internal decisions regarding Tibetan refugees. It is argued that the then Government of Nepal suppressed the Khampa Rebellion due to strong pressure from the Chinese Government. Since that time, Nepal has been stricter in checking the entry of Tibetan refugees and has taken steps to control the involvement of Tibetan refugees in anti-China protests in Nepal. This decision will also affect the already narrow life space and lead to further alienation of the Tibetan refugees. For example, after the protest the Government of Nepal closed down two refugee-related offices in Kathmandu (Joshi 2011). Besides this, as mentioned above, Nepal is in a weak position to provide resources and spaces to enable the refugees to get a sense of psycho-social and material security for a fulfilled life. If the frequency of refugee-police clashes increases, it creates unrest in the community and may augment negative attitudes between the host population and the refugees.

b. Bhutanese refugees in Nepal

The Bhutanese refugees were displaced by the Kingdom of Bhutan in the early 1990s in a mass exodus of about one-sixth of its population. Over 105,000 Bhutanese refugees have been living in seven different refugee camps in Nepal, with some others living outside the camps. Unlike the other refugees in Nepal, the refugees from Bhutan are very similar to other Nepalis. Almost 97 per cent of the refugees are ethnic Nepali although other non-Nepali ethnic groups like Sharchop, Drukpa, Urow and Khenpga are also present. All the refugees understand Nepali and speak it as their first or second language. A majority are Hindu (60 %), followed by Buddhist (27%), Kirat (10 %) and Christian (CORC 2007).

Their main concern is about their future livelihoods and about the prospectus of return to Bhutan from where they originated. In response to their needs, in March 2008 the UNHCR began a multilayer resettlement to third countries including the United States, Canada, Denmark, New Zealand, Australia, the Netherlands and Norway. Since then, over 75,000 refugees have left the refugee camps (Refugee processing center 2012).

Their chief insecurity in Nepal is related to the resettlement process. This resettlement process created conflict between the people who wanted to go to these third countries and those who wanted to return to Bhutan. According to the UNHCR (2010), more than 80,000 registered refugees have expressed interest in resettlement whereas rest of them demand the right to return to their country of origin. They want to be allowed to cross into India to reach Bhutan from Nepal, but the Indian authorities have objected although they allowed to enter Nepal via India in 1990s. Around 1,500 of the Bhutanese refugees had spouses of Nepali origin and hence had their process for resettlement stalled (CORC 2007). Due to this situation they had to incur family separation and an uncertain future. Their identity as a 'Bhutanese refugee' already alienates them from the larger Nepali society. Formally, the lack of documents hampers their full participation in the community alongside Nepali citizens. Though there is formal and informal recognition of their existence and history a fairly commendable acceptance by Nepali society, their alienation in camps certainly creates some barriers to open acceptance. Similarly, the lack of documents also means that they are less empowered to determine the path and independently shape their future without confinement. This lack of documentation also leads to psychosocial insecurity as it denies a normal identity, as well as full participation in Nepal equal to any citizen of Nepal a stigma-free recognition.

c. Somali refugees in Nepal

At present there are 72 Somali Refugees in Nepal (NIDS and NCCR North- South 2011) who are under the care of the UNHCR as the Government of Nepal does not recognise them as refugees. Unlike other refugees in Nepal they are not settled in camps or provided with food rations and the help only consists of educational and medical assistance and a monthly allowance of USD 67. Under the present conditions, they can neither get jobs nor receive documents to continue their journey and thus they remain virtually entrapped. On top of everything, they have to pay an amount of USD 6 monthly as a fine for overstaying their visa. Though they feel physically safer in Nepal than in Somalia, many refugees perceive that the Nepali community discriminates against them and they have had to bear verbal and physical threats (ibid). Though they have been in Nepal for a significant time, they are unable to participate in a collaborative and constructive way in the community due to the socio- cultural and language-related differences. Only the children can speak Nepali and can thus be important agents for integration. Nepal has to reconsider its position as a host to this population. Supporting the Somali refugees is an additional burden to bear in the absence of a clear policy and adequate funding to provide them with a proper solution. Due to dissatisfaction, these refugee groups are putting forward their frustration in the form of demonstrations against the Government of Nepal. There have as yet been no riots between them and the police of Nepal and no interference by the Government of Somalia. Yet as the numbers and the frustration grow, there could be incidences which would undermine the security of the refugees themselves as well as create disturbances to the host communities. As yet there have been no incidences where the refugees have posed threats to the host community or had any effect on the bilateral relationship between Nepal and Somalia. However, the Government of Nepal has not been able to internalise this role of host and take steps accordingly.

7.5.3 Nepal as a migration transit hub and its growing link with illegal activities

One of the most overlooked positions of Nepal is its position as a transition hub - a situation where it is neither an origin nor a destination country. Due to relatively relaxed migration policy, Nepal offers easy mobility for foreign nationals within its borders. Due to this, Nepal may be used as a safe haven for illegal activities like money laundering, illegal drugs trading and smuggling of counterfeit currencies.

There are several reports that show that Nepal is becoming an important hub for different kinds of illegal activities, though it is neither a country of origin nor a destination country. As shown above, these activities have a large geographical outreach from Nepal to India, Peru, Bangladesh and now Bangkok and the USA. As the visa rules are less strict in Nepal for South Asian nationals than for example in Pakistan, Bangladesh and India, it is likely that more such activities will be carried out in Nepal. As illegal activities increase, there may be a rise in other criminal activities related to the larger crimes in Nepal.

Additionally, Nepal is becoming a new route for the narcotic drugs trade. Its position near countries like Afghanistan and Pakistan, major hubs of drug production and India which is famous for drug dealings, has already made it insecure. New arrests show that Nepal is being used by dealers from countries as far away as Thailand and Peru.

This growing position of Nepal as a meeting hub for illegal activities has still not been internalised in Nepal. The overt focus on labour migration and the failure to see this important position and its link with crime will have dire situations for human security.

Such increasing incidences of illegal activities involving Nepal will have implications for the country's human security. As NTS Asia (2007, p6) notes, "while poverty cannot be identified as a definitive cause for terrorism, it is a significant element in making populations vulnerable to carefully designed campaigns that promote radical views". The same argument may apply to resorting to illegal activities, which may lead to the increasing degradation of the human security of the person involved, as well as the proliferation of crime in the broader society.

Due to the lack of employment opportunities in Nepal, many youths only plan for the short term. The large availability of illegal jobs which bring 'easy money' may lure Nepali youths. This increase has already been observed; for example, the number of Nepali people arrested for drug dealing rose from 706 in 2007-2008 to 1,432 in 2008-2009 (CBS 2010). As Nepal has a high rate of migration, it may be easy for Nepalis to establish international connections and get involved with large criminal networks; thus threatening Nepali society and the wellbeing of the individual themselves. In addition, the flow of money for criminal activities is made easier by the Hawala system and is on rise at the Nepal-India border. As brokers are located primarily in the Middle East, Africa and Asia, it is easy to transfer cash for illegal activities across the globe. Mikilan (2009) notes that once a fully-fledged money market instrument, today the Hawala system is used mostly for migrant worker remittances and is controlled by various mafias. He believes that "the Indo-Nepal border is one of the most illegally trafficked borders in the world due to its openness (Indians and Nepalis are not required to show identification), length (approximately 1800 kilometres), generalised condition of lawlessness and strategic location as an overland trade route crossroads between West Asia, China, India and Southeast Asia" (p 4).

7.6 Conclusion

The link between human security and migration has re-emerged in recent times especially after the elaboration of the concept in 1994 by the Human Development Report. For Nepal, this nexus has great relevance given the present understanding of security issues in migration. While a large focus is placed on labour migrants and their security from a humanitarian perspective, there are other aspects of migration which necessitate that the migration-human security nexus in Nepal be revisited. This chapter aims to contribute to a better understanding of the position of Nepal in the migration circle and its link with security, showing that though largely portrayed as a labour sending country, Nepal plays many different roles as host, transition country and hub for the meeting of migrants from different parts of the world.

Besides, there is the process of internal migration, both voluntary and forced. All these types of migration will have implications on the human security of both the migrants and the non-migrants. However, the current outlook towards migration from the concerned sectors is very foreign employment-oriented and thus overlooks these important dimensions of migration, their outcomes and their relations to the human security of the concerned population. As Nepal is increasingly caught in the migration trajectory of various types, the human security of the migrants as well as that of the host country population will be affected.

Due to the lack of employment opportunities in Nepal, many youths only plan for the short term. The large availability of illegal jobs which bring 'easy money' may lure Nepali youths. This increase has already been observed; for example, the number of Nepali people arrested for drug dealing rose from 706 in 2007-2008 to 1,432 in 2008-2009 (CBS 2010).

References

Alkire S. 2003. *A Conceptual Framework for Human Security. Working paper 2.* Centre for Research on Inequality, Human security and Ethnicity (CRISE). Oxford: University of Oxford.

Bourdleu P. 1977. *Outline of a theory of practice.* Translated by Nice R. Cambridge: Polity Press.

Brooks R, Waters J. 2011. *Student Mobility, Migration and the Internalization of Higher Education.* Hampshire: Palgrave Macmillan.

CBS [Central Bureau of Statistics]. 2010. *Statistical Pocket Book of Nepal.* Kathmandu: Central Bureau of Statistics.

CORC [Cultural Orientation Resource Centre]. 2007. Bhutanese Refugees in Nepal. COR Centre Refugee Backgrounder no 4. Washington D.C.: Cultural Orientation Resource Centre.

Foner N. 2000. *From Ellis Island to JFK: New York's Two Great Waves of Immigration.* New York: Russel Sage Foundation.

Foucault M. 1975. From Discipline and Punish: The Birth of the Prison. New York: Vintage Books Available at: http://foucault.info/documents/disciplineAndPunish/foucault.disciplineAndPunish.panOpticism.html; accessed 17 July 2010.

Ghimire A, Gurung P. 2011. Migration Issues in South Asia: A draft report submitted to the Special Project Mobility, Migration and Movement of the Swiss National Centre of Competence in Research NCCR North-South.

GiddensA. 1984. *The constitution of society: Outline of the Theory of Structuration.* Cambridge: Polity press.

Hall T. 1998. *Urban Geography.* London: Routledge

Heisbourg F. 1991. Population Movements in Post-Cold War Europe. *Survival* 33:31-43.

Huda S. 2006. Sex Trafficking in South Asia. *International Journal of Gynecology and Obstetrics* 94:374-381.

Huysmans J, Squire V. 2009. Migration and Security. *In*: Dunn C, Mauer M, Victor M, editors. *Handbook of Security Studies*. London: Routledge.

IOM [International Organisation for Migration]. 2010. *World Migration Report 2010. The Future of Migration: Building Capacities for Change*. Geneva: International Organisation for Migration.

IOM [International Organisation for Migration]. 2011. World Migration Report: *Communicating Effectively about Migration.* Geneva: International Organisation for Migration.

Joshi R. 2011. *Tibetan Settlements in Thangboche and Jawalakhel. A draft report submitted to the Nepal Institute for Peace*. Kathmandu: Nepal Institute for Peace.

Kicinger A. 2004. *International migration as a non-traditional security threat and the EU responses to this phenomenon*, Central European Forum for Migration Research Working Paper 2/2004.

Korn D. 1999. Exodus within borders: An introduction to crisis of internal displacement. Washington D.C.: Brookings Institutions Press.

Leaning J, Arie S. 2001. *Human Security Report 2000*. New Orleans: USAID

Loescher G. 1992. Refugee Movements and International Security. *Adelphi Papers*. **Martin P, Widegren J.** 1996. International migration: A global Challenge. *Population Studies* 51(1):1-18.

Miklian J. 2009. *Illicit Trading in Nepal: Fuelling South Asian Terrorism*. Working Paper No. 3. Oslo: Peace Research Institute Oslo.

NIDS [Nepal Institute of Development Studies] and NCCR [National Centre of Competence in Research] North-South. 2011. *Nepal Migration Yearbook 2010*. Kathmandu: Nepal Institute of Development Studies and South Asia Regional Coordination Office of the Swiss National Centre of Competence in Research (NCCR North- South).

Norbu D. 1996. *Tibetan Refugees in South Asia: A case of peaceful adjustment, refugees and Regional Security in South Asia.* Regional Center for Strategic Studies. New Delhi: Konark Publishers

NTS-Asia. 2007. *Non Traditional Security: Challenges in Asia- What role for multilateralism? A report by Consortium of Non traditional Security Studies in Asia (NTS-Asia)*. New York: NTS-Asia and International Peace Academy.

Refugee Processing Centre. 2012. More than 75,000 refugees settled so far. available at: www.wrapsnet.org/home/tabid52/articletype/articleview.

Rudolph C. 2003. Security and the Political Economy of International Migration. *American Political Science Review* 97(4):603-620.

Rudolph C. 2006. *National Security and Immigration.* Stanford: Stanford University Press.

Sarkar S. 2011. Karachi link to fake Indian Currency in Nepal. Available at: www. inewsone.com/2011/05/07-; accessed 10 January 2011.

Torpey J. 2011. *The Invention of Passport, Surveillance, Citizenship and the State.* Cambridge: Cambridge University Press.

Truong TD, Gasper D. 2011. Transnational migration, Development and Human Security, *In:* Truong TD, Gasper D, editors. *Transnational migration and Human Security: the Migration-Development-Security Nexus.* Heidelberg: Springer.

UN [United Nations]. 2008. *Illicit Drug Trends in Pakistan.* Islamabad: United Nations.

UNHCR [United Nations High Commission for Refugees]. 2010. Country Operations Profile-Nepal. *UNHCR.* www.unhcr.org; accessed 1 May 2010.

UNIFEM [United Nations Development Fund for Women] and People's Forum. 2009. *Mahila ko Surakshit Baideshik Rojgar: Kanun ra Kanun Karanwayan Sanyantraharu ko Prabhavkarita. A Report.* Kathmandu: United Nations Development Fund for Women and People's Forum.

Vincent C, Ball S. 2006. *Childcare choice and class practices: Middle-class parents and their children.* London: Routlege

Weiner M. 1993. *International Migration and Security.* Boulder, C.O.: Westview Press.

****

Chapter 8

Climate change: A challenge to human security

Batu Krishna Uprety

8.1 Introduction

Climate change means a change of climate, attributed directly or indirectly to human activity, which alters the composition of the global atmosphere. Climate change thus differs from natural climate variability observed over comparable time periods (Climate Change Secretariat 1992). Change might occur in the climate system - the atmosphere, hydrosphere, biosphere and geosphere and in their interactions - through natural and anthropogenic activities (ibid).

Human security is the new dimension that is linked with and understood as having close relations with climate change. Human security is the condition when individuals and communities have the option to avoid or adapt to risks to meet their basic needs and rights, have the capacity and freedom to exercise these options and can actively participate in attaining these options (GECHS 1999). Human security is also a state that is achieved when and where individuals and communities have the options necessary to mitigate or adapt to threats to their human, environmental and social rights.

Climate change is a natural process. This change has made the Earth habitable to human beings and other life forms. The proverb 'slow and steady wins the race' could be understood as a process and a lesson that provides opportunities to enhance understanding that climate change happens, should happen and will continue to happen. The current concern is the scale and magnitude of such happenings. Global warming, accelerated through anthropogenic emissions of greenhouse gases of varying global warming potentials, has been the major concern in recent years as atmospheric concentrations of greenhouse gases have significantly increased after the Industrial Revolution. The United Nations Framework Convention on Climate Change (UNFCCC) and the Kyoto Protocol (KP) are the legally-binding international instruments to address the adverse effects of climate change. Several decisions have been made for the effective implementation of the UNFCCC and the KP during the last seventeen and seven years respectively.

The observed effects of climate change are more pronounced in recent years and thus pose a new and emerging threat. This article examines the causes and consequences of climate change and outlines measures taken to address them, keeping human security concerns in perspective.

8.2 Greenhouse gases

Greenhouse gases have different warming potentials. All greenhouse gases (see Box 8.1) are expressed in carbon dioxide equivalent ($CO_{2\text{-eq}}$), where the global warming potential of CO_2 is taken as one unit. Based on the warming potentials, one ton of methane emission is equivalent to 21 times (21 tons) of CO_2 emissions. One ton of nitrous oxide emission is equivalent to 310 tons of CO_2 emissions (MoPE 2004). At the seventh session of the Conference of the Parties serving as the Meeting of the Parties to the KP (COP/MOP or CMP), it was decided to include Nitrogen Trifluoride in Annex A (Climate Change Secretariat 2011).

Prior to the 1850s, the concentration of Greenhouse gases in the atmosphere was not at an alarming level. The Industrial Revolution increased the usage of fossil fuels and correspondingly, greenhouse gases emissions. The present rate of temperature rise indicates an increase of possibly 4°C by the end of the century (WB 2010).

Box 8.1 Greenhouse gases

- Carbon dioxide (CO_2)
- Methane (CH_4)
- Nitrous oxide (N_2O)
- Hydrofluorocarbons (HFCs)
- Perflurocarbons (PFCs)
- Sulphur hexafluoride (SF_6)
- Nitrogen trifluoride (NF_3)

Source: Compiled by the author

People, particularly in developed countries, consider that society and ecosystems might adapt to a global temperature increase of 2°C above its preindustrial level. If temperature rise is maintained at 2°C, it might be possible to reduce a significant loss of ice caps and limit the increase of floods, droughts and forest fires (ibid). The noticed change in climate system was highlighted by scientists some three decades ago. The observed scenario shows a rapid change in climate systems. Experience indicates that recent years are becoming hotter. Taking into consideration the repeated happenings of the devastating nature of climate-induced disasters, climate change has accelerated continued threats to human beings, life-forms and life-support systems, according to an Intergovernmental Panel on Climate Change (IPCC) special report on 'Managing the Risks of Extreme Events and Disasters to Advance Climate Change Adaptation', published in 2012.

The World Development Report (WB 2010) states that for nearly 1 million years before the Industrial Revolution, the carbon dioxide (CO_2) concentration in the atmosphere ranged between 200 and 300 parts per million (ppm). Over the past 150 years, levels have been far above that range at 387 ppm (ibid). The earth has on an average warmed up by 0.8°C from pre-industrial levels. Models project that the global average temperature will increase to between 2.5 and 7°C above pre-industrial levels by 2100. Even a temperature rise of 2°C will have tremendous effects on human life and life-supporting systems due to frequent and stronger weather events, including additional stress on water, food security, health and biodiversity. This is a clear indication that predicted temperature rises will have tremendous impact on human security and resources on which human beings depend upon for survival.

Anthropogenic emissions of Greenhouse gases will continue to accelerate change in climate systems. This accelerated change might affect agriculture production and food security, water and energy security, increase snow and glacier melt and decrease glaciations. This will accelerate shifting vegetation and the frequent occurrence of diseases. In other words, climate change will induce extreme events such as droughts and floods, which will pose threats to the very survival of human beings, livelihoods and the function of life-supporting systems, the basic elements of human security. In this context, greenhouse gases emissions are the root causes of climate change and require urgent action to safeguard life and life- supporting systems and to ensure human security.

8.3 International initiatives to address climate change

As climate change and human security are increasingly inter-linked, a genesis of international initiatives should urgently address them in an effective, efficient and transparent manner. There is a consensus at the scientific level that the world is becoming warmer principally due to human activities and/ or increased Greenhouse gases emissions. This has resulted in increased pressure on basic necessities such as food, water, air and energy. Global warming is challenging sustainability and putting additional pressure on human security. Hence, our understanding of climate change should be enhanced.

At the first World Climate Conference in 1979, scientists discussed about the science and impacts of climate change and realised the need for urgent action to address the accelerated changes in the climate system. The Conference issued a declaration calling on governments to anticipate and guard against potential climate hazards (Climate Change Secretariat 2006). Scientific evidence has convinced the international community - politicians, decision-makers, planners, programme implementers and people at large - that climate change will not disappear in the twenty- first century. The Toronto Conference on the Changing Atmosphere recommended developing a comprehensive global framework convention to take necessary and timely actions to deal with the challenges and threats of climate change (ibid). The issue was taken up by the UN General Assembly which established the Inter-governmental Negotiating Committee (INC) open to all UN Member States in 1990 to draft the legally-binding instrument on climate change. Accordingly, the United Nations Framework Convention on Climate Change (UNFCCC) was drafted and its text was adopted in May 1992 in New York. The Convention was opened for signature at the Rio Earth Summit in June 1992. The Convention came into force in 1994. In order to make the Convention operational, the KP was adopted in 1997 during the third session of the Conference of the Parties (COP) to the UNFCCC (Decision1/CP.3). Hence, 9 May 1992 is the 'birth day' for addressing the impacts of climate change at the national, regional and global levels with short-, medium- and long- term approaches. On 11 December 1997, developed and industrialised countries committed to reduce greenhouse gases emissions; however, the United States of America - the major greenhouse gases emitter - did not ratify this Protocol.

In the 1980s and 1990s, climate change was discussed within the scientific community and a small group of climate negotiators. The Inter- Governmental Panel on Climate Change (IPCC), established in 1988, published the first assessment report in 1989 which led to increased understandings of climate science (Climate Change Secretariat 2006). The IPCC Fourth Assessment Report (AR4) published in 2007 brought a landslide change in the understanding of science and the impacts of climate change on a broader scale. According to the Report of IPCC (2007) warming of the climate system is unequivocal, as is now evident from observations in global average air and ocean temperatures, widespread melting of snow and ice and rising global average sea level. The 13th session of the COP to the United Nations Framework Convention on Climate Change (UNFCCC) in Bali, Indonesia, adopted the Bali Action Plan (BAP) with the understanding that the Kyoto Protocol alone does not provide sufficient basis to solve the emerging threats of climate change. There are some milestones regarding the implementation of the UNFCCC at the global level (Box 8.2) that made the international community realise the urgent need for reducing greenhouse gases emissions and thus reducing the impact of climate change on human beings and natural resources.

Box 8.2 Major events on climate change

1979: First World Climate Conference (scientists' recommendations to take actions at the international level)

1988: Establishment of Inter-governmental Panel on Climate Change and publication of assessment report

1992: Adoption of the UN Framework Convention on Climate Change

1995 : COP1 to the UNFCCC (Berlin mandate to develop a Protocol)

1997 : COP3 to the UNFCCC (adoption of the KP with commitment of developed country Parties to reduce green houses gases emissions by 5.2 per cent at 1990 level by 2012)

2001 : COP7 to the UNFCCC [package of decisions for Least Developed Countries (LDCs) – LDC work programme, guidelines for the preparation of the National Adaptation Programme of Action (NAPA), establishment of LDC Expert Group and LDC Fund]

2005 : CMP1 to the Kyoto Protocol and formation of the Ad Hoc Working Group on further commitment to the KP (to decide on second commitment period, i.e. for post-2012 period)

2007 : COP13 to the UNFCCC adopted Bali Action Plan to deal with greenhouse gases emissions for longer period

2009: COP15 to the UNFCCC and Copenhagen Accord

2010 : COP16 to the UNFCCC with decision on Cancun Adaptation Framework, Green Climate Fund and National Adaptation Plan

2011 : COP17 to the UNFCCC and extension of the Kyoto Protocol including decision on Ad hoc Working Group on Durban Platform for Enhanced Action to develop legally binding instrument beyond 2020 period

Source: Compiled by the author from various sources

International mechanisms for enhancing people's understanding of the impacts of anthropogenic greenhouse gas emissions and of appropriate mitigation measures, along with the compliance of developed countries (greenhouse gas emitters) to provide additional funding and technologies to 'climate vulnerable' countries, would possibly contribute to improving human security from climate change impacts in countries like Nepal.

8.4 The emission gap

At the Copenhagen Climate Change Summit 2009, the Heads of States and Heads of Governments focused on how to keep temperature rise below and/or at 2^{0}C. The Least Developed Countries, including Nepal and the Small Island Developing States stressed the need to keep the temperature rise below 1.5^{0}C, taking into consideration climate vulnerability and observed effects of climate change.

The United Nations Environment Programme (UNEP) conducted a study on the current level of greenhouse gases emissions and published the Emission Gap Report in 2010 to consider the possibility of reducing temperature in line with the Copenhagen Accord (UNEP 2010). The study shows that emission levels of approximately 44 gigatonnes of carbon dioxide equivalent ($GtCO_{2eq}$) (range: 39-44 $GtCO_{2eq}$) in 2020 would be consistent with a "likely" chance of limiting global warming to 2°C. Under business-as-usual projections, global emissions could reach 56 $GtCO_{2eq}$ (range: 54-60 $GtCO_{2eq}$) in 2020, leaving a gap of 12 $GtCO_{2eq}$ (Figure 8.1). However, it is feasible to bridge the remaining gap through more ambitious domestic actions related to greenhouse gas emission reductions. These actions would also require international climate finance and technology transfer.

The UNEP study report stressed an expected 'gap' in 2020 between emission levels consistent with a 2°C limit and those resulting from the Copenhagen Accord pledges (UNEP 2010, p 10). Climate systems are greatly affected by anthropogenic greenhouse gases emissions and the situation is becoming worse every year. An increase in climate-induced disasters including diseases will greatly affect human security and challenge the very survival of life. Unless the emission gap is bridged, the impact of climate change on human beings, livelihoods and natural and constructed resources will continue to be a threat.

Figure 8.1 The emission gap

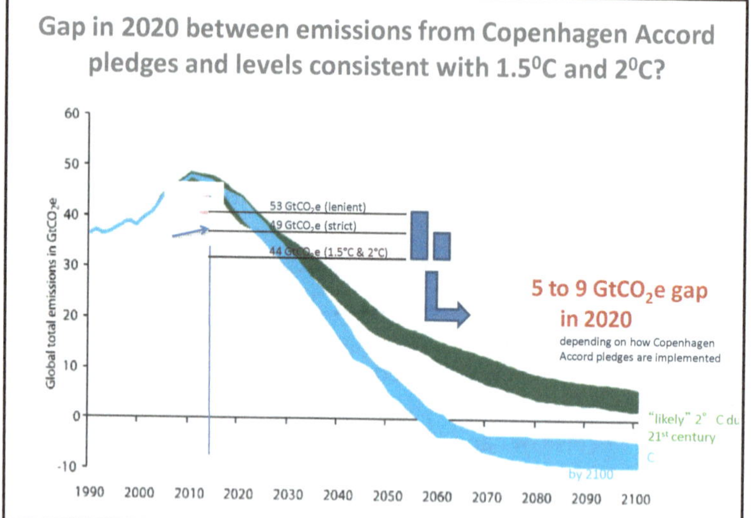

Source: UNEP (2010)

This piece of information on emission gaps provides a strong basis for sizeable decreases in greenhouse gas emissions. A reduction in greenhouse gas emissions will have multiple benefits for human beings to live in harmony with nature. It will equally help to safeguard human life and help human adapt to climate change risks.

8.5 Climate change and human security

Climate science makes it clear that global warming is increasing and will have unprecedented effects. Links exist between climate change effects and human security, but their scope and implication are poorly understood. There are several arguments which show that climate change can potentially undermine human security. The degree to which societies are vulnerable to climate change depends on the extent to which parts of the population are dependent on natural resources and ecosystem goods and services, the extent to which the resources and services they rely on are affected by or sensitive to climate change and their capacity to adapt to changes in these resources and services for their continuous supply. But climate change risks are only a small part of what constitutes human security. Climate change might accelerate resource conflict within and outside political boundaries, as well as increase poverty and even violence that pose risks to well-being. The effects of climate change transcend national boundaries and people are required to understand nature's level of tolerance to it (Dahal 2011).

Economic assessment of the losses and benefits caused by climate change and climate-induced weather events and disasters might help people to better understand the upstream-downstream linkages and importance of life-supporting systems. IPCC (2012) estimated annual losses from weather- and climate-related disasters at a few USD billion in 1980 to above USD 200 billion in 2010. It is difficult to value and monetise many impacts of climate change such as the loss of human life, cultural heritage and ecosystem services. Information and knowledge on economic loss of elements of human security would draw attention to protect life support systems from climate change impacts. It is expected that pricing lost resources will depend upon the value and importance attached to them at generic, country-specific and area-specific levels (sometimes the value of life is also related to/determined by social wellbeing/status). Such assessment will provide convincing results to better establish the linkage between climate change and human security. Furthermore, climate change impacts will not be location-specific, particularly for high- value resources, but will be on a wider scale (transboundary, regional and global).

Extreme weather events and climate change have brought additional threats to mountains and downstream communities and people depending upon the mountain resources. The increased amount of short-time precipitation in the hills and mountains will reduce the absorbing capacity of nature and its resources, which could result in downstream flooding and increased occurrences of landslides in the upstream. Glacier lake outburst flood-induced disasters might equally claim lives and properties downstream including public property such as infrastructure (roads, bridges, hydropower plants etc.). It might also create transboundary impacts and might increase conflict amongst neighbours. The Himalayan ecosystem which is highly vulnerable to climate change is equally an important resource for the densely populated Gangetic plane. Change in temperature and monsoon rainfall has brought critical challenges to conventionally defined state-centric security (Dahal 2011). Similarly, the Intergovernmental Panel on Climate Change (IPCC) states that "there is a high confidence that changes in heat waves, glacier retreat and/or permafrost degradation will affect high mountain phenomena such as slope instabilities, movement of mass and glacier lake outburst floods" (IPCC 2012, p 13). Fossil fuel-dependent development does not recognise the limits of natural systems and brings insecurities to human and other life-forms and ecosystems.

8.5.1 Climate change impacts in Nepal

The Climate Change Risk Atlas 2010 ranked Nepal as the fourth most vulnerable country out of 170 countries worldwide to climate change (Maplecroft 2010). This statistic indicates that Nepali people are insecure from global climate change phenomena. Nepal is climate-vulnerable not because it emits high amounts of Greenhouse gases but because climate change does not recognise political boundaries.

In the early 2000s, Nepal emitted only 0.025 per cent of global greenhouse gas emissions (MoPE 2004). Nepal has experienced an average annual increase of 0.06°C temperature for the period of 1974 - 1994 based on the analysis of observed temperature of 49 stations (Shrestha et al. 1999). For 45 weather stations of Nepal analysed over the period from 1975 to 2006, the annual rate of average temperature rise was 0.04°C (PA 2009; Figure 8.2). Both data are sufficient to understand the observed warming trend in the country. The northern part of the country is facing higher temperature increase and the number of hot days and nights has increased.

Figure 8.2 Average annual maximum temperatures (1975-2006)

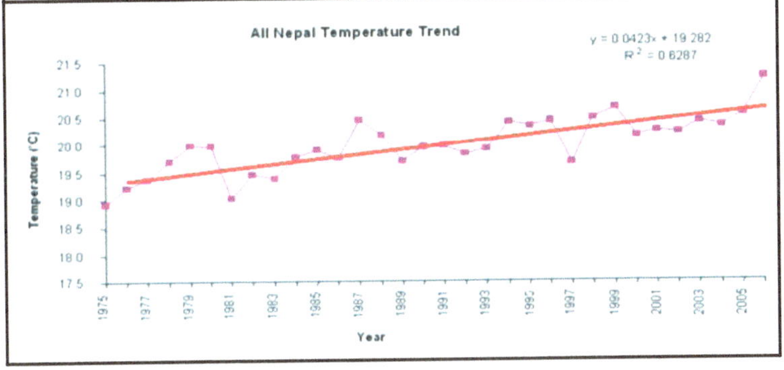

Source: PA (2009)

Some inter-annual variations in monsoon rainfall have been observed. Based on the analysis of records between 1976 and 2005 from 166 weather stations around Nepal, annual precipitation trends reveal a positive trend in annual rainfall except for Mid-Western Nepal (PA 2009; Figure 8.3). Annual average summer precipitation has increased by 15 to 20 per cent in the Mid-Hills and Tarai but it is declining in the Far- and Mid- Western regions. Post-monsoon precipitation is increasing in most of the Mid-Western and southern parts of Eastern and Central/Western Nepal.

Figure 8.3 Precipitation trends (1971-2006)

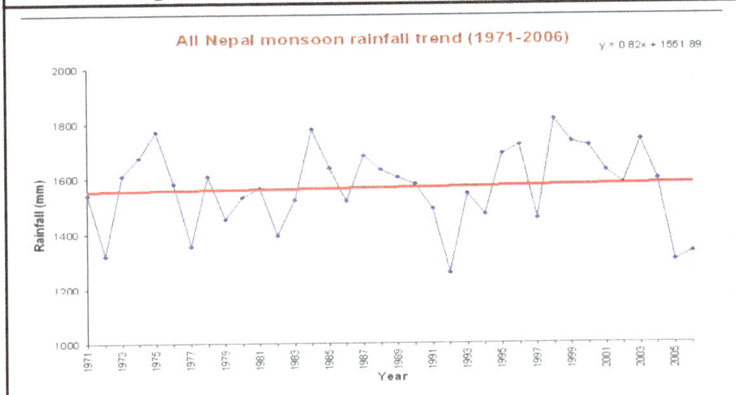

Source: PA (2009)

Climate vulnerability has increased threats. Nepal's National

Adaptation Programme of Action document of 2010 has identified Mid- and Far-West Nepal as climate-vulnerable, taking into consideration the combination of landslides, flood, drought and glacier lake outburst flood vulnerabilities (Figure 8.4).

Figure 8.4 Climate vulnerable districts of Nepal

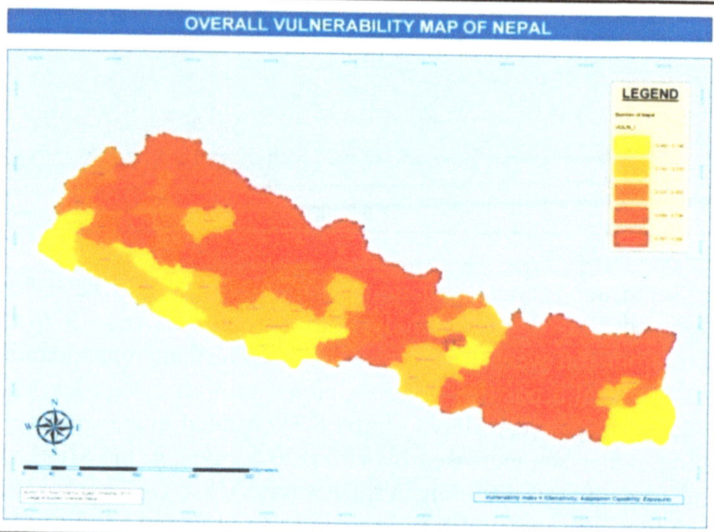

Source: MoE (2010)

The consequences of climate change and extreme weather events are visible. Glaciers are retreating at a faster rate in the last few decades. A majority of glaciers in the Khumbu Region retreated by 30-60m between 1979 and 1989 and the glacier surface thinned by nearly 12m. Out of 2323 glaciers lakes inventoried, 330 have expanded to areas larger than 0.02 km^2, and are still expanding (Bajracharya and Mool 2005). Glacial retreat in Nepal can reach 20m per year, resulting in a six-fold growth of glacial lakes (CNCCC 2007). 'Vertical tsunamis' might occur due to lake outbursts and will affect people, their livelihoods and ecosystems both upstream and downstream. The retreat of Glacier AX010 in Shorong Himal, eastern Nepal is visible and remarkable. The pictures are self-explanatory.

Studies carried out in the Imja, Tsho Rolpa and Thulagi Glacial Lakes in 2009 indicate serious risks of outburst, although not immediate, requiring risk reduction measures as soon as possible. Some of the visible effects of climate change in the mountains are:

1. The existing rate of snow and glacier melt might increase water in Nepal's river system by about 5.7 per cent until 2030 and decrease by 28 per cent by the end of this century (Chaulagain 2007).
2. There is an increase in the number of climate-induced 'refugees'. For example, about 150 people in Mustang district have migrated from the uplands to the lowlands due to water scarcity. Drinking water scarcity has been emerging as a major threat in many hill districts of Nepal.
3. About 1.9 million people are vulnerable to climate change and an additional 10 million Nepali people are increasingly at climate risks (MoE 2010). Every year more than 1 million people are directly impacted by climate-induced disasters such as drought, landslides and floods in Mid- and Far West Nepal.
4. More than 4,000 people have died in Nepal over the last ten years in climate-induced disasters, which have caused economic losses of about USD 5.34 billion (MoE 2010).

Nepal's National Adaptation Programme of Action documents communities' observations and experiences regarding rising temperature, shifting agro-ecological zones, increased variability (timing, duration and intensity) in precipitation and changes in the amount and timing of snowfall (MoE 2010). The National Adaptation Programme of Action also documents community observations on shifts in wind and increases in the number of extreme events including droughts, floods and avalanches. The above information helps to classify Nepal as one of the major climate 'hot- spots'. These threats have increased human insecurity.

8.5.2 Climate-induced human insecurity

As mentioned above, the impacts of climate change have been pronounced in a number of areas like water, agriculture, forests, tourism, infrastructure and human health (MoE 2011). These sectors are closely linked with human development, ecosystem functioning and the country's overall socio-economic development. Climate variability, extreme weather events, flood and drought have direct impacts on food production and energy security. In other words, climate change has imposed an additional burden on human life and resources. The possible increases in human insecurity associated with climate change and/or climate-induced disasters in agriculture, water and biodiversity sectors are briefly described below:

a) Climate change and agriculture: Increasing agricultural productivity and production is a perennial policy and strategy of Nepal to ensure food and nutrition security. Each periodical plan emphasises increasing agricultural GDP. For example, the annual agro-GDP growth rates were targeted to increase from 2.6 to 3.6 per cent and annual per capita food grain production from 272 kg to 322 kg (NPC 2007 as cited in MoE 2011). However, food productivity has not increased. The World Food Programme estimated that 43 of Nepal's 75 districts faced a food deficit; 23 districts were chronically food insecure (Nepal Food Security Bulletin 2010 as cited in MoE 2011).

In Nepal, more than 60 per cent of households do not produce sufficient food to feed their families and about four-fifths of landless households have food insufficiency for 10-12 months of the year (MoE 2011). The food insecure people are subsistence farmers and the disadvantaged include female-headed households. Food availability, food access, utilisation and stability are the major determinants to measure food security (ibid). Frequent droughts, floods and landslides continue to affect crop production. Any shift in agro-ecological zones may affect productions of crops and livestock from possible invasion of new weeds, diseases and pests.

Increased temperatures will likely reduce growing season and productivity, increase evapo-transpiration and irrigation water shortages and also lead to an increase in pests, diseases and invasive species. Drought will impact on paddy production as summer paddy is water-loving. Heavy rainfall will also flood the paddy fields and affect other crops that require a moderate amount of water. The primary impact will be the decline in food production and its secondary impact might be migration due to decreased food availability which has a direct bearing on human security. Nepal's rice yield declined in 1972, 1976, 1977, 1979, 1982, 1986, 1992, 1994, 1997 and 1999, at times when the monsoon rain was lower than the normal (1450mm). There is a positive correlation between rainfall and rice yield (Figure 8.5; Nayava 2008 as cited in MoE 2011).

Figure 8.5 Rice yield (kg/ha) and rainfall (mm)

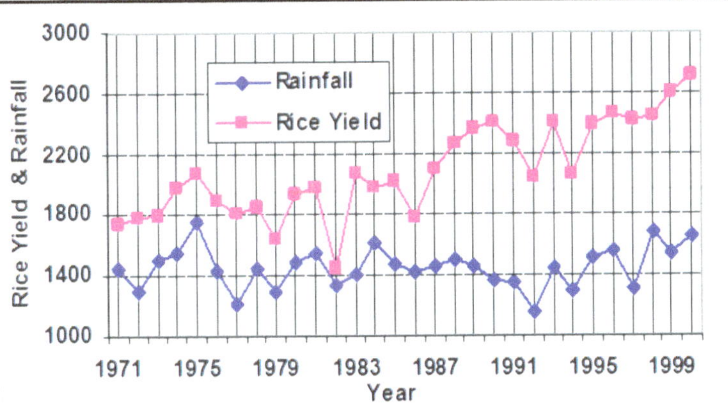

Source: Nayava 2008 as cited in MoE (2011)

Every year floods damage crops, household assets and public property. In 2007, floods and landslides rendered more than half a million people food-insecure (IDMC 2008 as cited in MoE 2011). Agricultural production was made further insecure by the impact of climate change on irrigation demand. The projection indicates that an increase in temperature by 3°C would increase irrigation water demand annually by 11 per cent, keeping other parameters constant (MoE 2011). Nepal has yet to introduce pre- disaster preparedness measures to increase coping capacities and ensure food security. In a nutshell, climate variability and weather extremes will continue to have adverse impacts on the agricultural sector. A decline in food production would result in human insecurity.

(b) Climate-induced water insecurity: Major water sources are glaciers and monsoon rainfall. An uneven distribution of daily precipitation prevails in rainy season. Sometimes, 10 per cent of the total annual precipitation occurs in a single day (Alford 1992) and 50 per cent of the total annual precipitation was recorded within 10 days (Dahal and Hasegawa 2008). The average annual rainfall ranges from only 163mm at Lomangthan (Mustang) to 5,244mm at Lumle (near Pokhara) thereby indicating a significant variation of rainfall across a similar landscape within a few kilometres in the same development region (MoE 2011). The total average annual runoff from all 6000 rivers is estimated at about 225 billion m^3, with only an estimated 15 BCM (billion cubic metres) used for economic and social purposes (WECS 2005). In addition, about 8.8 BCM is also available in the shallow and deep aquifers (ibid). However, accessibility to clean and safe water is a major concern.

Frequent extreme events and uneven rainfall has increased floods, drought and debris flows in the Tarai and valleys, while landslides and spring evaporation are prominent in the mountains. A study predicts that the total water availability in Nepal will increase from 176 km^3/ year to 178 km^3/year in 2030 and then drop to 128 km^3/year by 2100 (Chaulagain 2007). In case of glacier lake outburst floods, the situation might worsen further. Nepal has experienced 10 glacier lake outburst floods that originated in Tibet. For instance, a glacier lake outburst flood in 1981 damaged sections of the highway between Zhangzangbo Gully and the Sun Koshi Power Station as well as the Friendship Bridge on the Bhote Koshi River, causing economic losses of about USD 3 million in Nepal (Bajracharya and Mool 2006). If glacial lakes burst, increased water volume washes away property and infrastructure and threatens the existence of human beings as well.

Climate change will increase the intra-annual variability of stream flow. The high intensity of rainfall will increase flood frequency and discharge. Water-induced disasters have claimed lives and destroyed property and infrastructures every year. The Department of Water Induced Disaster Prevention in 2006 estimated that water-induced hazards cause about 300 deaths and infrastructure damage worth USD 9 million each year. Similarly, landslides and floods are perennial problems in the mountains and plains respectively, and are further triggered by uneven rainfall distribution.

Nepal has promoted run-off-the-river type hydropower plants and these plants are highly vulnerable to the effects of stream flow changes, water availability and quality, particularly high sediment load during the rainy season. Similar effects have been noticed in the irrigation sector. Climate change will adversely affect water resources and use, thereby further making the life of the Nepali people more difficult, particularly in terms of clean energy supply, availability of safe and sufficient drinking water and food production. It will impose additional stress on hydro-electricity generation and will lead to energy insecurities and further disturb social harmony due to stress on drinking water (including increased collection time). In a nutshell, climate-induced water insecurity will be a major threat for Nepali people in the years to come.

(c) Climate change and biodiversity insecurity: Biodiversity contributes to the maintenance of ecosystem dynamics, food security, livelihoods and cultural and spiritual practices. Forests are important for food, fodder, fuel, fibre and fertiliser including timbers and oxygen. They also provide goods and services. In Nepal, several factors including over- and/or unregulated forest use and habitat loss have adversely affected biodiversity. Climate change is a new threat to biodiversity. The change in temperature and precipitation will continue to affect biodiversity both positively and negatively. Climate change might lead to the extinction of location-specific species and/or species having low tolerance and limited range of geographical habitat. Some species with a high geographical distribution might invade and destroy the diverse habitats, including high value medicinal and aromatic plants. Climate change might also promote speciation (creation of new species). Drought-induced forest fires will increase greenhouse gases emissions and impact on the productivity and diversity of forests.

Biodiversity insecurity is closely linked with livelihood insecurity. The rise in temperature and change in rainfall will likely increase the occurrence of pests and diseases and reduce productivity. The National Adaptation Programme of Action documents that density, frequency and dominance of plant species such as Panch aunle (Dactylorhia hatageria), Amala (Emblica officinalis), Ritha (Sapindus mukurosii), Timur (Xanthoxylum armatum) and Bel (Aegle marmelos) are declining and shifting to higher altitudes and that grass production has declined sharply in low rainfall areas (MoE 2010). Grass species like Kukhure suli, a weed that grows in mustard farms in the Tarai, has disappeared (NCVST 2009). Seasonal changes have also resulted in early sprouting, flowering and fruiting of some plants. A decrease in the length certain species ripen, even species with healthy populations, has resulted in lower productivity (MoE 2011).

Temperature rise will likely accelerate the upward shifting of the tree line, might change plant composition, increase invasive alien species and/or the emergence of new temperature-resistant species and change wildlife habitat (MoE 2011). If valuable plants that are used for subsistence living disappear from one area, people depending upon them would find it difficult to meet their demands. New species which develop might or might not be useful to human beings and ecosystems and might compel people to migrate from their homeland in search of better livings.

The most visible impact of temperature change and extended dry spells is increased forest fires. Both crown and surface fires destroy grasses, shrubs and trees and kill insects, birds and wild animals. Forest fires also reduce NTFPs (non-timber forest products) production and increase carbon emissions. Predictions show that out of 15 vegetation types, Nepal will have only 12 remaining types when CO_2 levels double (MoPE 2004). A temperature rise of two degrees Celsius and a 20 per cent increase in precipitation would change vegetation patterns (ibid). Temperature increase in the sub-alpine and alpine regions would push vegetation as much as 500m upward. Nilogandhe (Ageratum houstonianum), for example, has begun to appear up to an elevation of 900m in Western Nepal (NCVST 2009). The impact will be severe on ecosystem goods and services and subsequently on wild relatives of agricultural crops.

Climate change will equally affect aquatic ecosystems and species and sensitive fauna and flora. Temperature rise increases humidity in river valleys, which creates a favourable environment for diseases and pests. Beetle infestations have increased in the utis plant (Alnus nepalensis) in the lower hills of the Koshi Basin (Ghimire 1985 as cited in MoE 2011). In 2009, Eastern Nepal's cardamom yield was reduced by 60 per cent due to an unknown disease and another unknown disease affected the roots of orange trees, affecting production (MoE 2011).

Although Nepal has yet to start research and scientific studies into the impacts of climate change and weather events on both wild and domesticated biodiversity, people's perceptions and understanding demonstrate increased impacts on specie and ecosystem biodiversity. In a nutshell, human security largely depends upon biological resources (to meet food demand including ecosystem goods and services), water and energy but these elements are greatly impacted by increased frequency of extreme weather events and temperature rise.

8.6 National initiatives to address climate change

Nepal's greenhouse gas emission is insignificant. It has adopted a policy to develop and use clean, renewable and hydropower energies, which do not emit Greenhouse gases. As a Least Developed Country (LDC) Party to the United Nations Framework Convention on Climate Change (UNFCCC) and the KP since 1994 and 2005 and having no commitment to reduce Greenhouse gases, Nepal's efforts are directed to adapt to climate change and reduce its impacts on life and life-supporting systems.

Some initiatives such as the development of certain instruments and capacity enhancement that might reduce human insecurities are summarised below.

Nepal became a Party to the United Nations Framework Convention on Climate Change (UNFCCC) in 1994. Between 1994 and 2006, Nepal prepared the initial national communication (INC) report and shared with parties in 2004. It also promoted, as usual, renewable energies. Between 2007 and 2009, Nepal concentrated its efforts on developing fundable projects, raising awareness and promoting institutional and coordination mechanisms. In 2008, Nepal accessed Least Developed Country (LDC) Fund, including support from the United Kingdom's aid agency DFID and Denmark's aid agency DANIDA, for National Adaptation Programme of Action preparation. Similarly, preparations of the second national communication and technology needs assessment, including development of a pilot programme for climate resilient, were initiated. In 2009, solid foundations were laid to implement activities to address climate change impacts in Nepal: a high level coordination mechanism was established, a regional conference on climate change was organised, a cabinet meeting was held at Kalapathar (Mount Everest Base Camp) and participation at the Copenhagen Climate Change Conference was at the level of Head of the Government.

Climate change activities were scaled up in 2010 and 2011 by establishing the Climate Change Management Division (CCMD) in the Ministry of Environment in 2010, approving the National Adaptation Programme of Action in September 2010 to implement the most urgent and immediate adaptation actions and also approving the Climate Change Policy and National Framework for Local Adaptation Plan for Action as an operational instrument for the National Adaptation Programme of Action implementation in 2011. These initiatives have led to further understanding about climate-impacted sectors and areas, as well as the planning and implementation of activities which reduce impact and contribute to attaining the objectives of human security. With this context in perspective, Nepal's climate change responses have been summarised as follows (Uprety 2011).

(a) Compliance with the commitments: As a part of sharing information on greenhouse gas emissions and mitigation and adaptation actions and other activities, Nepal finalised its initial national communication report in July 2004 which, 'inter alia', documented its share of greenhouse gas emissions at only 0.025 per cent of the global level (MoPE 2004). As a follow-up to this process, Nepal is preparing the second national communication to record sector-based greenhouse gases emissions, mitigation options and adaptation needs. Nepal is also assessing technologies required to address climate change impacts which will help identify, prioritise and use technologies for climate adaptation and mitigation which will in turn reduce climate change impact and ensure human security.

(b) Coordination mechanism and institutional strengthening: Climate change is a cross-cutting issue and requires coordinated efforts for desired results. There are three or four tiers of coordination mechanisms. The Government of Nepal constituted a Climate Change Council (CCC) in the autumn of 2009 under the chairmanship of the Prime Minister for policy coordination and guidance. The 28-member Council is also represented by eight independent experts. Within the last two-and- a-half years, the Climate Change Council met nine times and provided guidance to streamline initiatives that address climate change impacts.A high-level coordination committee was constituted in 2011 under the chairmanship of the Minister for Environment to ensure coordination on activities related to the Pilot Programme for Climate Resilience (PPCR). Similarly, a Multi-stakeholder Climate Change Initiatives Coordination Committee (MCCICC) was formed in mid-2010 to promote functional level coordination among stakeholders and streamline activities to address the impacts of climate change. The formation of project-specific steering committees and technical committees is a common phenomenon in Nepal. The establishment of the Climate Change Management Division with three sections (Climate Change Section, Climate Change Council Secretariat Section and Clean Development Mechanism Section) and nine permanent positions is a long-term initiative and will contribute to promoting the link between climate change and human security.

(c) Policy focus: Nepal is one of the few countries to have a separate policy on climate change: the Climate Change Policy was issued by the Government of Nepal (GoN) in January 2011. The policy focuses, 'inter alia', on climate adaptation and disaster risk reduction, resilience, low carbon development pathways and climate-friendly resource management to minimise the impacts of climate change on human beings, livelihoods and ecosystems. It equally focuses on accessing climate finance, promoting research, technology development and transfer and enhancing people's participation. The Policy intends to channel over 80 per cent of the total programme or project-based fund received for climate change into field- level activities. Effective implementation of the policy will open multiple avenues to promote human security by addressing climate change impacts.

Nepal has already adopted a clean energy development path by maximising the development and operation of hydro-power projects.

Recent policies also focus on renewable energies, approaches to low carbon development and carbon sequestration in forests (NPC 2011). These approaches provide additional opportunities to reduce energy and biodiversity insecurities.

(d) National adaptation programme of action and local adaptation plan for action: As a Least Developed Country, Nepal has prepared the National Adaptation Programme of Action to mainstream and implement the most urgent and immediate adaptation actions. Started in May 2009, the National Adaptation Programme of Action was prepared within 16 months through extensive consultation and was approved by the government in September 2010. Community-based adaption actions will contribute to address human security issues, as National Adaptation Programme of Action basically focuses on implementing integrated actions to develop the adaptive capacity of climate-vulnerable communities and the resources on which they depend. The Local Adaptation Plan for Action will contribute to meet the 'twin' objectives of implementing adaptation actions to increase productivity through a structured and cost- based plan and integrating adaptation options into sectoral, district and national planning processes and plans. The commitment of 14 donors and development partners to support climate change-related activities will help in making development climate-friendly and meeting people's basic needs such as food, water, energy, fodder, cloths and medicines - major elements of human security.

(e) Programmes and projects: The translation of national and international commitments into action requires field-level implementation to know what works and what does not in the Nepali soil. With this understanding, Nepal has adopted a multi-pronged approach to secure funding and address the adverse impacts of climate change on the mountains, people and their livelihoods and life-supporting systems.

Nepal is the only country to access funding from the Climate Investment Fund for Pilot Programme for Climate Resilience (PPCR), scaling up Renewable Energy Programme (SREP) in low income countries and REDD+ (Reducing Emissions from Deforestations and Forest Degradation). The PPCR will focus on making watershed management activities climate- resilient and developing human resources to make sectoral development plans and programmes climate-resilient. The SREP focuses on developing small hydropower projects and micro-energies including biogas, micro- hydro and solar. Economic assessment of the losses and gains from climate change will likely provide additional data and information on sectors and geographical areas affected by climate change and the investment required to reduce insecurities.

(f) Benefitting from the clean development mechanism: Human security can also be promoted by securing funding from carbon trade, as Article 12 of the Kyoto Protocol provisions for such trade between developed and developing countries through the Clean Development Mechanism. Developed countries will benefit from purchasing emission reduction credits from developing countries as per their compliance requirements and developing countries will benefit from selling such credits generated from Clean Development Mechanism programmes and/ or projects which contribute to attaining sustainable development goals. This scheme thus contributes to reducing greenhouse gases emissions and ensuring energy securities.

As of April 2012, the Designated National Authority (The ministry of Environment, Science and Technology) has approved Project Design Document (PDD) of 15 Clean Development Mechanism Projects totalling to annual 401,245 ton of carbon (CO_2-eq) for trade (personal communication). In August and September 2011, the CDM-Executive Board has issued CER (certified emission reduction) of 92,278 tons of carbon (CO_2-eq) for biogas projects (personal communication with Government officials).

(g) Conferences and meetings: In order to enhance knowledge and share information and experiences, Nepal has been organising regional and international conferences, workshops and meetings since 2009 (Box 8.3). It also organised a Summiteers Summit on 11 December 2009 in Copenhagen to draw the attention of the international community to the impacts of climate change on the Nepal Himalaya, including International Expert Consultation on Climate Change in September 2010 and April 2012.

Nepal's efforts regarding climate change matter a lot amongst the 48 least developed countries (LDC) and confidence has been shown to Nepal to function as the Chair of the LDC coordination group for 2013 and 2014.

Although the above initiatives do not focus directly on human security, they are the building blocks that provide a broader platform to enhance understanding on climate change, its impact on life and life-supporting systems and promote the conservation of resources required for human development. Awareness of efforts to address the adverse impacts of climatechangewould lead to developed, revised and amended instruments to promote human security. In this context, the above initiatives will help people, at different levels, to direct activities to promote human security by addressing the adverse impacts of climate change in an effective and efficient manner. In other words, these initiatives could be counted and valued for further understanding issues and concerns related to human security and act individually, jointly and collaboratively.

Box 8.3 Major national initiatives on climate change

1994	:	Party to the UN Framework Convention on Climate Change
2004	:	Preparation of Initial National Communication
2005	:	Party to the Kyoto Protocol
2009	:	Establishment of Climate Change Council, Regional Conference on Climate Change (from Kathmandu to Copenhagen), Cabinet meeting at Kalapatthar COP15 participation by Head of the Government
2010	:	Establishment of Climate Change Management Division MCCICC, LEG 18 meeting and NAPA endorsement
2011	:	Climate Change Policy, National Framework on Local Adaptation Plan for Action and CDM global workshop CDM DNA forum and CDM regional workshop
2012	:	International Conference of Mountain Countries on Climate Change approval for 401,245 ton of carbon for trade annually

Source: Compiled by the author from various sources

8.7 The way forward

The discussion presented with the proceeding section clearly demonstrates the potential climate change risks and its impacts on the human security and livelihood of the Nepali people. Climate change poses a serious human security challenge. General understanding of the adverse impacts of climate change on different sectors such as agriculture, forestry, water resources, health, infrastructure, biodiversity and tourism has increased in recent years. People are increasingly concerned with their losses from unseasonal and unusual climate-induced disasters such as the Seti River flash flood in May 2012. People with financial resources and the technical and technological capacity have opportunities to secure themselves, their livelihoods and resources.

In Nepal, ground-breaking work is being completed on climate adaptation. The pre-requisites for addressing climate-induced human insecurities such as institutional and coordination mechanisms, policies and tools are in place. The effective implementation of climate change policy as a national development agenda would develop the country's adaptive capacity and resilience to climate change risks. It seems that options and opportunities exist to benefit from the climate change regime. There is a need for doubling or quadrupling activities at different levels. The need is to 'act now, act together and act differently' so that the impacts of climate change on agriculture, forests, water, energy, tourism, health and other sectors are better understood and accordingly addressed. This ideal requires enhanced political guidance, new and additional financial resources, technology development and transfer and capacity building to deliver services effectively.

The challenges and threats of climate change to different facets of human security need to be better understood to find, select and implement coping strategies. Then, commitment could be translated into action in the spirit of the Climate Change Policy, National Adaptation Programme of Action and Local Adaptation Plan for Action. Climate adaptation and resilience should be internalised in the planning and implementation at different levels. Promoting low carbon development pathways, research and development into the economic losses and gains from climate change and developing instruments along with the provision of finance and technology would contribute to securing and protecting life, livelihoods and life-support systems.

As mentioned above, climate change impacts could be addressed and human security could be ensured through increased finance, the use of climate-friendly adaptation and mitigation technologies and building human capacity. This is possible through the rational mobilisation of domestic and external resources, including human resources. Finance could be accessed by establishing a national entity such as a Climate Change Fund. An autonomous and semi-governmental Climate Change Centre, if established in the spirit of the Climate Change Policy, might provide better opportunities to holistically and scientifically address climate change impacts and ensure human security and/or climate security in Nepal.

It is now understood and established that climate change has accelerated and will pose significant risks to social-ecological systems in many parts of the world. Challenges and threats will continue to affect human security. There are linkages between elements of human security and climate change, but these linkages are poorly understood and require further research.

References

Alford D. 1992. *Hydrological aspects of the Himalayan region.* Kathmandu: International Centre for Integrated Mountain Development.

Bajracharya SR, Mool PK. 2006. *Impact of global climate change from 1970s to 2000s on the glaciers and glacial lakes in Tamor Basin, Eastern Nepal.* Kathmandu: International Centre for Integrated Mountain Development.

Chaulagain NP. 2007. *Impacts of climate change on water resources of Nepal: The physical and socioeconomic dimensions.* [Doctoral Thesis]. University of Flensburg.

Climate Change Secretariat. 1992. *United Nations Framework Convention on Climate Change.* Bonn: Climate Change Secretariat.

Climate Change Secretariat. 2006. *United Nations Framework Convention on Climate Change Handbook.* Bonn: Climate Change Secretariat.

Climate Change Secretariat. 2011. *Report of the Conference of the Parties serving as the meeting of the Parties to the Kyoto Protocol on its seventh session, held in Durban from 28 November to 11 December 2011.* Bonn: Climate Change Secretariat.

CNCCC [China National Committee on Climate Change]. 2007. *China National Report on Climate Change.* Beijing: China National Committee on Climate Change.

Dahal DR. 2011. Climate Change and Security in South Asia.. Kathmandu: New Spotlight.

Dahal RK, Hasegawa S. 2008. Representative rainfall thresholds for landslide in the Nepal Himalaya. *Geomorphology* 100:429-443.

GECHS [Global Environmental Change and Human Security]. 1999. Global Environmental Change and Human Security: *GECHS Science Plan.* Bonn: International Human Dimensions Programme on Global Environmental Change.

IPCC [Intergovernmental Panel on Climate Change]. 2007. *Climate Change 2007: The Scientific Basis.* Working Group I contribution to IPCC (Intergovernmental Panel on Climate Change) 4th assessment report. Cambridge: Cambridge University Press.

IPCC [Intergovernmental Panel on Climate Change]. 2012. *Managing the*

Risks of Extreme Events and Disasters to Advance Climate Change Adaptation- Summary for Policymakers. A Special Report of Working Groups I and II of the Intergovernmental Panel on Climate Change. Geneva: World Meteorological Organisation.

MoE [Ministry of Environment]. 2010. *National Adaptation Programme of Ac- tion*. Kathmandu: Ministry of Environment.

MoE [Ministry of Environment]. 2011a. *Nepal Country Report: Climate Summit for a Living Himalayas: Bhutan 2011*. Kathmandu: Ministry of Environ- ment.

MoE [Ministry of Environment]. 2011b. *Status of Climate Change in Nepal*. Kath- mandu: Ministry of Environment.

MoPE [Ministry of Population and Environment]. 2004. *Initial National Communication to the Conference of Parties of the United Nations Framework Convention on Climate Change*. Kathmandu: Ministry of Population and Environment.

NCVST [Nepal Climate Vulnerability Study Team]. 2009. Vulnerability through the Eyes of the Vulnerable. Climate Change Induced Uncertainties and Nepal's Development Predicaments.Boulder: Institute for Social and Environmental Transition (ISET), Nepal and Institute for Social and Environmental Transition (ISET) Colorado.

NPC [National Planning Commission]. 2011. *Three Years Plan (2011-2013)*. Kathmandu: National Planning Commission.

PA [Practical Action]. 2009. *Temporal and Saptial Variability of Climate Change over Nepal (1976-2005)*. Kathmandu: Practical Action..

Shrestha AB, Wake CP, Dibb JE, Mayewski. 1999. Maximum Temperature Trends in the Himalaya and Its Vicinity: An Analysis Based on Temperature Records from Nepal for the Period 1971-1994. *Journal of Climate* 12:2775-2786.

UNEP [United Nations Environnent Programme]. 2010. *The Emission Gap Report*. Nairobi: United Nations Environnent Programme.

Uprety BK. 2011. *Climate Change: Living with the Threats*. Kathmandu: Image Nepal.

WB [World Bank]. 2010. *World Development Report, 2010. Development and Climate Change*. Washington, D.C.: World Bank.

WECS [Water and Energy Commission Secretariat]. 2005. *Nepal Water Plan*. Kathmandu: Water and Energy Commission Secretariat.

****

Chapter 9

Political insecurity and armed conflict: A threat to human security

Geja Sharma Wagle

9.1 Definition of political security

Political security is one of the important dimensions of human security which deals with the sovereign principles of democratic and human rights, human dignity, political freedom and protection from state repression. According to the definition of human security, political security is concerned with whether people live in a society that honours their basic human rights, follows the rule of law and ensures political freedom. A repressive state, conflict and violence might undermine security and the political rights of citizens and therefore pose political threats to citizens. In fact, political threats include political and human rights violations and violence stemming from conflict, as well as arbitrary behaviour, a corrupt and repressive government, unpredictable institutional settings, a poorly functioning judiciary and a lack of enforcement of the rule of law generally associated with 'freedom from fear'. The concept of political security is also the security of an individual from violence and political suppression by the state. In fact, the main objectives of human security are peace and harmony in society and the individual freedom and security of citizens (UNDP 1994).

According to the definition of the United Nations (UN) on human security, an individual or citizen of any nation is the referent point of security so that political security equates to the security of an individual regardless of his/ her nationality, race, ethnicity, religion, culture, gender, sexuality, class or adherence to any other group or community (Thakur 2008). Therefore, security scholars argue that the definition of political security is freedom from fear where people should be able to live in a society that honours their basic human rights, follows the rule of law and protects political rights. In fact, sources of political threat and insecurity are the state and security agencies. In order to counter the threat of political repression, people require that their rights be respected and they require protection from military dictatorship or abuse, political or state repression, the practice of torture, ill treatment or disappearance and from political detention and imprisonment (ibid).

If citizens are to be protected from political suppression, fundamental human rights need be respected by the state because human rights recognise the dignity inherent in every person as a human being and at the most basic level seek to protect an individual's right to life. Human security scholars argue that human security should be built upon and strengthened through human rights and political freedoms, which are fundamental components of human security and human dignity. Along with authoritarian regimes, political suppression of the people and human rights violations by the state, poverty, unemployment, discriminatory laws and social practices, as well as a lack of opportunity and justice, are the principle sources of conflict, human rights violation and political insecurity (Tadjbackhsh and Chenoy 2008).

Political security is a highest priority in human security and most states and governments (primarily democratic states and governments) have followed the principles of political security. But political suppression, human rights violation, systematic torture, ill treatment and disappearance are still serious challenges across the world, so protecting people against state repression and human rights violation remains a fundamental issue. Mostly governments repress people brutally during civil war, political revolution, people's revolt and conflict, often on the pretext of ensuring peace and the security of the people and property. These attempts to remain in power undermine the fundamental principles of political security, democratic principles, human rights and the rule of law.

9.2 Differences among political security, community security and personal security

It might be considered that political security, community security and personal security are similar, but according to the definition as defined by the UN report 1994 on human security, they entail significantly different meanings. Personal security aims to protect people from physical violence, whether it is from the state, non-state actors, criminal and violent groups or individuals. In fact, the greatest source of anxiety and fear for a citizen is violent crime and conflict, meaning that any citizen of any country wants to be secure from physical harm and crime. These threats encompass threats from the state through physical torture, threats from other states (wars), from international or cross-border terrorism, from other groups (ethnic or religious conflicts), from individuals or gangs (street violence), domestic violence against children (abuse, prostitution, labour) and even violence against oneself (suicide or drug abuse). Hence, the political dimension of human security is generally associated with 'freedom from fear' and best measured through proxy indicators and qualitative perception studies (UNDP 1994; Tadjbackhsh and Chenoy 2008).

Community security refers to the security of communities from violent conflict. This idea implies a rather wider definition than individual security and it emphasises a particular conflict. It aims to protect people from the loss of traditional relationships and values and from sectarian and ethnic violence. The political, social and economic rights of traditional communities, in particular, minority ethnic groups, are often threatened by ruling and dominant communities. Community security, in which the integrity of cultural diversity is threatened, requires security from oppressive traditional practices, treating women harshly, discrimination against ethnic or indigenous groups and refugees, group rebellion and armed conflicts. The UNDP's 1994 definition of 'community security' could also be included in this category, which designates both the security of the community as regards its identity and practices and the security of the individual against possible threats from the community such as discriminatory practices (UNDP 1994). According to the UN report 1994, about half of the world's states have experienced some level of inter- ethnic strife. The UN declared 1993 the Year of Indigenous People to highlight the continuing vulnerability of the 300 million aboriginal people in 70 countries, as they face a widening spiral of violence (ibid).

9.3 The interrelationship of political security, conflict and human rights

Political security, conflict and human rights are not only closely interrelated, but they are also inseparable in many respects. In fact, political insecurity, conflict and human rights violations are by-products of each other. Countries, societies and communities which are violence- and conflict-ridden might be a result of human rights violations and political suppression by the state; likewise, human rights are often violated and people's rights suppressed as a result of war, conflict or revolt. Therefore, political insecurity is an immediate result of war, violence, conflict, political suppression and human rights violation.

Conflict-ridden, conflict-affected, under-developed, developing and post- conflict countries have a vicious circle of war, violence, conflict, political insecurity and suppression, human rights violations, lack of justice and security and political instability. And all of these events have a chain effect in society. Therefore, to ensure political security, all kinds of violence should be ended and the government and security agencies should follow the rule of law, respect the fundamental principles of human rights and not suppress political opponents on any pretext. The Universal Declaration of Human Rights states that each person has the right to live a life without fear and human rights defenders, at the most basic level, seek to protect an individual's right to life.

Therefore, governments must respect the fundamental principles of human rights by protecting the right to live a dignified life.

Conflict and violence have negative and long-lasting effects on human rights and human security. After a conflict ends, on average a society takes more than 10 years to return to the level of human rights observance before the conflict (WB 2011). It is necessary that democratic polity, systems and governments respect the fundamental values of the rule of law, human rights and the political freedom of the people to ensure the political security of all citizens.

9.4 The global context of armed conflict and political insecurity

The twentieth century was dominated by the legacy of devastating world wars, independence movements, colonial strugglesand ideological conflicts so that those wars and conflicts seriously undermined the fundamental principle of people's political security and the peace and harmony of society. But following the end of the Cold War, there have been significant positive developments in terms of political security and global peace and security, in large part because most of the former colonial countries became independent and have since adopted democratic systems. As a result, the numbers of inter-state and civil wars have decreased and intra- state and ethnic conflicts have increased significantly. Comparing the data of wars and conflicts from 1900 to 2008, the declining numbers are really significant and positive which is a welcome development for global peace and political security of the people. Since 1991-92, when there were 21 active major civil wars; since 2002, the number has steadily fallen to less than 10 per year. Major civil conflicts (those with more than 1,000 battle deaths per year) increased during the post-colonial and Cold War era, peaking in the late 1980s and early 1990s (WB 2011). The following figure indicates the trend of wars and conflicts:

Figure 9.1 Civil wars peaked in the early 1990s and then declined

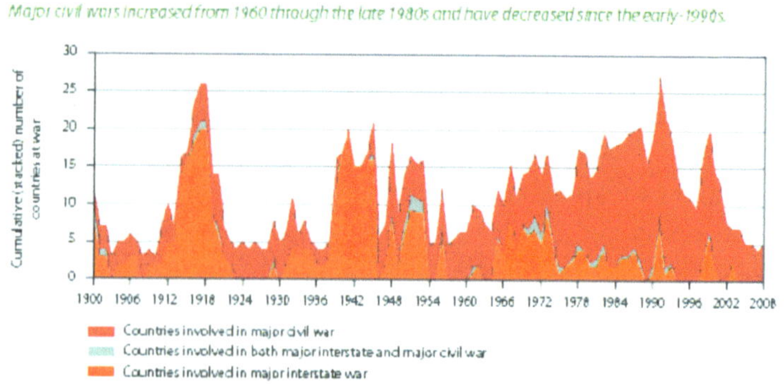

Source: Uppsala/Prio Armed Conflict Harbom and Wallensteen 2010; Lacina and Gleditsch 2005 as cited in WB (2011)

The number of conflicts has decreased in the twenty-first century; however, as a result of the Arab Uprising, the number of extra-judicial killings, human rights violations, political suppressions, abductions and extortions is on the rise in 2011 and 2012. Therefore, political security is and will remain a serious global issue in the years to come. The international community has been strongly raising the issues of political suppression and has been appealing to the respective countries' governments to respect the fundamental principles of people's rights and political freedoms.[1] In addition, new threats have emerged in the twenty-first century including terrorism, ethnic conflict, identity politics, organised crime, human and drugs trafficking and civil unrest (WB 2011).

Although the number of wars and casualties has decreased since 2000, the dynamics of war, conflict and violence have become much more complex, unpredictable and dangerous. Therefore, one of the challenges of the twenty-first century is to maintain social, cultural and religious harmony and establish sustainable peace by addressing the multi-dimensional issues of intra-state and ethnic conflict. Even security experts and policy makers of

[1] Escape from Syria'. 2012. Time. 19 March.

the global super power, the United States (US), have defined the emerging trends conflict and security of the twenty-first century as complex and unpredictable:

> *The international strategic landscape of the twenty-first century is shaped by complex and contradictory forces. The world is characterised by turmoil and changing patterns of state-to-state relationships as well as conflicts within states caused by ethnic, religious and nationalistic differences have become commonplace. The integration of national interest into meaningful national security policy has become more difficult. In this new environment, US national security policy and priorities have become complicated, often ambiguous and even inconsistent, not because of the immediate threat of a major conventional war but rather the unpredictable, uncertain and confusing characteristics of the international arena (Sarkesian et al. 2008 p.3).*

9.5 Political suppression and political insecurity in the Nepali context

Nepal's history since the 1940s is a history of political revolution and political suppression and the nature of the Nepali state and its agencies is suppressive and coercive so that the political security of the Nepali people is still a serious problem. The Nepali people and political parties have been fighting for democracy, their political rights and freedom, the rule of law and human rights since 1940 but governments have been suppressing those political movements, undermining the political security of the Nepali people.

The Nepali Congress (NC) and Communist Party of Nepal have been fighting for democracy and political security. They fought against the autocratic and despotic Rana regime and to establish democratic system in the 1940s. The Rana rulers tried to suppress the movement by arbitrarily and brutally killing and/or detaining a number of Nepali people and by mobilising the army to suppress the people's revolution. But they failed and democracy was established in 1950 as a result of the people's movement (Gautam 2009; Adhikari 2002).

In 1960, King Mahendra took power, imprisoned then Prime Minister B. P. Koirala, as well as the speaker of the House of Representatives, ministers and leaders of the NC and imposed the autocratic Panchayat[2] system. Subsequently, the NC announced a movement against the king's coup to reestablish democracy and the Nepali people's political rights and freedoms (Rose 1971). The movement was, however, brutally repressed by then Royal Nepalese Army (RNA)[3] and a significant number of leaders and cadres of the NC were killed or imprisoned during the movement. The NC again launched an armed struggle to topple the king and establish democracy in 1973 but once again, King Birendra mobilised the army. Consequently the army arbitrarily killed and imprisoned the leaders of the NC, challenging the fundamental principles of democracy and human rights (Adhikari 2002).

The Communist Party of Nepal [CPN] (Marxist and Leninist) launched a 'armed rebellion' to put an end to the Panchayat system and establish 'people's democracy' in 1971, but again the movement was brutally suppressed by the king by mobilising the security agencies (Mishra 2001; Fisher 1998). Political parties kept fighting against the despotic Panchayat regime and the rulers kept suppressing the movement during the 30 years of the regime. Therefore, it was a black period for political security, freedom and human rights. During the course of the political struggles, a number of leaders and cadres of political parties lost their lives. Therefore, fighting against the Rana and Panchayat regimes was the politics of sacrifice and ultimately and martyrdom, because the despotic regimes followed all sorts of political suppression disregarding the people's political security (Gautam 2009; Adhikari 2002; Fisher 1998; Rose 1971).

The NC and the CPN (Marxist and Leninist) launched a peaceful people's movement in 1990 to establish democracy, the rule of law and human rights, including political security. The king and Panchayati rulers tried to suppress the movement

---

2 An autocratic system imposed by King Mahendra.

3 The Government of Nepal has changed the name of the Royal Nepalese Army into the Nepal Army thereby amending the Military Act 1959 on 26, September 2006. The author has used the term – the Royal Nepalese Army (RNA) before September 2006 and thereafter the Nepal Army (NA).

by mobilising the security agencies, but could not suppress it. Democracy was established in 1990 as a result of the continuous struggle of the political parties and the Nepali people. Following the advent of democracy, the Nepali people became sovereign and independent and enjoyed their political freedom so that the government respected the universally accepted principles of human rights and political freedom.

When King Gyanendra took power on 1 February 2005 and imposed an authoritarian regime, thus suspending democratic principles and values, the rule of law and human rights, the political parties and the CPN (Maoist)[4] joined hands to establish democracy by overthrowing the king by signing the Twelve Point Agreement and fighting against the king. King Gyanendra mobilised the security agencies (the Nepal Police and the Armed Police Force) including the RNA to contain and suppress the peaceful people's movement of 2006. The security agencies tried to contain the movement by killing, torturing, arresting and beating the people. As a result of the suppression, 24 Nepali people were martyred and thousands of Nepalis were arrested and tortured. The international community strongly raised the issue of gross human rights violations and requested the government to respect the human rights and political security of the Nepali people. Ultimately, King Gyanendra agreed to hand over power to the Nepali people and democracy was established in 2006. Following this decision, the state adopted many security policies so that the Nepali people enjoyed political freedom and political security (Nisthuri 2007).

9.5.1 Political Insecurity during the maoist insurgency

Not only during the despotic Rana and Panchayat regimes, but also even after the establishment of multi-party democracy

---

4 The CPN (Maoist) and the Nepal Communist Party (Unity Centre) united in January 2009 and the name CPN (Maoist) was changed into the United Communist Party of Nepal (Maoist) [UCPN (Maoist)]. Two breakaway factions of the CPN (Maoist) kept its name CPN (Maoist), one led by Matrika Yadav and another led by Mohan Baidya (Kiran). The author has used the term 'CPN (Maoist)' before unification and the 'UCPN (Maoist)' after the unification.

in 1990 and the promulgation of a democratic constitution, the legacy of political conflict and suppression still existed as a residue of Nepali society. When the CPN (Maoist) declared the 'People's War' on 13 February 1996 to establish a 'people's democracy' by putting an end to multi-party democracy and constitutional monarchy, political insecurity and state's suppression reached its peak. The CPN (Maoist) started an armed insurgency from the Hill districts (Gorkha, Rolpa, Rukum, Salyan, Sindhuli, Jajarkot, etc.) by attacking local police posts and cadres of opposition political parties (in particular, the NC and the Communist Party of Nepal Unified Marxist Leninist (CPN UML). In the aftermath of the Maoist's armed attacks on security agency personnel and other people, the government decided to mobilise the Nepal Police (NP) to control the armed, illegal and unconstitutional activities of the CPN (Maoist) (Kandel 2011). The NP initiated 'Romeo' and 'Kilo-Sera Two' operations in those districts to control the Maoists' activities by following aggressive and coercive strategies by mobilising excessive forces. Yet despite the NP's aggressive and coercive strategy undermining the fundamental principles of political security and human rights enshrined in the Constitution, the government could not control the CPN Maoist's armed activities. Instead, the local people heavily criticised the extra-judicial killings, arbitrarily arrests, torture and human rights violations by the government (ibid).

The CPN (Maoist) also followed counter-military strategies to restrain the government's operations and they also undermined the people's political rights and freedoms. Their retaliation tactics included the issuance of death warrants and the killing of a number of innocent people accused of spying against the people's war. The CPN (Maoist) also followed the much-debated 'annihilate strategy' against their political opponents (Dixit 2011). Because of the aggressive military strategy and counter-strategy of both sides, 81 people including security personnel were killed in 1996. Out of this figure, 59 people were killed by the state and 22 were killed by the CPN (Maoist) (INSEC 1997).

When the Maoist insurgency posed serious challenges, the government wanted to mobilise the army against them (Shrestha 2004); however, it was believed that King Birendra did not give consent to mobilise the RNA so the government established the Armed Police Force (APF) on 24 October 2001 as a paramilitary force (Bhattarai and Wagle 2010). The government mobilised the APF but it could not control the armed activities. Two days after the CPN (Maoist) attacked and overran an army barracks in Dang district on 24 November 2001, the government declared a state of emergency against the CPN (Maoist) on 26 November 2001, declaring them 'terrorists' (Kandel 2010).

When the government declared the state of emergency and mobilised the RNA, the conflict became increasingly violent, with the irreversible loss of ever more casualties. Extra-judicial killings, arrests, torture, disappearances and human rights violations were regular activities of both the security agencies and the CPN (Maoist) cadres during the emergency, with the numbers of abuses reaching a peak between 2002 and 2004. A total of 13,347 Nepali people lost their lives during the insurgency (13 February 1996 to 21 November 2006) (INSEC 2008). According to INSEC, 8,393 Nepali people were killed by the state and 4,954 Nepali people, including security personnel, were killed by the CPN (Maoist). In addition, there was a huge loss of public property and infrastructure. The following table divulges the numbers of human casualties, forced disappearance, displaced families, abductions and other abuses.

Table 9.1 The number of deceased, disappeared, displaced and abducted persons from 13 February 1996 due to the armed conflict (Numbers as of July, 2011)

S.N.	Title	Number
1.	Deceased persons	17,828
2.	Disappeared persons	1,452
3.	Displaced families	22,863 (89,171 persons)
4.	Abductions	2,985
5.	Widows	9,000
6.	Injured	1,737
7.	Orphans	242
8.	Individual property damaged	14,438
9.	Disabled	5,912
10.	Imprisoned and judicial custody	1,415

Source: The Ministry of Peace and Reconstruction

The reason for the high intensity of armed conflict was the breakdown of the ceasefire, the termination of the peace talks of 2001 and 2003 and the declaration of the state of the emergency which resulted in heavy fighting between state security agencies and the CPN (Maoist) fighters. Not only extra-judicial killings, arrests, torture and human rights violations high at this time compared to other periods, forced disappearances too were common. A total of 1,452 Nepali people disappeared in a decade, most of them during the state of the emergency (INSEC 2007). Consequently, Nepal was ranked as first in the year 2003 in the world for disappearances so that national and international human rights institutions including the UN and Amnesty International strongly raised issues of extra-judicial killings, arrests, torture, forced disappearances and gross human rights violations in international forums and appealed to the government and the rebels to respect the fundamental principles of human rights and international humanitarian laws including the Geneva Convention (Dixit 2011).

9.5.2 Political insecurity during the madhes movement

Following the success of popular people's movement 2006, the CPN (Maoist) joined the political mainstream by renouncing violence and establishing the Democratic Republic. It was believed that the state would be a more politically secure and became human and people's rights- friendly country. But even following this transition, the legacy of political revolt and violence by the political parties, groups and communities and political suppression by the state has remained a crucial problem which continues to pose a serious threat to human security.

When the government promulgated the Interim Constitution on 15 January 2007, the Madheshi People's Rights Forum (MPRF) burned the document the very next day, demanding Nepal should be a federal state. The MPRF also called a Madhesh Bandh from 17 January against the Constitution which developed into religious and communal violence. Therefore, the government followed a coercive security policy and mobilised excessive security forces, undermining the political security of the people. As a result, a Madhesh movement activist, Ramesh Mahato of

Siraha district, was killed on 20 January 2007 by Maoist cadres and the movement took a devastating turn. There were clashes between the CPN (Maoist) cadres and Madheshi activists. Whereas the Madhesh movement had originally called for federalism, it turned towards political and communal violence (in particular the Madheshi activists against the CPN (Maoist) and the Madheshi people against the Pahade[5] people) (Wagle 2011).

As a result, 27 Nepali people (some Madheshi activists and the rest CPN [Maoist] cadres) were killed in the violence in Gaur of Rautahat district on 21 March 2007. Following the Gaur incident, violence spread across the Tarai. There were gross violations of human rights. Because of the communal violence and security problem, hundreds of thousands of Pahade-origin Tarai people left the Tarai and went to Pahad. A total of 51 Madheshi people lost their lives during the Madhesh movement (Wagle 2011, p 177). The Madhesh movement broke the centuries-old social, religious and cultural harmony of the Nepali society which had immediate and will have longer-term negative impacts in Nepali society.

9.6 Nepal's peace building process as a means of ensuring political security

The People's Movement of 2006 heralded significant political change in the history of Nepal and laid the strong foundation for Nepal's democratic transformation, restructuring the state and providing space for conflict resolution, political security and sustainable peace. Yet the historic movement of 2006 not only established the Federal Democratic Republic by putting an end to the 238-year old monarchy, but also ended the decade-long armed conflict by bringing the rebellious CPN (Maoist) into the political mainstream through a peaceful dialogue process (Kandel 2011). Nepal's peace process formally started when the government and the CPN (Maoist) signed the Comprehensive Peace Agreement (CPA) on 21 November 2006, but the peace process had informally already begun following the signing of the

---

[5] Hill Origin People

Twelve-Point Agreement between the then Seven Party Alliance (SPA) and the CPN (Maoist) on 22 November 2005 and the success of the People's Movement in 2006. In fact, the Twelve-Point Agreement between the SPA and the CPN (Maoist) had established strong landmark foundations for political parties to fight for democracy and peace whereby the parties had agreed to fight jointly against King Gyanendra's unconstitutional and autocratic move of 1 February 2005 (Gautam and Manandhar 2008).

Following the signing of the CPA, the government and the CPN (Maoist) agreed to manage the Maoist Army Combatants and their arms and signed another agreement -the Agreement on Monitoring of the Management of Arms and Armies (AMMAA) on 8 December 2006. Under the provision of the CPA, the CPN (Maoist) agreed to renounce violence, follow the rule of law, honour universal human rights principles and democratic norms and values (Martin 2010). Furthermore, the CPN (Maoist) agreed to put their combatants into 28 different cantonments and store weapons in containers under the supervision of the United Nations Mission in Nepal (UNMIN). UNMIN began the task of verifying the arms and armies on 15 June 2007 and completed it on 27 December 2007 (ibid).

As per the provision of the Article 145 of the Interim Constitution, on 28 October 2008 a Special Committee (SC) for the Supervision, Integration and Rehabilitation of the Maoist Army Combatants was formed under the leadership of then Prime Minister Pushpa Kamal Dahal 'Prachanda' to expedite the integration and rehabilitation process. In addition, a Technical Committee (TC) was formed on 16 April 2009 to advise and support the SC to carry out its mandate. However, the Dahal-led government could not achieve any significant progress on peace process. The government led by Madhav Kumar Nepal started the process of discharging the disqualified combatants on 7 January 2010, a process which ended on 8 February 2010[6] The UCPN (Maoist) formally handed over the cantonments

6 Seven-Point Agreement and challenges for its implementation. 2011a. Policy Paper of the Nepal Institute for Policy Studies 6. November.

and the combatants to the SC for Supervision, Integration and Supervision on 22 January 2011 at Shaktikhor of Chitwan District. The following Table illustrates some important efforts which have taken place in the course of the peace and the constitution writing process (NIPS 2011a).

Table 9.2 Agreements among major political parties and important decisions of the Government of Nepal and Parliament

S.N	Agreements	Date signed	Signatories parties/ remarks
1	Twelve-Point Agreement	22 November 2005 (7 Mangsir 2062)	The Seven Party Alliance (SPA) and the CPN (Maoist)
2	Restoration of Parliament through the Royal proclamation	24 April 2006 (11 Baisakh 2063)	King Gyanendra
3	Proclamation of the House of Representatives	28 May 2006 (14 Jestha 2063)	Endorsed by the House of Representatives
4	Ceasefire Code of Conduct	26 May 2006 (12 Jestha 2063)	Krishna Prasad Sitaula on behalf of the Government of Nepal and Krishna Bahadur Mahara on behalf of the CPN (Maoist)
5	Interim Legislature-Parliament including the CPN (Maoist)	15 January 2007 (1 Magh 2063)	The Government of Nepal, the CPN (Maoist) and political partics
6	Interim Government including the CPN (Maoist)	1 April 2007 (18 Chaitra 2063)	-
7	Joint Letter to the United Nations	9 August 2006 (24 Shrawan 2063)	The Government of Nepal and the CPN (Maoist)
8	Comprehensive Peace Accord (CPA)	21 November 2006 (5 Mangsir 2063)	Prime Minister Girija Prasad Koirala on behalf of the Government of Nepal and CPN (Maoist) Chairman Pushpa Kamal Dahal 'Prachanda'
9	Agreement on Monitoring of the Management of Arms and Armies (AAMMA)	8 December 2006 (22 Mangsir 2063)	Krishna Prasad Sitaula on behalf of the Government of Nepal and Krishna Bahadur Mahara on behalf of the CPN (Maoist), witnessed by the UN Representative Ian Martin

S.N	Agreements	Date signed	Signatories parties/ remarks
10	Promulgation of the Interim Constitution 2007	15 January 2007 (1 Magh 2063)	The Interim Government
11	Arrival of UNMIN	23 January 2007 (9 Magh 2063)	The Government of Nepal and the CPN (Maoist)
12	Start of the verification process of the Maoist Army Combatants	15 June 2007 (1 Ashad 2064)	UNMIN carried out the verification process
13	Completion of the verification process of the Maoist Army Combatants	27 December 2007 (12 Poush 2064)	UNMIN completed the verification process
14	Constituent Assembly elections	10 April 2008 (28 Chaitra 2064)	The Government of Nepal
15	Formation of the Special Committee (SC)	28 October 2008 (12 Kartik 2065)	The Government of Nepal
16	Agreement to discharge disqualified combatants	16 December 2009 (1 Poush 2066)	The Government of Nepal and the UCPN (Maoist)
17	Start of the discharge process	7 January 2010 (23 Poush 2066)	The Ministry of Peace and Reconstruction and the United Nations Development programme jointly carried out the discharge process
18	Completion of the discharge process	8 February 2010 (25 Magh 2066)	Completion of the discharge process
19	The UCPN (Maoist) formally handed over the cantonments and the Maoist Army Combatants to the SC for Supervision, Integration and rehabilitation	22 January, 2011 (8 Magh 2067)	The Government of Nepal and the UCPN (Maoist)
20	Seven-Point Agreement	1 November 2011 (15 Kartik 2068)	UCPN (Maoist) Chairman Pushpa Kamal Dahal 'Prachanda', NC President SushilKoirala, CPN (UML) Chairman JhalaNathKhanaland on behalf of Joint Madhesi Democratic Front, Bijaya Kumar Gachchhadar

Source: Compiled by the author from various sources

Despite the divergent opinions among political parties on the integration and rehabilitation process, a historic Seven-

Point Agreement was signed among the major political parties on 1 November 2011. As per the Seven- Point Agreement, the Secretariat of the SC conducted the regrouping of the Maoist Army Combatants from 18 November to 30 November 2012. A detailed study of the Maoist Army Combatants opting for integration, voluntary retirement and rehabilitation is provided below. The table below also gives brief information of the Maoist Army Combatants and their weapons during the verification process and shows the disqualified combatants in number.

Table 9.3 Facts and figures regarding the maoist army combatants' registration, verification, regrouping process and number of arms

Registration and verification process	
Total number of registered Maoist Army combatants	32,250
Total number of combatants verified by UNMIN	19,602
Verified male combatants	15,756 (80.37%)
Verified female combatants	3,846 (19.63%)
Total number of weapons registered and stored in the containers	3,475
Absentees, automatically considered as disqualified combatants, during the verification process	8,640
Disqualified combatants	
Under the age of 18 as of 25 May 2006 (considered minors)	2,973
Late recruits	1,035
Total disqualified (minors + late recruits)	4,008
Outcome of the Regrouping process	
Total number of Maoist Army Combatants	19,602
Total number of combatants opting for integration	9,705
Total number of combatants opting for voluntary retirement	7,365
Total number of combatants opting for rehabilitation	6
Dead, suspended and deserters	94
Total	**17,170**
Number of combatants absent in the regrouping process	**2,432**

Source: Compiled by the author from various sources

Following the signing of the CPA and when the CPN (Maoist) joined the political mainstream, the decade-long war formally came to an end and much-needed peace prevailed. The number of human casualties declined and the government stopped arresting and torturing the people, ensuring the political security of the people. The Maoist Army Combatants were confined within the cantonments and their weapons were stored in containers under the supervision of UNMIN. The CPN (Maoist), by and large, abided by the CPA despite some incidents. Hence, the security situation today is improved compared to the conflict period (1996 to 2006). The Nepali people have started to enjoy their political rights and freedoms regardless of their political affiliation, caste, ethnicity, language, gender or religion.

Despite the achievements after the CPA, Nepal's security situation has not improved satisfactorily because of the legacy of the decade-long conflict and deep-rooted culture of political insecurity. In particular, the unlawful and anarchic activities of the CPN (Maoist) and activities of illegal armed outfits have created serious problems for peace and security across the nation. The UCPN (Maoist) established the Young Communist League (YCL) right after the CPA, inducting their military commanders and tried to develop it as a parallel law enforcement agency. The YCL tried to take the law into its own hands with the result that it has created serious chaos, anarchy, terror, human rights violations and political insecurity. Likewise, the indefinite general strike called on 1 May 2010 by the UCPN (Maoist) to topple down the Madhav Kumar Nepal government created serious political insecurity, terror, instability, chaos and a potential political conflict among political parties. The Maoist leadership even called upon the Maoist Army Combatants confined within the cantonments to take to the street. But ultimately the UCPN (Maoist) withdrew the general strike and the nation was spared hazardous political conflict.

9.7 The state of political insecurity and impunity after the CPA

Following the signing of the CPA, the decade-long armed conflict came to an end, but the security situation remains critical and volatile. The media still report incidents of extra-judicial killings, arrest, torture, human rights violations, kidnapping, extortion and threats by the state, the CPN (Maoist) and other armed and illegal outfits across the country (NIPS 2011b). Law enforcement agencies cannot perform their duties and responsibilities effectively to ensure peace and security and the rule of law is not prevailing. The Tarai is more vulnerable than the Hill and Mountain regions because of the activities of armed and illegal outfits across the border (ibid).

According to the reports of INSEC, a Nepali human rights organisation, a total of 4,481 people have been killed by the state, the CPN (Maoist) or other groups since the signing of the CPA in 2006: 926 in 2006, 551 in 2007, 541 in 2008, 473 in 2009, 459 in 2010 and 377 in 2011. The number of killings is decreasing but threats remain. Seven journalists have been killed and more than 1000 incidents have been recorded by the Federation of Nepalese Journalists since the signing of the CPA.[7] According to the report, in 2011, 12 people were killed by the state whereas 89 people were killed by unidentified armed groups and 59 were abducted. The year before, 117 people were killed by unidentified armed groups and 83 people were abducted. Furthermore, human rights defenders have been killed, abducted, beaten, given death threats and their properties captured (INSEC 2012). The following Table reveals the grave situation of extra-judicial killings, arrest, torture, human rights violations, kidnapping, extortion and threatening.

Table 9.4 Killings and human rights violations after the signing of the CPA

S.N.	Type of violation	2006	2007	2008	2009	2010	2011	Total
1	Killing	926	551	541	473	459	377	3327
2	Injuries	2833	835	1017	701	424	272	6082
3	Arrest and Torture	3160	429	294	215	135	94	4327
4	Beatings	1676	1494	1623	1327	843	457	7420
5	Threats	1659	681	767	636	548	112	4403
6	Right to Assembly	13033	1215	2494	553	256	387	17938
7	Racial Discrimination	189	273	671	217	69	72	1491
8	Women Rights	314	427	472	664	618	648	3143
9	Child Rights	347	4451	707	1219	525	413	7662
10	Economic, Social and Cultural Rights	265	429	182	200	141	33	1250
11	Inhuman Behaviour	118	84	33	68	37	19	359
12	Abduction	22978	1007	729	281	185	144	25324
13	Death in Jail	-	-	-	2	-	9	11
14	Death in Detention	1	4	-	1	-	2	8

Source: INSEC (2007, 2008, 2009, 2010, 2011, 2012).

[7] Interview with Jagat Nepal, Secretary of the Federation of Nepalese Journalists in June 2012.

Following the CPA, the Maoist Army Combatants demobilised in 28 different cantonments and disarmed as they stored their weapons in containers under the supervision of UNMIN. Those combatants are now undergoing the process of integration, rehabilitation and voluntary retirement. Nepal did not follow the fundamental principles of the internationally acclaimed and established best practices of conflict resolution and peace building process, in particular, integration and rehabilitation processes. Therefore, Nepal's fragile and elusive peace process has taken more than five years

-and it has not been completed yet. Even after the end of the decade- long armed conflict, the legacy of violence and crime are inherent in Nepali society. Unfortunately, it seems that violence and criminality have become integral part to society and that the conflict has destroyed the values and cultures of social harmony. In fact, the culture of violence is deeply rooted within society.

Ensuring justice to conflict victims and punishment to perpetrators is a key challenge to the state in a post-conflict context. After the signing of the CPA, impunity has been pervasive in Nepal. Some of the major problems are the lack of transitional justice and the culture of pervasive impunity. The government and political parties should have promoted the culture of the rule of law and strengthened public security to ensure peace and security. The government should have already formed and activated the much-needed commissions as envisioned by the Interim Constitution and the CPA - the Truth and Reconciliation Commission (TRC) and the Commission to Investigate Forced Disappearances (CIFD) - to provide justice to the victims and bring perpetrators before the law.

Despite the Supreme Court directives and the National Human Rights Commission (NHRC) recommendations, the government has not yet constituted the commissions. The people accused of being involved in serious human rights violations have not been punished and the orders of the Supreme Court have not been honoured by bringing the culprits to justice. Political parties, the NHRC and national human rights institutions have been drawing attention to human rights violations, transitional justice and impunity issues, but none of the governments have listened to them and taken a decision towards addressing the issue. Therefore, the successive governments were not accountable and answerable to the people and were not followed the rule of law and internationally acclaimed democratic and transparent practices.

Taking serious note of Nepal's human rights situation and pervasive impunity, the United Nations High Commissioner for Human Rights, Navi Pillay presented a report to the 19th session of the UN Human Rights Council in Geneva on 21 March 2012. She warned that Nepal would be placed on the list of countries breaching international treaty obligations if Nepal opts for amnesty for conflict-era crimes. The report further pointed out that obstacles remain in ensuring a human rights framework: 'Lack of accountability for human rights violations, whether perpetrated during the conflict or after, remains entrenched. During the year, there were moves to withdraw cases from courts and efforts to provide amnesties and pardons, including within the framework of future transitional justice mechanisms'.[8]

Instead of taking a sincere step towards giving justice to victims and punishment to perpetrators, the government has itself promoted the culture of impunity time and again by making controversial decisions. The Babu Ram Bhattarai-led government made a controversial decision on 1 November 2011 to recommend Bal Krishna Dhungel, a Maoist CA member, for presidential pardon, arguing that the murder is alleged to have committed was a 'political' case related to the conflict era, which could be forgiven as per the provision of the CPA[9] The District Court, Okhaldhunga, had on 10 May 2004 condemned Dhungel to life imprisonment and ordered the confiscation of his property, terming him a 'murderer' of Ujjan Kumar Shrestha of Okhaldhunga. The Supreme Court upheld the district court's

[8] For detail see, The Kathmandu Post .UN report decries deal on amnesty. 22 March 2011.

[9] For detail see Weekly Newspaper. Nepali Times. The lords of impunity. 11 November. 2011.

verdict on 3 January 2010.[10] Likewise, on 4 September 2011, PM Bhattarai appointed UCPN (Maoist) Polit Bureau member Prabhu Sah to the post of Minister, despite his alleged involvement in the murder of Birgunj-based Bishwa Hindu Yuva Sangh leader Kashi Tiwari in 2010.[11]

Likewise, UCPN (Maoist) Polit Bureau member Agni Sapkota was appointed Information and Communication Minister on 4 May 2011 despite charges relating to his involvement in the abduction and murder of Arjun Lama in Kavre district in 2005. The national and international human rights communities had urged not to appoint any individual accused of human rights violations[12] Even the Office of the High Commissioner for Human Rights, Nepal (OHCHR-N) expressed concern over the appointment of Sapkota. The OHCHR-N issued a statement, mentioning that "this decision contradicts Nepal's commitments, as expressed during the Universal Periodic Review process, towards accountability for serious human rights violations and abuses committed during the conflict and reinforces the culture of impunity in Nepal"[13]

To put an end to pervasive impunity and ensure justice to victims, Nepal should ratify the Rome Statute of the International Criminal Court. The country has not ratified this Statute because of the double standards of political parties and successive governments from 2006. Had Nepal signed the ICC, perpetrators would have been punished. The International Criminal Court was adopted by the UN in July 1998 and entered into force in July 2002. As of October 2010, 114 countries had ratified the Statute. The ICC, like many of its predecessor tribunals, seeks to prosecute individuals rather than states (Beswick and Jackson 2012). Thus, the ICC is designed to respect state sovereignty in situations where states are willing to act responsibly to

---

[10] ibid.

[11] For detail see Weekly Newspaper. Nepali Times. Impunity from impunity. 14 October. 2011

[12] For detail see National daily. The Republica. OCHR-N concerned over Sapkota's appointment. 5 May. 2011

[13] Ibid.

fulfill their obligations to international justice. States that are party to the Statute and accept the standing of the Court can refer cases to the ICC for investigation, as can the UN Security Council (ibid).

9.8 The interrelationship between political security and Nepal's security policy

Political security and national security policy are not only closely interrelated, but are in many respects also inseparable. In fact, policies are the foundation and backbone for intended results and act as guidelines for governments and security agencies. In this way, national security policy is the foundation and guideline for political security. The government and security agencies alone cannot achieve the intended result in the absence of appropriate and relevant national security policy. But unfortunately, Nepal does not have a written comprehensive national security policy.

Had Nepal had a well-defined appropriate national security policy to deal with internal and external security threats, there might not have been so much loss of life and property during the movements and conflicts in the past. Nonetheless, the successive governments and political parties have not paid due attention to drafting a national security policy in the past even after the establishment of the Federal Democratic Republic in 2006. Instead, successive governments have still been following ad hoc and traditional security approaches to deal with security policies, with the result that they have failed to promote the much-needed democratic culture of political security, sustainable peace, the rule of law and human rights.

In fact, in the absence of a comprehensive written national security policy, successive governments have been misusing the security agencies for their own political interests and convenience and to protect their regime and retain power. Had the government drafted a people-centric and human rights-friendly security policy clearly defining the roles and responsibilities of the security agencies and then there would have been fewer chances to misuse the security agencies in the past. Given the political and security context of Nepal, it is pertinent to draft a national security policy addressing a wide range of security issues as soon as possible to ensure the political security of the Nepali people in line with human security.

Probably having realised this fact, the political parties have been raising the issues prominently following the declaration of the Federal Democratic Republic in 2006. The CA members have also strongly raised these issues in the CA and Legislature-parliament and have demanded to draft a new national security policy addressing internal and external security challenges. In particular, the CA members have comprehensively discussed national security policy in the National Interest Preservation Committee and the Committee on State Restructuring and Distribution of State Power and they have suggested the government to draft a national security policy following consultation with concerned stakeholders. The National Interest Preservation Committee drafted its preliminary report on national security policy in line with human security and submitted it to the CA. Even the Nepal Army (NA) drafted a report on national security and submitted to the National Interest Preservation Committee in 2008. The NA had also suggested redefining Nepal's national security policy in line with human security (Bhattarai and Wagle 2010).

Given the sensitivity of security and the urgency of the issues, the government led by Madhav Kumar Nepal constituted a five-member Cabinet Committee under the leadership of then Defence Minister Bidhya Devi Bhandari on 24 December 2009 to draft policy papers on national security policy, democratisation of the army and strengthening and reforming law enforcement agencies under the Ministry of Home Affairs (MoHA)[14] The Committee drafted and submitted its reports to Prime Minister Nepal on 2 August 2010, demonstrating that the government and political parties realised for the first time that Nepal should

---

14 The government constituted a five-member committee led by then Defence Minister Bidhya Devi Bhandari. Its members were then Home Minister Bhim Rawal, Culture Minister Dr. Minendra Rijal, Law Minister Prem Bahadur Singh and Minister without portfolio Laxman Lal Karna.

have a comprehensively written national security policy to ensure peace and security, which is a welcome and positive step. However, the Committee did not consult with concerned stakeholders during the drafting process and these documents have not been brought into the public domain. These documents are still under the consideration of the Cabinet as confidential documents (NIPS 2011b). And none of the successive governments have taken any initiatives to finalise and implement the documents.

The policy drafting process should be inclusive because security is not an exclusive domain of the government; thus, the government should consult with concerned stakeholders during the drafting and finalisation processes. In fact, security is the prime concern of the people because according to the definition of human security the people are the referent point of security. Therefore, the government should consult with political parties, security agencies, members of Parliament, parliamentary committees, security experts, civil society, human rights activists and the media, incorporate their feedback, then finalise the documents.

If a government drafts a security policy in isolation without consulting concerned stakeholders, that policy will not be people-centric and rights- friendly. The policy might even be a weapon to suppress the people. Therefore, the government should consult with concerned stakeholders and finalise the policies as soon as possible in order to ensure the people's political security. The policy should be people-centric and rights-friendly, recognising the people as the referent point of security and embracing the seven fundamental aspects of human security i.e. economic security, health security, food security, environmental security, personal security, community security and political security.

9.9 The role of the government and security agencies in ensuring political security

The government and security agencies are responsible for ensuring peace and political security. The government drafts the policies, rules and regulations, the Parliament adopts them and the security agencies implement them.

According to the existing rules and regulations of the government, the security agencies, in particular, the NA, the NP, the APF and the National Intelligence Department (NID), are responsible for maintaining the peace and security of the nation and the people. The NA is responsible for national security, including national unity, territorial integrity and people's sovereignty. Likewise, the NP is a law enforcement agency responsible for public security. The APF is a paramilitary force that looks after border security and armed conflict. The NID is responsible for information collection and analysis with regards to national security and public security.

Analysing the political history of Nepal and the facts and figures of the past, the army and the police have been suppressing the people through extra-judicial killings, violating human rights, the excessive use of force, arresting political opponents. These actions have seriously challenged the political security and political rights of the people during political movements, insurgencies and conflicts since the 1940s. When the APF was mobilised against the Maoist insurgency, it brutally repressed the people. Therefore, the UN, the NHRC and national and international human rights organisations have been raising the issue of human rights violations in international forums and they have been calling upon the Nepali governments to respect the people's political security of the people and basic principles of the rule of law and human rights. The Government of Nepal and security agencies should seriously take into account these concerns and should respect the basic principles of political security, the rule of law and human rights.

Security agencies must implement the decisions and directives appropriately, according to existing rules and regulations by not violating the basic tenets of political security, the rule of law and human rights. The security agencies should be professional, competent and effective to appropriately implement those policies, rules and regulations because professionally sound, effective and competent security agencies which are accountable to the people will best serve the nation's and people's interests. The security agencies should act upon the decision of the government of the day regardless of the ideology of the ruling party. Likewise, security agencies should be accountable to the government and should implement democratic principles and values and political and human rights friendly. The government should not misuse the security agencies to oppress political opponents and competitors under any pretext. Therefore, the government should properly enhance the professionalism of the security agencies and train them in human rights- friendly policies.

The government should clearly redefine the role of the NA, the NP, the APF and the NID for three reasons. Firstly, there is some level of duplication and overlap among the security agencies as per the existing practice. Secondly, the role of security agencies has changed and to some extent been diminished by the changed political and security context of the global and national arenas. Thirdly, the role and structure of security agencies should be restructured in line with the Federal Democratic Republic.

The government and security agencies are responsible for ensuring political security, but political parties are also equally responsible for this matter. It is quite relevant in the Nepali context because political parties themselves fight for democracy, human rights and political security. But when they reach in power; they themselves suppress the people on the pretext of peace and security of the people. Therefore, unless the political parties respect the fundamental principles of political security and follow the rule of law and human rights, it is impossible to ensure people's political security.

9.10 Conclusion

Given the fact that political security is the most important dimension of human security, the government should ensure the political security of the people by respecting their fundamental political rights, individual freedoms and liberty. We can draw the conclusion that political security is a basic right of every citizen according to the definition of human security and that ensuring political security and peace is the primary duty of any state. Therefore, the government and security agencies must embrace and follow the basic principles of human security to ensure political security. The state is the source of political insecurity and suppression, so the state should be responsible and accountable to the people by embracing democratic principles and values and following the principles of human security. The state must not suppress its people under any pretext and must respect the rule of law and follow human rights.

Following the peaceful resolution of the decade-long armed insurgency and the entry of the CPN (Maoist) into the political mainstream, the security situation is improving but it is not conducive for human security and sustainable peace. The Nepali people have breathed the fresh air of peace and harmony after the CPA but their political and human security is still under threat. The nature of the state is still; to some extent, repressive and the security agencies are coercive. Therefore, Nepal has witnessed a number of extra-judicial killings, political suppression, human rights violations, excessive use of force, extortion and intimidation even after the signing of the CPA. Taking into account these facts, the government and political parties should take significant steps and policy decisions to ensure political security. The government and political parties are yet to understand that political security is an integral part of a democratic polity and human security.

Nepal is passing through a historic transition from a unitary kingdom to a plural, democratic, multi-religious, multi-lingual, multi-ethnic, multi- cultural, republican, federal, secular, sovereign and modern nation- state, embracing the aspirations of the Nepali people. During this historic transformation process, there are many political, social, economic, security and cultural issues that need to be restructured in line with the changed political, security and social context. There are two reasons why Nepal's national security policy should be redefined in line with human security to ensure political security and sustainable peace. Firstly, there has been a fundamental policy shift in security studies; and secondly, a significant change in the political and security context of Nepal. Hence, the government should draft a new national security policy in line with human security and the changed political and security context of Nepal following comprehensive consultation with political parties, security agencies, civil society, security experts and media. The new policy should embrace the fundamental principles of democratic values, the rule of law and human rights by ensuring the political security of the people.

Nevertheless, political security cannot be ensured by merely drafting security policies because those policies need to be implemented in practice. As the government and security agencies are responsible for implementing these policies, the role of security agencies is vital and crucial. Security agencies, therefore, must embrace the fundamental concept of human security and follow the security policy of the government. Likewise, security agencies should be people-friendly, rights-friendly and must abide by the constitution, follow the rule of law and respect human rights. Security agencies should not suppress the people under any circumstance and the government should not use excessive force to contain the people.

The ever-growing culture of impunity and ineffective law enforcement agencies are major hindrances to political security and justice. The trend of human rights violations and crimes persists in Nepal, primarily because of the deep-rooted culture of impunity, which responsible political parties and the government continue to nurture. The residue and legacy of armed conflict should be brought to an end and the culture of reconciliation, cooperation and non-violence should develop among people, ensuring much-needed political security and sustainable peace.

References

Adhikari SM. 2002. *The History of the Nepali Congress*. Kathmandu: Bhudi Puran Prakashan.

Beswick D, Jackson P, editors. 2012. *Conflict, Security and Development*. London and New York: Routledge.

Bhattarai R, Wagle GS, editors. 2010. *Emerging Security Challenges of Nepal*. Kathmandu: Nepal Institute for Policy Studies.

Dixit KM. 2011. *Peace Politics of Nepal*. Kathmandu: Himal Books.

Fisher JF. 1998. *Living Martyrs: Individuals and Revolution in Nepal.* New Delhi: Oxford University Press.

Gautam B, Manandhar C, editors. 2008. *Peaceful Transformation of the Maoist Struggle.* Kathmandu: Martin Chautari.

Gautam R. 2009. *Nepal's Democratic Movement and the Nepali Congress, Krishna Kumari Adhikari and Shree Ram Shrestha.* Kathmandu.

INSEC [Informal Sector Service Centre]. 1997. *Criminalization in Nepalese Politics.* Kathmandu: Informal Sector Service Centre.

INSEC [Informal Sector Service Centre]. 2007. *New Roadmap and Challenges of Transition.* Kathmandu: Informal Sector Service Centre.

INSEC [Informal Sector Service Centre]. 2008. *Upheavals of Peace process.* Kathmandu: Informal Sector Service Centre.

INSEC [Informal Sector Service Centre]. 2009. *Challenges of Constitution Drafting process.* Kathmandu: Informal Sector Service Centre.

INSEC [Informal Sector Service Centre]. 2010. *Hurdles of peace process.* Kathmandu: Informal Sector Service Centre.

INSEC [Informal Sector Service Centre]. 2011. *Enmeshed Peace process.* Kathmandu: Informal Sector Service Centre.

INSEC [Informal Sector Service Centre]. 2012. *Power Obsession delays peace.*Kathmandu: Informal Sector Service Centre.

Kandel SK. 2011. *Maoist: Revolt Debate and Transformation.* Kathmandu: Pairabi Prakashan.

Martin I. 2010. *Nepal's Peace Process at the United Nations.* Kathmandu: Himal Books.

Mishra BC. 2001. *From Jhapa Movement to the Division of the CPN (UML).* Kathmandu: Sunaulo Bihani Abhiyan.

Mishra BP. 2009. *The Nepalese Peace Process.* Kathmandu: Fine Print.

NIPS [Nepal Institute for Policy Studies]. 2011a. *Seven-Point Agreement and challenges for its implementation.* Policy Paper. Kathmandu: Nepal Institute for Policy Studies.

NIPS [Nepal Institute for Policy Studies]. 2011b. *Emerging problems of public security and its solutions.* Policy Paper. Kathmandu: Nepal Institute for Policy Studies.

Nishthuri B. 2007. *19 Days: A Diary of the People's Movement 2006.* Kathmandu: Modern Books.

Rose LE. 1971. *Nepal Strategy for survival.* Bombay: Oxford University Press,

Sarkesian SC, Williams JA, Cimbala JS, editors. 2008. *US national security: policy makers, processes and politics.* New Delhi: Viva Books.

Shrestha CB. 2004. *Nepal Coping with Maoist Insurgency: Conflict Analysis and Resolution.* Kathmandu: Chetana Lokshum.

Tadjbackhsh S, Chenoy AM. 2008 (2nd edition). *Human Security Concepts and Implications*. London and New York: Routledge.

Thakur R. 2008 (4th edition). *The United Nations, Peace and Security*. Cambridge: Cambridge University Press.

UNDP [United Nations Development Program]. 1994. *Human Development Report*. New York: Oxford University Printing Press.

Wagle J. 2011. *Madhesh Movement: Achievement and Challenges 2011*.Kathmandu: Third Alliance.

WB [World Bank]. 2011. *Conflict, Security and Development*. Washington DC: World Bank.

****

About the authors

Adhikari, Damodar a governance expert, holds a doctoral degree in decentralised governance from the University of Dortmund, Germany. He received a joint Masters in Regional Development Planning and Management from the University of the Philippines and University of Dortmund. Dr Adhikari has more than 24 years of experience in designing, managing and implementing large plans and programmes and providing technical assistance to government agencies and international development organisations. His areas of technical expertise include analysis and design of public policy; health sector reform; local governance, decentralisation and federalism; institutional development; development planning and management; public-private partnerships; sector-wide approach (SWAp); and programme monitoring and evaluation. Currently, Dr Adhikari has been working as Senior Technical Advisor of Global Health in RTI-International and providing technical assistance in programme design and management, governance, health systems and policy reform in a number of countries in the Asia region. Dr Adhikari has published three books and eight journal articles on governance issues and health sector reform and has contributed to numerous conferences.

Bhattarai, Rajan is Chair of the Nepal Institute for Policy Studies (NIPS). He has completed his doctorate from the School of International Studies at the Jawaharlal Nehru University in New Delhi. He has a Masters in International Studies and General Diplomatic Practice from the School of Oriental and African Studies, University of London. Dr Bhattarai has co- edited two books - Changing Security Dynamics in Nepal and Emerging Security Challenges of Nepal - both published by NIPS. He is also an author of Geopolitics of Nepal and International Response of conflict Transformation. Number of his articles have been published in journals and magazines inside and outside the country. Dr Bhattarai served as a Foreign Policy Advisor to the Prime Minister of Nepal from May 2009 until February 2011. He has served as a co-general secretary of the Asian Students Association from 1993 to 1996 in Hong Kong. He also worked as a secretary of the International Department of the CPN (UML) one of the major political parties in Nepal. Dr Bhattarai is also a regular columinist on number of national dailies.

Bishokarma, Nirmal Kumar is a PhD Candidate at Kathmandu University, Nepal and Swiss National Centre of Competence in Research (NCCR) North-South. His research focuses on food security, resource scarcity and exclusion issues. Mr Bishokarma has 15 years experience working for the Nepal Livelihoods and Forestry Programme of the UK's Department of International Development, the United Mission to Nepal and German Development Cooperation (GTZ) supported project. He has published half a dozen English articles in peer-reviewed journals published in Nepal on the subject of the social and institutional aspects of food security, resource scarcity, political conflict and natural resource management.

Ghale, Yamuna holds MSc in Ecological Agriculture from Wageningen University, The Netherlands. She has gained over 20 years of professional experience in the field of agriculture and natural resource management, food security and trade, gender and social inclusion. Her long association with organisations like SNV-Nepal, ICIMOD, Action Aid International Nepal and Swiss Agency for Development Cooperation/Embassy of Switzerland has enriched her understanding, commitment and competence in the field of food and agriculture. Mrs Ghale has contributed in many international, regional, national and local level workshops, conferences as a panellist, moderator and special invitee. She has authored and co-authored several books, journals, newsletters and local newspapers in the field of her competence. She is associated with many national and international networks such as NEPAN, FIAN, WOCAN, WLCN, ASON, ACOS etc.

Ghimire, Anita is a post-doc fellow at the Swiss National Centre of Competence in Research (NCCR) North-South with a PhD from Kathmandu University. Her research interest is on migration, conflict, livelihood and sociological theories. She has publications on the livelihoods of internally- displaced persons from sociological perspectives. Her doctoral thesis was on the livelihoods of internally displaced persons. Her present research focuses on 'Migration and Development' and 'Migration and Mobility' in South Asia. She can be contacted via: bhattarainitu@ gmail.com.

KC, Sony holds an MA in Human and Natural Resources Studies from Kathmandu University and an MA in English Literature from Indira Gandhi National Open University. Currently, she is a Secure Livelihoods Research Consortium's Research Programme Officer on Livelihoods, Basic Services and Social Protection in Post-Conflict Nepal. Her major areas of interest are social protection and its implications in Nepal and gender mainstreaming in research. Ms KC was a recipient of the NCCR North-South Student Fellowship 2010 for her Master's thesis titled 'Analysing the Roles and Challenges of Women in the Tourism Sector of Nepal - An ethnographic study of Western Nepal'.

Khatiwada, Yuba Raj is currently the Governor of Nepal Rastra Bank. He has held the position of Vice Chairman of the National Planning Commission, Government of Nepal (June 2009 to March 2010). He has also served the United Nations as Senior Economist in the UNDP Regional Centre, Asia-Pacific for three years (2006 - 2009). Before that, he was a Member of the National Planning Commission, Government of Nepal for nearly three years (2002- 2005). He is a career central banker with more than 20 years' experience working with Nepal Rastra Bank at different levels. He holds a Masters degrees in Economics and public administration from Tribhuvan University, Nepal and a Ph. D degree in Economics from the Delhi School of Economics at the University of Delhi. He has undertaken a number of research studies and authored many articles and a few books on macroeconomic policies, development and poverty.

Upreti, Bishnu Raj holds a PhD from the Netherlands. Dr Upreti is a senior researcher on conflict management and is known in this field nationally and internationally. He has written and/or co-edited 28 books on conflict, peace, state-building and security and frequently published in peer- reviewed international journals and anthologies. Besides research, he is also teaching at Kathmandu University. Earlier, he has worked as a Research Fellow at King's College London and Surrey University, UK. He is engaged with policy-makers, politicians and the national and international media on Nepal's armed conflict and peace process. Dr Upreti is member of the advisory boards of different national and international organisations. He is currently the South Asia Regional Coordinator of NCCR North-South, a global research network active in addressing the challenges to sustainable development. Corresponding email address to Dr Upreti is bupreti@nccr. wlink.com.np

Uprety, Batu Krishna graduated in plant science. While working with the government for nearly three decades, he institutionalised the Environmental Impact Assessment (EIA) system by developing and implementing guidelines and manuals and strengthened climate change activities in Nepal by preparing NAPA, National Framework on LAPA, Climate Change Policy and status papers for climate negotiations, including by accessing climate finance, developing coordination mechanisms and promoting carbon trade. Mr Uprety used to teach EIA and environmental policies at the post-graduate level and has published books on EIA, environment conservation and sustainable development, including some articles on strategic environmental assessment, EIA, climate change and biodiversity in journals.

Wagle, Geja Sharma is Project Coordinator for the Nepal Institute for Policy Studies. Security scholar Wagle did a Masters degree in sociology from Tribhuvan University and is also a research fellow at the University of Birmingham of the United Kingdom. He is a co-editor of the book Emerging Security Challenges of Nepal published by NIPS in 2010. He served as Advisor to the Prime Minister in 2001 and 2002. He worked as a consultant for the Department for International Development Nepal. Mr Wagle writes regularly for Nepali newspapers and international journals and magazines on security, peace and strategic issues.

****